ISLANDER

PATRICK BARKHAM was born in 1975 in Norfolk and is a features writer for the *Guardian*. He is the author of *The Butterfly Isles: A Summer in Search of Our Emperors and Admirals*, which was shortlisted for the Ondaatje Prize, *Badgerlands: The Twilight World of Britain's Most Enigmatic Animal*, which was also shortlisted for the Ondaatje Prize and the Wainwright Prize, and *Coastlines: The Story of Our Shore*. *Islander* was shortlisted for an Edward Stanford Travel Writing Award and for a BBC *Countryfile* Magazine Award. Patrick Barkham lives in Norfolk.

'Like the water between his islands, Barkham's book shimmers – with curiosity, wisdom, cleverness, and wonder. He's shrewd, merry and generous; a splendid shipmate and yarn-spinner, and the perfect companion as you shuffle together along a beach' Charles Foster, author of *Being a Beast*

'Enchanting and lyrical, *Islander* is a book of many wonders; a book of coasts and heartlands, of peripheries and interiors – and a profoundly moving portrait of our natural world' Nicholas Crane, *The Making of the British Landscape*

'Barkham visits all sorts of weird and wonderful people on each land and paints a vivid and at times idiosyncratic picture of life cut off from mainland Britain, but he also seriously examines the perennial appeal of island life for many. Barkham is an engaging guide . . . [whose] strengths are his evocative nature writing and his literary resear~~ch~~ ~~...~~ ~~visito~~rs and history to hi~~...~~ ~~...~~ and nuance where~~...~~

D0301188

ISLANDER

A JOURNEY AROUND OUR ARCHIPELAGO

PATRICK
BARKHAM

Illustrated by Emily Faccini

GRANTA

Granta Publications, 12 Addison Avenue, London, W11 4QR

First published in Great Britain by Granta Books, 2017
This paperback edition published by Granta Books, 2018

A CIP catalogue record is available from the British Library

9 8 7 6 5 4 3 2 1

ISBN 978 1 78378 190 4 (paperback)
ISBN 978 1 78378 189 8 (ebook)

www.granta.com

Typeset in Garamond by Avon DataSet Ltd, Bidford on Avon, Warwickshire
Printed and bound by CPI Group (UK) Ltd, Croydon, CR0 4YY

For my archipelago, Milly, Esme and Ted

CONTENTS

Compton Mackenzie's Islands

The Isle of Man, holidaymaker 1891–1910
Capri, built house, resident 1913–20
Syra and other Aegean isles, Greece, wartime service 1915–18
Herm, The Channel Islands, owner 1920–23
Jethou, The Channel Islands, owner 1923–30
Shiants, The Hebrides, owner 1926–36
Island on the River Beauly, Scotland, leased house 1930–33
Barra, The Hebrides, built house, resident 1933–45

Note

The British Isles: the geological archipelago of Great Britain, Ireland and their smaller islands (does not include the Channel Islands).

Britain: in this book I use 'Britain' as a synonym for the United Kingdom of Great Britain and Northern Ireland (does not include Ireland, the Isle of Man or the Channel Islands).

INTRODUCTION

It begins with a jolting ride on a *flakmoped*, a three-wheeled motorbike designed for carrying loads, like me. I've travelled all day: car, plane, train, bus and then a smooth ferry across limpid water to Runmarö, one of the thirty thousand islands, islets and rocks of the Stockholm archipelago. Here, I clamber into a tray mounted high on the front of the bike, which belongs to a hoverfly obsessive called Fredrik Sjöberg. Sea breeze in my face, engine-roar in my ears, I'm carted in this strange contraption up a track between pine woods, around a corner, past dinky wooden houses and tiny wild meadows that smell of honey. Golden fritillaries glide between giant thistles, calm blue water peeps through the trees in surprising places, always unexpectedly close, and Sjöberg nods at everyone we pass. Arrivals in a new place are often exhilarating, but the fifteen square kilometres of Runmarö are something else. Yellow lichen shines like the sun from granite-grey rock. There are wild strawberries, speedwell and a deep peace, only broken by a mistle thrush repeating three notes. Sjöberg likens the island to a Sunday afternoon. This miniature universe simply seems right. It feels like home.

As the hours pass according to a slow, small-island rhythm, I start to wonder. Did I want to be here – or somewhere like it – for ever? I was born on an island but I'm sure that my character has been shaped more by living in an era of globalisation than by Britain's status as a nation surrounded by water. I read *Robinson Crusoe* and *The Swiss Family Robinson* as a boy but I've never fantasised about being cast away. I've never totted up my own Desert Island Discs and certainly never hankered after an island of my own.

And yet, twenty-fours hours on Runmarö causes me to reconsider. Big places are blurry but small islands are pin-sharp. They are as distinct as people, in my mind. Memories of small islands are like recollections of lovers, tinged with affection, nostalgia and a sense of impossibility. My first love, when I was a toddler, was Scolt Head, an uninhabited tidal island off the Norfolk coast where I spent early family holidays. We also holidayed on the long thin island of Öland, in Sweden.

My young adulthood was hardly Robert Louis Stevenson, or Paul Gauguin discovering a playground in the South Seas, but the most memorable trips of my early journalistic career were to tiny islands in the South Pacific. One was a dystopia: Nauru, which I visited in 2001 when the Australian government created an offshore prison for refugees on this ruined tropical rock. The other was a utopia, the coral archipelago of Tuvalu, which is being drowned by climate change. Here I travelled to Funafuti (airport code: FUN), hired an old motor-bike and skidded along the gravel roads without a helmet, giddy with small-island magic, mournful that it was imperilled. More recently, while researching a book about Britain's coastline, the most compel-ling experiences always seemed to be found on our great wealth of small islands: Lindisfarne, Lundy, Brownsea, Northey. Small islands are, by very definition, eccentric – away from the centre – and they are populated by people who seem unconventional to those confined to the mainstream. In this way they hold out an invitation, but also pose a challenge to us.

On Runmarö, Sjöberg demonstrates how to catch a fly with a tubular device he describes as part flute and part opium pipe, but he also reveals illuminating glimpses of his defiantly sedentary existence. He shows me a ripple of rock running through his waterside garden, a trace of limestone among the predominant granite; this anomaly brings an unusual abundance of flowers, and 180 species of hoverfly. We walk through the woods. Runmarö may be a special place but it is typical of the rural periphery of Western Europe too. Its small farms are overgrown now, food imported from elsewhere, and its flowery meadows are becoming forests again. Sun-loving species such as butterflies are falling extinct; beetles are returning to the woods, beavers are back and so too is the sea eagle.

Sjöberg is the author of a memoir called *The Fly Trap*, which is as small and dazzling as his island home. He grew up in the environmental movement but he's a bit of a contrarian. There's too much doom and gloom about extinction, he thinks; he hates 'nature reserves' and he's relaxed about 'invading' alien species that outcompete native creatures. He also ponders the boundaryless character of the modern human world. We are oppressed by so much freedom, he believes, and this makes the limitations of small-island life particularly appealing. Small islands are a liberation from choice. They are also a trap.

Sjöberg wonders why he chooses to enisle himself in a low wooden house overlooking the water. Does it make him think differently about the world? Or does he choose to live there *because* he thinks differently about the world? Either way, I suspect he senses that his original way of thinking and his life set apart from the mainstream are intimately entwined.

When I return home to my bigger island, *The Fly Trap* inspires me to read a fable about small-island lovers. Sjöberg is a fan of 'The Man Who Loved Islands', a short story by D.H. Lawrence about a wealthy young idealist who acquires a small island as a sanctuary. Lawrence's fictional hero, who is called Mr Cathcart, buys a haven of gorse, blackthorn and granite, four miles in circumference, somewhere beyond the British mainland. For a while, he adores his island home, working alongside the thirty-odd people who are his tenants and employees. Soon, though, he realises one inescapable truth about small islands: living on a rock surrounded by the ocean is prohibitively expensive. His capital disappears in renovations. Projects fail. 'His' islanders quietly mock and exploit him.

Our hero's solution is to downsize. He takes his most faithful carpenter, and a widow and her daughter to keep house for him, to a smaller island. For a while he finds peace, and compiles a list of every flower in this tiny place. Things take a typically Lawrentian turn, however, for our island idealist sleeps with the widow's daughter, Flora. She has a child, and the man who loves islands realises that he has sabotaged his quest for peace. So he removes himself once more, to a concrete hut on a bleak island-rock on which he no longer does anything but dream, living alongside a cat, and then alone. He sleeps, hallucinates and, eventually, goes mad and dies.

It is a simple story of disillusionment and, like the best kind of fable, niggles away at the reader. Sjöberg, who hoped the story's title would answer his question Why an island?, was disappointed when he first read it. Then he found himself returning to it, repeatedly, and marvelling at its truths about nesomanes, as John Fowles calls small-island lovers, small-island existence, and life itself.

Struck by these themes, I do not immediately realise that virtually every detail in the story is taken from real life. The man who loved islands, Mr Cathcart, was a real man, a friend, fellow writer and rival. Compton Mackenzie is barely known outside Scotland these days and is not much remembered within it. The name rings a bell for those who have watched the film or read the book *Whisky Galore* – his 1947 tale of fictional islanders salvaging thousands of bottles of whisky from a wartime shipwreck – but I wonder why he is not better known. He was admired by Henry James, Virginia Woolf, F. Scott Fitzgerald and George Orwell. He averaged more than a book each year of his long life, an unceasing flow of four million published words, including ten – ten! – volumes of autobiography he penned in his eighties. He also played a major role in many of the great events of the twentieth century – he was a brilliant spy in the First World War, an inventor of bureaucracy, a founding father of the Scottish Nationalist Party (despite being born in England), a pioneer of music journalism, and an early entertainer on BBC radio and television. Here was a feted author and brilliant raconteur, a handsome if rather bird-like man with a mop of black hair that his friend Eric Linklater once likened to a raven shot on its nest. Sir Compton Mackenzie was clever, witty, well connected and celebrated in his lifetime. Now, less than five decades after his death, he is virtually forgotten. Are islands something to do with it?

The island-infatuation of idealistic, extravagant, egotistical, foolish and tragic Mr Cathcart – or Compton Mackenzie – fascinates me. Why did Lawrence write so unsparingly about a friend? What became of their friendship? And how did Mackenzie's life on small islands actually unfold? I also ponder the universal truths in Lawrence's brief exploration of small-island life. His story reveals the lure of islands for idealists, the clash between dreams and financial reality, and the tension between an individual's need for liberty and his or her need for society. In Lawrence's view, the past is unusually present on small islands. They are dangerously seductive places for people seeking to escape the mainstream who swiftly discover they cannot escape themselves.

I wonder if Lawrence is correct. To find out, I decide I must take my lead from the man who loved islands. Like Cathcart, and like Mackenzie, I will travel through the archipelago that is the British Isles, moving from large island to medium-sized island to tiny island. I won't merely shadow Mackenzie but our paths will cross as I follow his trajectory, seeking ever smaller islands and the essence of what it is to be an islander.

The cliché is that Britain is an island nation, but it is, of course, several nations that share innumerable islands. We might count six thousand, or more if we include riverine islands, man-made islets or rocks revealed by the tide. Of these, about 132 islands are permanently inhabited. We are all islanders, but some are more islander than others.

'No man is an Island, entire of itself;' wrote John Donne, famously, 'every man is a piece of the Continent, a part of the main; if a clod be washed away by the sea, Europe is the less.' I see what he is saying but I'm with the novelist and island-lover John Fowles, who argued that in fact a small island is closely analogous to an individual person. J.M. Barrie took a similar view: 'To be born is to be wrecked on an island,' he wrote in the preface to R.M. Ballantyne's *The Coral Island.* A small island can be an illuminating metaphor for a person's life.

People may be islandish but islands are also like people. A distinct place that we can encompass in a glance without coming close to grasping its complexity may be the planet's closest geological approximation to a person. A few square miles of small island looms far larger than the equivalent pocket of land on the mainland. Small islands are celebrities; they become public figures laden with reputations and attributes they may or may not actually possess. Visitors become fans who feel like they own a piece of them. And so everyone seems to have a strong view about which islands I should visit. People tell me I must go to Jura for George Orwell or Piel for its pub or Eel Pie on the Thames for its coterie of rock stars. When I mention the Scilly archipelago, I lose count of the number of people who recommend that I visit Bryher, or warn me away from Tresco. I choose a longlist and change my mind. I shy away from recommendations; I can feel myself becoming a small-island contrarian.

Eventually, I decide on these eleven islands, a list that may look idiosyncratic but that is bound by two loose rules: a geographical spread within (and slightly beyond) the British archipelago, and my decision not to revisit places I've written about in my previous book, *Coastlines.* The eleven places represent the various ways we have used small islands over the centuries – both for real and in our imagination. These small islands have been havens for ourselves and destinations for our money, for parties, prisoners, holidays, dreams, national identities and fictions.

They also lay bare our relationships with other species. Small islands are simplified ecosystems – there are usually fewer species of animals and plants – which makes it easier for us to make sense of the astonishing complexity and interrelatedness of living things. Our impact on other terrestrial species on small islands is often obvious and profound. Extinctions occur rapidly when we overburden a small place surrounded by sea with development, or let loose invasive new species.

Today, our planetary dominance has, in effect, turned Earth into an archipelago of tiny islands: wild nature or pristine habitat exists only in fragments where species are more vulnerable than ever to obliteration. At least real small islands can be havens for wildlife too: species once ubiquitous on mainland Britain, such as the corncrake, now survive only on its peripheries. There is space for nature in places that are not so easily exploited to meet our own economic desires.

This vision of the small island as a pristine paradise is one not shared by most humans in recent history. In the past, islands have mostly been seen through the same lens as Daniel Defoe's in *Robinson Crusoe*. They are wild places that must be tamed; prisons for castaways and condemned men, replete with external dangers and internal challenges to sanity. In the human world, they often become nightmarish places of incarceration, as Napoleon on St Helena, Alfred Dreyfus on Devil's Island and Nelson Mandela on Robben Island would testify.

Gradually, though, the spectre of the prison island has been banished by the popularisation of Jean-Jacques Rousseau's romantic idea that islands are a perfect locale for the blossoming of the solitary self. The publication of Lawrence's short story, in 1928, may mark the pinnacle of this island love, but an urge to escape to small islands pulses through recent history, usually during times of crisis. When the mainland or mainstream is in crisis, people look to the periphery for escape or inspiration. Many of us are looking there right now. Are small-island values – robust self-sufficiency, for instance, or an integrated, neighbourly community – passé, or are they more pertinent than ever? Small islands may offer a critique of our larger island life, but might they also provide salvation for our epoch?

I want to meet human and non-human islanders and listen to their stories. Through this island-hopping, I would like to reveal the unique character of small islands and small-island life. My ambition is to travel in the spirit of the man who loved islands, alive to his romantic questing but stripped of his illusions. Here, at least, I have a head-start: I don't have the cash to pursue his vision of possessing an island of my own. I hope to reach the end of this book as an island-person on a tiny island off an island, finally understanding this island place, and an islander's place in the world, without going mad.

1

Man Is an Island

The Isle of Man, 221 square miles, population 85,000

'It seemed to pick the very money out of your pocket, as if it
were an octopus with invisible arms stealing from you in
every direction'
'The Man Who Loved Islands'

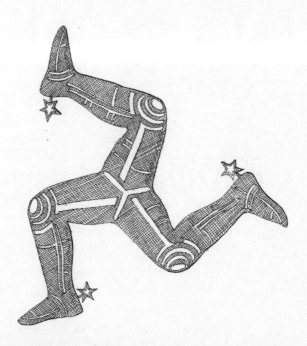

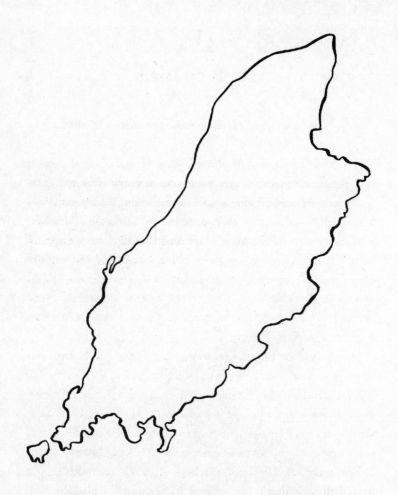

Night has fallen fast and a string of lights traces the grand crescent of Douglas promenade, pink sky and low mountains beyond. From a high hill to the south, the seaside capital of the Isle of Man looks as magical as it must have been to the eyes of Compton Mackenzie, who first visited the island as a boy in its heyday, the summer of 1891. 'There was something exotic about Douglas to my youthful imagination,' Mackenzie wrote, 'and those dance- and music-halls nestling in the rich foliage of the cliffs above the incomparable curve of that bay seemed like visions from *The Arabian Nights* when they were lit up by jewelled fairy lamps.'

From a distance, Douglas looks as vibrant as it was in the late nine-teenth and early twentieth centuries, when the Isle of Man was *the* holiday island paradise for the people of northern England. Steam-ships carried more than a million passengers to Douglas in 1933. Now, though, as I drive into its tidy streets listening to Manx Radio playing songs I haven't heard for twenty-five years – the lesser hits of Roxette, Des'ree and Huey Lewis and the News – there's not much sign of dance-hall razzle-dazzle. The seafront smells strongly of bladderwrack, and the waves hurl hunks of seaweed onto the broad prom where they are dodged by a smattering of Lycra-clad joggers and power-walking mums. Mighty stands of pampas grass thrust from prom gardens alongside spiky New Zealand cabbage palms, which locals have assimilated as 'Manx palms'. The promenade is lined with six-storey Victorian boarding-houses for long-vanished holidaymakers. Most have been turned into private apartments but a few hotels survive – the Trevelyan, the Rutland, the Empress, the At Caledonia – flashing pastel shades from another era. Beside them is the Palace Casino, an ugly magnolia-coloured building that was opened by Sean Connery at the height of James Bond mania in 1966. The Isle of Man was a vibrant destination during its daring reinvention in the 1960s, too. The casino is now a Best Western hotel as well. Holidaymaking is no longer really Man's business. But plenty of other things are. The island is quietly, discreetly, thriving. The backstreets of Douglas are lined with multi-storey car parks marked 'private', where Jaguars and Maseratis gleam in the half-light.

The Isle of Man is less than a quarter of the size of Lewis and Harris, which is the biggest British isle after Britain and Ireland. Man is smaller than Skye, Mull, Anglesey and Islay. It has fewer residents than the Isle of Wight and Jersey. Man's population of 85,000 makes it the size of Redditch in the West Midlands. And yet this apparently sleepy, superficially nondescript small island can claim to be wealthier – in material riches and culture – than any other small island in our archipelago. It is a far more significant presence within the British Isles than most provincial English cities three times its size.

If boats are holes in the water into which you throw money, islands are sea monsters that rise up and grab the cash from your hand. As the man who loved islands discovered, islands are incorrigible, reckless spendthrifts. Most small islands and their residents wallow in a state of perpetual insolvency. The Isle of Man is an exception. Profitable trade is at the heart of its founding legends and its current identity. When I first visit in 2015, Man is enjoying its thirty-first year of unbroken economic growth and recently overtook affluent Guernsey and Jersey to become the biggest economy of the islands known as the Crown Dependencies. How did a modest island that endures an unattractive climate at an unfashionable latitude become so rich?

Man harbours some interesting superstitions and I encounter the first when I take the island's A1 from east-coast Douglas to west-coast Peel, where I'm lodging for the evening. The road is empty of all traffic apart from a smart Volvo bus whisking two pensioners home, and a rat. When I mention this beast, islanders won't repeat its name: rats are 'long-tailed gentlemen' or R-A-Ts. There is a similar reluctance to discuss another three-letter word: T-A-X. Islanders like the term 'tax haven' even less. It was embraced by the Isle of Man's government in the 1960s, one islander tells me, when it was a forward-looking phrase like the 'white heat of technology'. Now it is a pejorative label, suggesting a place that deliberately creates advantageous tax laws to enable individuals from other countries to avoid paying their fair share. Alongside the TT, the Isle of Man's terrifying annual motor-cycle race held on a circuit of island roads, its tax arrangements are the source of its stature, and its infamy.

Man is situated in the centre of the Irish Sea, equidistant from England, Scotland and Northern Ireland. Until I hear the Manx Radio jingle, 'the nation's station', my slack mainland mind had assumed it was a British island. In fact, Man is a self-governing territory of the Crown. The British government is responsible for its defence and foreign affairs and has oversight of its laws but, as the Manx government states firmly on its website: 'The Isle of Man is not, and never has been, part of the United Kingdom, nor is it part of the European Union.' It claims to be a nation.

Culturally, Man is Celtic, and its Gaelic language, Manx, is kept alive even though English dominates today. Man was once part of a 'Kingdom of the Isles', along with the Hebrides. My first impression of its landscape is of a melange of all five countries you can see on a clear day from the top of its highest peak, Snaefell. Glen Helen with its beech trees turning ginger in late October could be a valley in the Lake District; lanes banked with gorse and huge hedges of fuchsia are like western Ireland; Peel's fine stone harbour reminds me of a Scottish port; the conifer plantations on Dalby Mountain possess the desolation of rural Northern Ireland; the pebble-dashed coastal suburbs are reminiscent of North Wales. And popping into view all around, always closer than expected, is the blue Irish Sea.

'Not so much itself but a scale model of something bigger,' declared Jonathan Raban, mercilessly, in *Coasting*, his illusion-stripping sail around Britain in the 1980s. Man's main line of work has always been a kind of smuggling, argued Raban. In the distant past, Manx fishing boats ferried tea, brandy and other taxed items over the sea to England. More recently, they profited from the gulf between island and mainland tax rates, he wrote, and 'trawled for English millionaires'. Another disparaging visitor, the late critic AA Gill, put it more crudely in 2006: the island's chief business, he declared, is 'money (laundering, pressing, altering and mending)'. Gill still hasn't been forgiven by locals when I visit.

Such perceptions infuriate its government and most of its people, who will point out that it is not a flash place. Man is not Monaco. I spy old farms with strange names – Baier Yude Noo – but no palatial houses and no fancy yachts. No one drips gold on my flight from Manchester, but then the super-rich don't take Flybe.

My first step in discovering how the Isle of Man has stayed financially afloat when other small islands have gone under is to meet Laurence Skelly, the minister for economic development. I thought it would be difficult to arrange an interview but the parliamentarians who sit in the Tynwald, which the Manx claim was established by the Vikings in 979 and is generally regarded as the world's oldest parliament continually in use, are more accessible than most rulers. Their home numbers are in the phone book. Still, driving into Douglas, which takes its name from *dubh glas*, 'black river' in early Gaelic/Manx, or possibly from the merging of its two rivers, the Dhoo and the Glass (the dark and the light), I'm surprised that Skelly keeps our appointment. The big stories on Manx Radio are the theft of pumpkins from a partially sighted woman's allotment just ahead of *Hop tu Naa* (Manx Halloween), and Skelly spending £276,000 to develop a 'world series' of the TT race that came to nothing. Callers are scandalised. 'This Laurence Skelly, he talks a lot and doesn't say a great deal,' says one Manxman. 'Mr Skelly has more spin than a fairground ride,' says another. A nonagenarian islander I meet reckons the current crop of politicians are Mirror Men: 'They always say they are looking into it.'

Despite the crisis, Skelly, a small man with a thatch of dark curly hair and a loose-fitting suit, is relaxed and expansive as he explains how the Isle of Man's economic success is embodied in its distinctive national symbol. Everywhere I travel on the island, I see a rather sinister-looking emblem: three bent legs extending from a central point. It's emblazoned across the airport carpet, on flags flying from front gardens, on the gable end of bungalows, on motels, ties, banks, lampposts and cartons of exceedingly creamy Isle of Man milk. This triskelion stands at the centre of the island's flag and is as ancient as any human trace on the island. The symbol was first identified in Malta six thousand years ago and features on the flag of another small island, Sicily. It moved north and is found in a megalithic tomb in Ireland dating from 3200 BC. Variations of its three interlocking shapes are relatively common in Celtic culture.

A joke from the 1930s reckons one leg is fleeing from Ireland, the second is kicking Scotland, while the third is bending to England. These days, this ancient symbol is deployed more assertively. Whichever way these symmetrical legs of Man are thrown, says Skelly, they always land on their feet, explaining the island's Latin motto, *Quocunque Jeceris Stabit*. 'We've had a lot of turmoil, with the English, the Scots, the Vikings. We're very fiercely independent. We're very proud.

But we're very innovative as well.' The triskelion has been turned into an ideal brand for modern Man, the resilient, adaptable home of restless global capital.

Like almost every other small British isle, the Isle of Man was founded upon farming and fishing. But, rather like Cornwall, it was also blessed with deposits of lead, zinc, silver, copper and tin. A significant mining industry was augmented by a late Victorian tourist boom that helped fund innovations such as its electric railway, which opened in 1893 and still takes tourists to the impressive red wheel at Laxey. This once pumped water from mines where six hundred men worked and it continues to slowly turn, the largest operational waterwheel in the world. The closure of the mines in the early twentieth century and the collapse of tourism around the Second World War left Man experiencing a post-industrial crisis earlier than most places. It found a solution earlier, too. And, unlike Cornwall, it was independent enough to experience a post-colonial awakening.

Man's population fell from a high of 55,000 in 1891 to 47,000 in 1961, as young Manx left to slog on sugar beet fields in East Anglia like Lithuanians do today. The arrival of a much older man on the island in 1959 helped transform its fortunes. Sir Ronald Garvey, Governor of British Honduras and then Fiji, looked to the British government like a safe pair of hands as Lieutenant Governor of the Isle of Man, the island's de facto chief executive and a comfortable retirement post for a colonial administrator. Home Office staff should probably have realised their appointment had gone troppo when Sir Ronald dispatched a Manx cat to replace the one they'd lost in Whitehall. (Compton Mackenzie also acquired a Manx cat, called Twinkle, when he was a student at Oxford.) Working closely with local Manx politicians, the rebellious Sir Ronald helped establish the island's pioneering casino. Then he suggested turning Man into a 'tax haven'.

When Man abolished the 'supertax' of the 1960s, Sir Ronald

appeared on the BBC, appealing to people to move to the island. Britain's Labour government was enraged that a 'British' island should openly tout itself as a home for the tax-avoiding rich, but Sir Ronald knew his target audience. As the Empire crumbled, thousands of colonial civil servants hankered after 'coming home'. There was one problem: they were repulsed by Britain's lax moral code and stiff tax code. The solution was to retreat, in their thousands, to an idealised, low-tax version of home. On the Isle of Man, and on the Channel Islands, they were free to build bungalows with sea views, give them African names and plant pampas grass to their heart's content. On Man, I meet a couple whose home was previously owned by an old colonial called Bunty who left behind a recipe for roast porcupine.

Newcomers on Man are called 'comeovers', but these migrants from the Empire earned another name: 'when-Is', as in 'When I was in Uganda we wouldn't stand for this sort of thing.' Even today, when only one or two old colonials are left alive, Manx spit out the term; the when-Is treated them like primitives, they say. But their arrival arrested decades of population decline, and by the 1970s the island was thriving. Crucially, it won the kind of devolution from the British government that, nearly sixty years on, Scotland has yet to achieve. 'That element of independence has been absolutely critical to the Isle of Man,' says Allan Bell, the long-serving former chief minister. 'Had we not had it, we'd be the equivalent of Harris and Lewis – largely depopulated and dependent on farming, fishing and tourism. Because we've got a degree of independence, we've been able to apply our own competitive tax rate over the last fifty years, we've had a stable population and grown our economy.'

A day after meeting Skelly, and after another straightforward email exchange, I'm granted an audience with Bell. He's a fit, tanned man with sharp blue eyes and close-cropped white hair who, at the time of our meeting, is still chief minister and a year away from retirement. Unlike some islanders, he does not sound defensive about his homeland. 'The biggest enemy the Isle of Man has these days is Google – you push a button and all this out-of-date crap comes up,' he says. He points out that both the Organisation for Economic Cooperation and Development (OECD) and David Cameron when he was prime minister announced that the island was no longer a tax haven.

As a young Manx, Bell went off travelling to a place with a similar reputation for being a tax haven – Gibraltar – because, and he laughs at this irony, he wanted to escape the finance industry. He eventually returned home and joined the Manx nationalists, driven by a visceral dislike of the wealthy when-Is whose desire to avoid tax was so radically changing Man's character. But small islands must accommodate their revolutionaries and small-island revolutionaries must embrace their accommodation, and Bell is not the only islander to shift from rebel to ringmaster. One of his ministers, Phil Gawne, was jailed in 1988 for setting fire to a house, a terrorist act by an anti-finance movement called Fo Sostyn, Fo Ordaag 'Under England, Under the Thumb'. The FSFO graffiti was sometimes interpreted as 'Financial Services Fuck Off'. 'I never actually burnt anything down,' says Bell, drily. 'I never had the opportunity.'

In the 1970s and 80s, Man's lightly regulated low-tax regime attracted bankers, accountants, lawyers and other financial professionals. They created thousands of shell companies and shell banks, 'paper' companies with headquarters that were no more than a postal address on Man. Many of these practices resemble the tax-avoiding schemes still undertaken today. 'Some of the characters we had over here smacked of the Wild West for a certain period,' admits Allan Bell.

Leaf through old newspapers and the Isle of Man crops up in so many court cases and banking scandals in the 1980s – from the Brink's-Mat robbery to the collapse of the Allied Irish Bank, to name two – that it is hard to believe the island was simply an empty vessel into which rogues poured their liquid assets. 'The smugglers themselves looked like chartered accountants do everywhere,' wrote Jonathan Raban in 1986. 'They wore coloured golf socks and thick spectacles, they went to the barber's once a fortnight, and were shyly boastful about their handicaps after-hours in the bar of the Admiral House on the prom.'

Raban clearly endured a horrid couple of weeks hanging out with ageing tax exiles on Man in the 1980s, but I don't think his excoriating portrait of Man as the acme of Little England applies today. Its miniature echoes of the mainland combine to create a unique and constantly surprising place. I drive south, past the bizarre juxta-position of airport and the island's top school, King William's, which looks like Hogwarts and is exceptionally convenient for the children of wealthy foreign families who fly in and board there. Pastures are lit in luminous green by the flashing west-coast light. The air is moist and perfumed – by heather on the purple uplands, by freshly cut lawn in the suburbs, and then by pungent dashes of seaweed flung by the waves onto shoreside roads. The sea is a constant presence, in all directions.

In the little fields, the island's Loaghtan sheep look like wild Green Men with their four spiralling horns, and I'm startled by the stumpy tail of a black Manx cat (the stump is a genetic deformity) as it crosses the road by a fuchsia hedge. I walk out on the low rocks of the Langness Peninsula where proposals for a golf course were defeated by a local campaign to save the only home of the rare Lesser Mottled Grasshopper, whose nearest other known colony is a baffling 450-mile hop away – in Holland. A Manx folk band composed a rather lovely song to save the grasshopper. These islanders won't be pushed about.

Everywhere I drive on Man looks neat and tidy but it hardly screams of the super-rich. If there's wealth here, it's hidden away. I begin to form a more accurate picture of that wealth only when I log onto a property website at my lodgings in Peel that night. I search for homes in Man's mainland equivalent, Redditch. There, the most expensive home is £925,000. Then I look at the Isle of Man. The top-priced house? A brand-new mansion marketed for £30 million. There are another 145 properties for sale above £1 million. Man is awash with mansions, tucked behind high hedges or a long way down private driveways.

Browsing through these palaces, I'm startled to discover a castellated stone building with fine views, on the market for £1.95 million. I passed it earlier in the day, hidden in seven acres of beeches, pines and monkey puzzles up a winding driveway above the A1. Greeba Castle is a substantial Victorian house, 'imposing', 'elegantly proportioned' and a 'gracious home of literary and historical stature' in estate-agent-speak. A 'medium-sized' villa, in the rather less rapt eyes of Compton Mackenzie, who crossed the Irish Sea again to call on its former owner, the popular novelist Sir Thomas Henry Hall Caine, in 1910.

This encounter between Mackenzie, then a struggling young actor, and Hall Caine, a blacksmith turned hugely famous and rather egotistical writer, may have been the moment that sparked the man who loved islands into life. Mackenzie's visit to the Isle of Man saw his life take a decisive turn, setting him upon a path to fame and fortune; and friendship, rivalry and finally a falling-out with D.H. Lawrence. After the First World War, a number of writers including Mackenzie and Lawrence sought to escape the strictures of society, or perhaps their own souls, via small islands. But neither Lawrence, nor any other individual in the twentieth century, could match the obsessive fervour of Mackenzie's pursuit of small-island life.

Unlike some compulsive collectors of islands, Compton Mackenzie was a mainlander, with no familial connections with small islands. He was born Edward Montague Compton Mackenzie, in Hartlepool in 1883, to a mother and father who were actors and were touring with their theatre company. But even in his childhood he felt the tug of island life. A slender, dreamy, dark-haired boy, he read *Treasure Island* 'in one glorious gasp' aged eight, devoured *Robinson Crusoe* and then *The Swiss Family Robinson*, 'which filled my fancy with the delight of living on a desert island'. The Isle of Man wasn't quite a desert island, but his childhood holidays there made a strong impression. These times on Man were a happy interlude during a privileged yet loveless childhood dominated by a disciplinarian nanny. Monty's parents were busy with their touring company, and his icy mother's notable lack of affection – even by late Victorian standards – shaped his life more than he cared to admit, and later encouraged him into the arms of Faith Stone, an actress five years older than Monty who first met him when he was a celebrated undergraduate at the University of Oxford.

'I saw the rose-leaf complexion, the small, pretty Cupid's bow mouth, the sloping poet's brow, and then the wan crooked smile,' she remembered. They fell in love and quickly married without either family's permission. Faith miscarried their son and they never had any children but stayed together, and oddly apart, for fifty-five years.

This clever, talented and directionless young man spent most of his twenties dabbling in crazes: for poetry, the law, even landscape gardening. He seriously considered, at different times, becoming a vicar, a playwright, an actor. He was twenty-seven when he made his fateful return to Man at the summons of Sir Hall Caine, who was considering him for a part in one of his plays. Monty took the paddle-steamer from Fleetwood and necked three bottles of Guinness in a futile attempt to avert seasickness. Hall Caine was a figure of great renown. Crowds used to gather outside his homes. An airport on the Isle of Man was named after him. A flavour of his self-importance still lingers in Greeba Castle's oak-panelled entrance hall with its lintel carved with the legend: 'H.C.1897. Here shall Ye See No Enemy But My Winter And Rough Weather'. Monty's account of their meeting is of a young tyro mocking a pompous old man.

'It's all so simple,' Monty remembered Hall Caine commenting on his writing life, in a dreamy, sepulchral voice. 'So simple, so utterly in keeping with the simple life of this little island, and if I may say so with the books I write here in complete seclusion.' The Isle of Man was actually enjoying the height of its Edwardian popularity as a fashionable holiday resort – Douglas was lauded as 'the Naples of the North' and boasted one thousand boarding-houses and dancing-palaces on its long promenade – so Monty's reply was a masterstroke of tact. 'One can imagine Aeschylus writing his plays in surroundings like this,' he said. 'Thank you, Mr Compton,' intoned Hall Caine, 'that is one of the nicest things ever said to me.'

Monty charmed his way into a part in Hall Caine's play, but *The Bishop's Son* was so bad that it closed after just one week. It also ended Monty's career as a professional actor and compelled him to apply himself to a writing career instead. Although he was dismissive of Hall Caine he was clearly attracted by the 'simple' creative freedom that novelist enjoyed on the Isle of Man. Finally, Compton Mackenzie found his focus: he poured his wayward energy into writing, and the next year his debut novel *The Passionate Elopement* was published to enthusiastic reviews. His third novel, *Sinister Street*, a two-volume *Bildungsroman*, was published in 1913. Monty's star was on the rise. 'Possibly a work of real genius,' declared Ford Madox Ford, who considered him alongside D.H. Lawrence and Ezra Pound as the English language's brightest young literary hopes. 'The future of the English novel is to a quite considerable extent in his hands,' opined the *Manchester Guardian* in 1915. Henry James hailed Monty as 'by far the most promising novelist of his generation' and suggested his talent outstripped that of Hugh Walpole – and D.H. Lawrence. Both *Sinister Street* and Lawrence's *The Rainbow* were suppressed by libraries and booksellers, scandalised by their sexual and homosexual themes. So it was inevitable that Monty and Lawrence, two years apart in age and bracketed together as *enfants terribles*, and rivals, should meet. Lawrence's childhood as the son of a Nottinghamshire miner was rather different from Monty's gilded, if emotionally starved, existence, but they became firm friends, bonding over their mutual love of small islands. Each egged on the other to ill-fated small-island adventures. But Compton Mackenzie did not realise that island-infatuation would cause their friendship's end.

The next morning, I glance up towards Greeba Castle again, hoping to catch a sense of that 1910 encounter between Mackenzie and Hall Caine on my way to Athol Street, the financial district of Douglas. Jonathan Raban found Athol Street's cracked plaster and pervading whiff of fish and chips more 'amiable' than the City of London or New York. Thirty years later, it is as immaculate and expensively paved as the Square Mile. Past the Isle of Man Bank with its separate gold door for 'Isle of Man premium banking' are rows of handsome Georgian houses bearing oblique silver plaques by their doors: Xela Holdings Ltd, Turnstone, Annexio, Milton Optimal.

A decade ago, 60 per cent of Man's gross domestic product was generated by these mysterious 'financial services', much like its then wealthier neighbours, Jersey and Guernsey. The banking crisis burst the bubble for these two Channel Island tax havens, but they also drove themselves closer to bankruptcy by desperately following the Isle of Man when it became the first of the Crown Dependencies to cut its corporation tax to zero in 2006 – alongside a 20 per cent top rate of income tax, no stamp duty, no inheritance tax and a tax cap so no individual pays more than £120,000 per year.

When Jersey followed Man's lead, its government lost a far greater proportion of its income in doing so. You out-thought them, I had remarked to Allan Bell. 'Oh absolutely, Jersey, our poor-relation country cousin.' Bell had beamed, enjoying the joke against a rival island blessed with sunnier geography and more millionaires. 'They thought that financial services would carry them safely into the future. Perhaps it's because we were the poor relation, we've had to fight harder to attract new business here. We've had to be innovative. That is now imbued in our national character. Rather than having eighty-five thousand accountants clinging to a rock, it's a fully rounded country.'

Some might consider online gambling a lucky last throw of the dice; others prefer to say that the Isle of Man landed on its feet again, identifying alternatives to conventional financial services more quickly than did Jersey and Guernsey. A quarter of Man's economy is now e-business, mostly betting. Young Manx work through the night as Far Eastern gamblers pour dollars into PokerStars or Full Tilt Poker. And there are other, stranger activities: Man has a thriving ship registry and is also among the top ten countries in the world for registering planes. It's big in space: four of the biggest ten satellite companies have offices on the island, selling 'slots' for satellites that orbit the planet. Laurence Skelly's favourite new economic sectors are 'fintech' (digital currencies and other new technologies which will 'disrupt' conventional banking) and 'cleantech' (renewable energy). Attracting investment to the wilder shores of the business world is how the Manx have survived.

This world of high finance is as opaque as the lives of the wealthy, but the entrepreneur Charlie Woolnough, who agrees to a chat in an Athol Street coffee shop, is unexpectedly open. He's a gangly man at the end of his thirties, loose-limbed and likeable. He grew up on the island and, like many young Manx, studied business and finance before moving to work in London hedge funds. Woolnough made it home because of the Internet. A business's face to the world is no longer an address in Mayfair, it's a website, he says. A huge part of any London business's outgoings are London wages and London rent. 'Why would you want to set up a business in London? The digitisation of the world allows people like me to do what I want to do from where I want to do it.' He continues to sit on the boards of hedge funds based in the City of London but has established his own Manx business, CoinCorner, on Athol Street.

Woolnough's business is one of about twenty-five digital or crypto-currency start-ups on the island, and he employs seven people. CoinCorner is an exchange for digital currencies such as Bitcoin, which was devised by an anonymous programmer now known to be an Australian computer scientist, in 2008. While old Manx pound notes – the Manx pound is in a currency union with the British pound – are still legal tender, entrepreneurs can also buy pints, artisan loaves and taxi rides here with bitcoins.

The key feature of a successful digital currency is to stop people duplicating it, and spending their money twice. Bitcoin's inventor created a revolutionary piece of technology called the 'blockchain': users' transactions are recorded simultaneously on a public ledger stored across everyone's computer. This record protects people using the currency. The blockchain thrills and terrifies the financial sector in equal measure. Digital currencies cut out the need for a middleman such as a bank. People can make peer-to-peer payments or overseas transfers without any bank charges. Digital or cryptocurrencies should prove particularly useful in the developing world, where billions of people lack access to a bank, or have to pay exorbitant fees. But critics fear they facilitate crime and money laundering, and could even bring down the financial system.

Cryptocurrencies are being developed on the Isle of Man because an almost autonomous small island can make its own rules. Man has moved more quickly than Britain. 'The Isle of Man government came out and said, "We support cryptocurrencies, it's not a huge threat to the global order, it's actually potentially got social benefits for a lot of people,"' says Woolnough. 'The Isle of Man has led the way with cryptocurrency regulation in Europe.' Digital currencies are not yet fully regulated here but, to stop money laundering, cryptocurrency companies are legally obliged to know their clients and report any suspicious transactions. 'Sure, you could regulate new industries straight away, but you'd kill them,' says Woolnough. 'Some degree of regulation is a good thing to keep bad people out of the industry, but the real key is not using a sledgehammer to crack a walnut.'

Woolnough's vision of the island is the same always-landing-on-your-feet stance of the triskelion. 'Whilst it would be lovely to be in a position to pick and choose your business, we don't have that luxury.' In other words, Man must move quickly to lure new investment to its shores to sustain itself. I feel rather sorry for the island, perpetually condemned to explore risky new areas of business knowing that, if it is successful, the big countries will, in City-boy terminology, eat their lunch. 'I wouldn't use the word "condemned,"' says Woolnough. 'We're perpetually incentivised to seek new things. If you're first to do something and do it well, people will stay here.' Ten years on from the globalisation of online gambling, big brands have stayed on the island. I wonder how loyal offshore businesses are to a place like Man but, as a Manxman, Woolnough declares his commitment. 'If you live on an island, you become acutely aware of the community. If a bank closes down, everyone feels it,' he says. 'I'd like to think that CoinCorner will still be on the Isle of Man in fifty years' time.'

Not everyone I meet on the Isle of Man hails its new economic landscape with the heartiness of entrepreneurs and politicians. Many locals seem to share the mainland's popular suspicion of globalisation and elites, but I am struck by the unity of belief in the island's right to create its own low-tax system. Everyone I speak to, young and old, conservative and liberal, native and comeover, seems to think the same. When I'm invited onto Manx Radio – word gets around very quickly in a small place – the DJ, Roger Watterson, gives me his patriotic talk-show spiel. 'Because this is a little place away from the mainstream of things there's a terrible assumption in the UK that the natives have got a bone in their nose and a grass skirt, but actually this place runs very well.' Its image is 'grossly unfair', he argues. 'The Isle of Man is better-regulated than the City of London, and the OECD will tell you that.'

I have dinner with a lovely couple, Liz Charter and Tim Earl. Like many people I meet during my explorations, they are small-island specialists. Liz worked on Orkney before Man; Tim grew up on Guernsey and runs wildlife tours to places such as South Georgia and the Falklands. I wrongly assume that they will be critical of their adopted home's financial arrangements. 'Most people are paying the 20 per cent that people pay in the UK,' says Liz. 'People on islands are extremely patriotic,' warns Tim. 'You shouldn't go around thinking that it's shady. It just isn't. We're not tax havens, we're low-tax areas.'

Tim makes an interesting point. He thinks that Man cutting its corporation tax to zero was its biggest mistake because it antagonised the British government, who began to reconsider its generosity towards the island.

In fact, an accountant from a small Fenland market town was the first person in Britain to scrutinise the Isle of Man's financial relationship with the mainland. Richard Murphy is an implausible mix: a fast-talking Norfolk accountant who has become a global expert on tax avoidance. He's hated as much as AA Gill on Man. 'They think that I persecute them, but I persecute all small islands,' he says breezily when I phone him. Man's ancient parliament is 'a glorified parish council', he claims. 'They're about as independent as Norfolk.'

Murphy has a different view of Man's economic miracle: it is a state-sponsored tax haven, he says. Just over a decade ago, he examined the island's long-standing arrangement with Britain called 'the common purse agreement'. This entitled Man to a share of the UK's customs and excise revenues (later VAT) in exchange for not charging import duties on items from Britain. Murphy performed a basic accounting exercise: he compared the amount of VAT that Britain collected as a percentage of GDP with the amount 'collected' by the Isle of Man. The island's figure was nearly three times Britain's. In fact, while VAT was then levied at 17.5 per cent, Man was recovering more than 17.5 per cent of its gross national income in VAT – a mathematical impossibility. But it *was* possible, Murphy realised, because the formula used to give Man a share of British VAT revenues in the common purse agreement was handing the small island £200 million each year. No wonder Man is in such fine fettle. How opulent might Redditch look if its 85,000 residents were given £200 million, *every year*?

Murphy concluded that Britain's generosity was a bizarre accident. The subsidy continued during Man's long boom because no Westminster bean-counter questioned it: 'Last year's number looked like this year's number.' But then Murphy drew it to the attention of the chief secretary to the Treasury. In 2009, the British government announced it would remove the VAT rebate – the £200 million subsidy. 'At that point, I was accused of killing babies on the Isle of Man.' Murphy sounds gleeful. 'I've never had a bigger impact on any government, ever, than I did on the Isle of Man.'

To get the islanders' side of the argument, I go back to Allan Bell, Man's former chief minister. Was Britain's scrapping of the VAT rebate fair? 'No,' Bell answers before I've finished the question. 'Not so quickly. There were no warning signs that they were even thinking about changing it.' The £200 million was a third of their income, he tells me. 'It was a savage blow. It was unilateral.' Man's government has resorted to cuts and an unpopular water tax known as the 'toilet tax', but there is still a future financial black hole. The size of the Manx state – with its smooth roads, good schools, shiny buses and extensive welfare state – looks a little socialist. 'We don't skimp on that side of things,' says Bell. The economic miracle is precarious and the former chief minister is not sure where his island will find its next profitable niche in the global economy. They are 'taking a chance' on cryptocurrencies, he admits, with no guarantee of success. 'With competition so fierce, we've got to look at everything.'

I'm not a tax accountant, and while I cannot authoritatively judge whether the Isle of Man is still a tax haven or not, both patriots and critics agree that it has gone straight, or straighter. 'They did tidy up their act,' says Richard Murphy. But Man still has secret companies (nearly 10 per cent of the 36,342 London properties owned by off-shore companies in 2015 were based there) and Murphy argues that its zero corporation tax is designed to undermine Britain's tax revenues. 'A tax haven is basically a place that will sell its legislation to the benefit of people not living there,' he says. 'That's really all they have to sell because the Isle of Man has nothing going for it. It's not got a great climate. It's the Lake District, once removed. Would I bother going there on holiday even if they didn't hate me? Not really.'

Allan Bell sees it differently: 'This old-fashioned concept of a tax haven which is a sand spit with a bunch of palm trees swaying in the wind and a lot of banks couldn't be further from the truth with the Isle of Man.' In 2013, alongside sand spits such as the Cayman Islands, the Isle of Man signed a tax agreement with the OECD. 'We have transparency on tax matters,' says Bell. 'The only thing we have is a competitive tax structure and without that tax structure we would not have the economy we've got today. The more powers a place has to control the economic levers, the more chance of economic survival they have.' The Isle of Man has not simply survived, it has flourished. But its flowering may only be a very specific bloom, offering itself for the picking by the fickle lords, ladies and anonymous shell companies of global capitalism.

I can't find any Manx islanders seriously rebelling against their lords, but there is a subtle subversiveness in the endurance of Man's older traditions. AA Gill's notorious judgement was that the island has 'fallen off the back of the history lorry to lie amnesiac in the road to progress'. Insularity is a classic characteristic of small-islanders and the Isle of Man can appear as it did to Gill but, actually, the meaning of the word 'anachronistic' rather suits it: full of curiosities that belong to another time. The past may be unusually prominent, but so is the future.

On the 'reactionary' ledger is the fact that homosexuality could be punished with a life sentence until 1992, and gay marriage was not permitted until 2016. Judges could hand down corporal punishment (the birch) and the death penalty until the 1990s. This sounds barbaric, but several Manx I meet argue that such laws belonged to 'the haunted wing of the Manx statute book' – relics that were never actually used. If an island judge had handed down a death sentence after the British parliament abolished the death penalty in 1965, the island would have been overruled by Britain; Man is less independent than it likes to believe.

On the forward-thinking ledger, the Isle of Man gave women the vote in 1881, nearly fifty years before Britain. It permitted heterosexual civil partnerships before Britain, it built *Peggy*, the first ever yacht, it was the first place in Europe to launch 3G mobile phones, and it established Europe's first non-smoking jail in 2009. (Crime on the island dropped 14 per cent after the new prison at Jurby opened, or rather closed, its doors. But desperate prisoners still found a way to beat the smoking ban – inspectors caught them rolling lint from tumble-driers and pubic hair in pages from their Gideon Bibles to create home-made cigarettes.)

On my penultimate day touring the island I notice that the stone walls around many homes are painted white, and driveways are sometimes decorated with white stones or pieces of quartz. I wonder why, until I discover that these had a mystical significance in pagan times, continued to be widely used in the Christian era, and are often found under the altar floor in early chapels, set there as good-luck charms. As D.H. Lawrence suggested, the past is more apparent in the present on small islands.

Heading to the south-western tip of Man, I bump into the ghost of Compton Mackenzie again as I peer over the cliffs at the boiling waters of Calf Sound. Beyond a huddle of grey seals lounging in the lethal currents with the casual air of gentlemen in a jacuzzi is the Calf of Man, a hummock of 616 acres filled with migratory seabirds and inhabited by two nature reserve wardens each summer. In 1930, Mackenzie nearly bought this tiny, tantalisingly unreachable island for £6,500. 'It did seem a tremendous bargain,' he wrote in his memoirs. Mackenzie loved Man for its Gaelic culture and 'almost independent status'. Unfortunately, he was £7,800 overdrawn at the time. Man was the island that got away but, in an odd way, it was the making of the man.

On my last day I drive north from Peel, where 'LSD' is scrawled at a bus stop. Over the central fells, the northern town of Ramsey takes its name from the Norse for 'river of wild garlic', but bears an air of despondency deepened by Stalinist-style seaside apartment blocks. Tranquil roads become even quieter as I enter the northern quarter of Man: a flat, fertile patchwork of small meadows, single-storey Manx cottages and yellowing sycamores.

This landscape is beautiful, unusual and, rather poignantly, vacated. There are a couple of afternoon walkers – 'Lovely day. No wind!' – and a pair of choughs at the Point of Ayre, the northerly tip, where currents collide beyond a beach of flat grey stones and bronze kelp. The seaweed feels like smooth wet leather and looks like it has been hammered in a smithy. Inland, huddled farmsteads are scenically derelict. Milking parlours rot. The left headlight of an abandoned Land Rover peeps from an abandoned barn by an overgrown pond. Cockerels strut all over the place: there are feral chickens galore because Man, like many small islands, lacks big mammals, so there are no foxes or badgers to munch them up.

At the village of Ballaugh, the old church has wonky gateposts like thick pencils, and the new church, completed in 1832, has a tower topped with four slender pinnacles shaped like the ears of a hare. I follow a bumpy track bordered by wind-torn beeches to a low cottage the colour of fungi. Inside lives Johnny Crellin.

A bright young Irish civil servant who heads up Man's Department of Agriculture told me he'd seen Johnny a couple of years ago digging a drainage ditch by hand and levelling it by eye. This is not crude labour, but highly skilled: because it is so flat here, a machine is not precise enough to create free-flowing ditches. The work he was doing was also remarkable because Johnny is now ninety-two.

I explain my mission to visit small islands around Britain. 'I feel a bit insulted to be called a small island,' says Johnny with characteristic humour. His clear blue eyes and dark-grey hair are neatly coordinated with his blue slacks and grey jumper.

I want to understand what the island was like before its current incarnation as an agile financial-services animal; and Johnny, who speaks Manx as well as English in Man's curiously unplaceable accent, shows how local traditions live on in the globalised era of Bitcoin. The Manx were much more concerned with folklore in Johnny's youth. He tells me about the islanders' veneration of hares. A few years after the war, his wife went to a fish shop and bought a hare. Later, she met an old Manxwoman. When Johnny's wife showed her the hare, she said, 'You'd never catch *me* eating my own grandmother.'

'All that was present, and it's still here – the old *haf* names for animals,' he says. *Haf* is Old Norse for 'ocean'. Sea-going people are often superstitious, and Manx seafarers didn't want to mention animals by their conventional names while at sea. So a hare was 'the fellow with long ears' and rats were 'long tails' or 'ringeys'. Johnny tells me of neighbours who swore they'd been accosted by 'the little people'. Man's willingness to acknowledge the possibility of fairies endures: a young islander tells me a story about a touring rugby team visiting the 'fairy bridge', where tourists must hail the fairies as they pass. The only rugby player who refused the ritual succumbed to terrible injuries in his next match.

Johnny grew up on these northern flatlands of Man. When he was young, he and his three younger brothers would cycle past Ellen Brew's house. 'She had second sight – she'd give you one of Wilfie's sixpences and tell you how the next few years of your life were going to be fulfilled. We were petrified.' Once they cycled past and the chain came off his brother Geoffrey's bike. 'It's Ellen,' he said, and refused to go that way for years. On another occasion, Ellen was holding a baby duckling when they cycled past; the next time, she had a baby chick. The boys thought she had transformed it and stopped visiting her. When they whizzed by on their bikes, she would shout, 'You boys, you're getting proud now.'

At school, Johnny was 'more or less tutored in the armed forces rather than in Shakespeare and Milton'. Manxmen made good soldiers and sailors. When I visit in 2015 and 2016, an unusual number of Second World War veterans still live on the island. Another I meet, Hector Duff, is ninety-six and driving all over, giving talks to schools about his years of service. 'I'm often asked who are the best soldiers and I say British, because I'm patriotic,' says Duff. 'Our people here are very reluctant to praise or thank them. I'm very, very proud of being a Manxman. You can be both: Manxman first, British second.'

Johnny spent the war at sea, escorting Atlantic convoys. 'Any sailor who came home to Britain with a pair of nylons could get what he wanted – it was an incredible state of affairs,' he laughs. After the war, he was keen to come home but walked out of the barracks in a cheap suit and with no job. He became an 'Efficient Deckhand' with the New Zealand Shipping Company. When he visited Australia, local girls asked him to settle there. He adopts an excellent Australian drawl: '"Why don't you become an Australian?" They found it odd that I didn't do that.' Instead, he attended agriculture college in Glasgow, identified some vacant land on Man's northern plains and ran a suckler herd. 'And that was it. For the first time in my life, I couldn't move.' He was happy. 'I was very tied down with the culture of the island. I could speak the language. I felt a Manxman.'

Violet came to the north of the island to nurse one of Johnny's brother's children, and they started courting. When Johnny's motor-bike broke down in a ford, she gamely waded out to dry land. Johnny was impressed. 'She didn't mind things like that. She was the sort of person that I thought, well, I could settle up with her. She was probably on the elderly side for getting married,' Johnny laughs again, 'but we got on very well. I married her.' They moved into their current house. Vi recently went into a home and has now passed away. Her yellow fleece jacket is drying on Johnny's old-fashioned wooden rack above the Aga. Johnny says he's washing her things, bit by bit, to take to a charity shop. It reminds me of Robinson Crusoe, who suppresses any emotion for his drowned shipmates, until he finds three hats, one cap and 'two shoes that were not fellows'. It is hard to let go of the clothes of our loved ones.

Johnny shows me his vegetable patch. It is divided into four sections, rotated, and surrounded by green grass to encourage worms and centipedes to enter the soil. He has another tip. 'All the household urine goes into the compost heap. That's very important. That's where mine goes, and Vi's when she was here.'

Johnny is self-sufficient in vegetables, the whole year round. But modern, financial Isle of Man, in the style of its much larger neighbour Britain, can no longer feed itself. Agriculture represents only one per cent of Man's economy. 'It's terrible,' says Johnny. He worries about all our futures: globalised industrial farming is 'using the soil up', depleting it of humus and denying us fresh, nutritious food too. 'I got a bag of prawns the other day. It had a picture of a trawler on it, a nice sea-going name. When I looked at the small print, it's farmed in India. You simply don't know what you are buying. People haven't the knowledge or skill now to have a vegetable garden.'

Is the Isle of Man a sustainable independent country?

'The question is now whether it is an independent country at all. We could quite easily call it West Lancashire although we have our own parliament and the three legs of Man and all the rest of it. It has a certain distinction.' And language. What's Manx for 'goodbye'? I ask through my car window. '*Bannaghty ort,* blessings on you,' says Johnny, grinning. As I turn down his avenue of gnarled beeches, he shouts: 'But it doesn't make you a bishop.'

Different villages are always closer to each other than I expect on Man, and the past feels closer too. I stop in the southerly village of Cregneash, with its traditional Manx cottages, thatch tied down against the wind. It was one of the last strongholds of Manx country life, and until the early twentieth century villagers stubbornly celebrated 'Old Christmas' on 5 January despite Britain having adopted the Gregorian calendar in 1752.

D.H. Lawrence acknowledged the persistence of the past on small islands in 'The Man Who Loved Islands', but it was Adam Nicolson who really developed this idea in *Sea Room,* his superb account of the entire human history of the Shiants, a tiny trio of Hebridean islands that his father purchased from a farmer who had bought them from Compton Mackenzie. 'It is a place in which many different times coexist, flowing at different speeds, enshrining different worlds,' writes Nicolson. He finds the deep past more nakedly present than in any other place: 'Little here is overlaid, as it is elsewhere, with the thick mulch of recent events.'

This does not make small islands living museums, replete with relics left behind by the faster-moving mainstream. Historians of Britain have typically drawn a line from Exeter to the Tees, according to R.H. Kinvig, the author of a history of the Isle of Man. South of this line is lowland, continental and of the future; the north-west is upland, Celtic and of the past.

But Kinvig argues that the Western Atlantic belt, exemplified by Man, has been not just a backward 'preserving' zone but an advanced 'receiving' zone at many moments in history. Neolithic Orkney was a major civilisation. The era of the Celtic saints, from the fourth to the eighth centuries AD, looks rather more civilised than the society promulgated by southern Anglo-Saxon heathens. Now, in the twenty-first century, I wonder if the Isle of Man is a tiny turbocharged Republic of Ireland, embracing a type of unfettered capitalism so as to race ahead of big and more intricately regulated nations. This brings futuristic elements to modern Man, but it would not be possible without the past, and the island's robust conviction that it deserves more independence than the average British isle.

My last encounter with the disorienting coexistence of ancient and modern on the Isle of Man comes in late afternoon, when I take a short walk through the low wet woodland of Ballaugh Curragh. Before it grew wild, it had been pasture; before it had been tamed by drainage ditches, it had been a lake. A vivid green path leads through the stunted silver willows, barely three metres high. Ditches on either side are filled with prehistoric horsetails. Ash and holly mark former field boundaries. The fells are curvaceously pretty to the south, patched in bracken the colour of wet rust. Into this empty echo chamber pours just one sound: the teatime complaining of cows being brought back to a distant yard.

As I pause to admire the ink-dipped ears of a hare in a surviving hay meadow, I spot the bulky haunches of a much larger grey animal beyond, its head bent in benediction to the lush sward. It turns to regard me, stiffly raising itself on two legs like a dinky bear, silvered on its front. I freeze, and eventually this bizarre beast slackens its body and continues to graze. It is a red-necked wallaby. In recent decades, these animals have escaped a wildlife park on the island, twice, and in a land without deer have found plenty to graze. One hundred now hop wild. In the willow woods, I startle another and it thumps slowly away, tail thudding on the ground as if in exasperation.

Pillowy clouds gather over the hills and cold air sinks around me, bringing the sickly-sweet scent of the last flowers of ivy. The clouds turn orange and then soften to pink. A posse of long-tailed tits move through the trees, bound together like fairy lights. I feel a rush of affection for the defiant inhabitants of what may be the ultimate small-island nation.

2

The Tomb of the Eagles

Mainland, Orkney, 202 square miles; and South Ronaldsay,
Orkney, 19 square miles, population 19,000

'It set you yearning, with a wild yearning; perhaps for the past,
to be far back in the mysterious past of the island,
when the blood had a different throb'
'The Man Who Loved Islands'

In a grey chalet-bungalow at the end of a long straight road that rolls up and down with the land, a middle-aged woman holds up a skull. It is fine and round and bronze in colour. Teeth still hang from the jaw. 'Is this a cast or real?' Kathleen MacLeod asks the five trippers gathered before a glass-fronted cabinet in the front room. 'Very, very real.' She answers her own question softly and as quickly as the wind. 'These are very special people. Part of the family. I've grown up with them. When I was little, I thought everybody had skeletons under the stairs. This one we call Jock Tamson, after an old Scottish saying, "We are all Jock Tamson's bairns."'

The Tamson skull belonged to a young Neolithic man, an inhabitant of the Stone Age, but Kathleen, who wears a Tomb of the Eagles polo shirt and moves between gravity and levity so seamlessly it is hard to tell which is which, prefers to say he lived here two hundred generations ago, which doesn't seem so long. She knows he died young because his wisdom teeth have yet to appear. One day, about five thousand years ago, his skull was placed in a stone tomb overlooking the lonely eastern cliffs of South Ronaldsay. Alongside Jock Tamson in this long-forgotten chamber were eighty-four other people, plus select bones from snipe, shag, crow, curlew, kestrel, goshawk, woodcock, puffin, raven, red grouse, mallard, little auk, eider duck, herring gull, black-backed gull, short-eared owl and oystercatcher. There was also one dog skull, deer antlers and, most significantly, the remains of fourteen sea eagles. Seventy eagle talons were also placed alongside the bones of different people: one man had five talons, another seven, another fifteen.

What role did sea eagles play on this Neolithic island? What bond did humans form with other species five thousand years ago? Was it as exploitative as ours? I itch to crawl into this dark tomb, into the past. I hope this place of death might help me understand alternative ways in which humans and wild animals have lived together.

Kathleen returns Jock Tamson to the cabinet with some reverence and brings out other artefacts, which we can hold: a fine stone hammer head with a perfect hole drilled through it, an eagle's talon, beads, and a smooth, heavy butcher's club, perfectly weighted for a right-hander. I put my fingernail into the curved mark on decorative pottery made by a Neolithic nail. 'These people weren't going hungry,' says Kathleen. 'They had time to make jewels.' She passes over half a chunky black ring, made from high-quality coal, and then triumphantly brings out the other half. 'Dad found half a ring in 1976,' she says. 'He found the second half ten years later. That's an archaeologist's dream – to find a second half.'

After eight hundred years of use, the Tomb of the Eagles was filled with rubble and then forgotten for four thousand years, lightly buried under the flowery sward at the south-eastern tip of the archipelago of Orkney. Kathleen's dad, Ronnie Simison, was born in 1921, a few years after fifty-two ships from the German fleet were scuttled in the waters of Scapa Flow. Ronnie was unusually inquisitive. If he came across a dead animal on the family croft, he would bury it, then excavate it months later to examine the bones. He'd spend hours studying bluebottles, or spiders. 'He watched everything – the plants, the insects, the birds, the waves and how they changed the landscape,' says Kathleen. 'If there'd been a bad storm he would go out and know the stones that the sea had upturned.' In 1958, requiring a fence for his cattle, Ronnie wandered out for a bit of slate. You see these slender stones around Orkney, sometimes foraged from ancient monuments, making cheap corner-posts for a farmer. Near the cliffs, where sandstone is pushed into a slanting formation, he spotted several horizontal stones, going against the grain. He pulled up the turf around them and found a beautiful cache of possibly ceremonial tools. A few days later he returned, dug a little, and discovered a black hole. It was dark. He fished a cigarette lighter from his pocket and flicked it on. Two dozen skulls grinned back. What a thrill. He must have been excited. 'I don't think you see Orcadian farmers excited,' says Kathleen, drily. 'Even when things are going well.'

Word spread. Kathleen and her sister, Freda Norquay, who are now the guardians of the Tomb of the Eagles and run it as a tourist attraction, remember the doctor and policeman coming over the hill to take a peek. Carefully, Ronnie began digging at the tomb. The home he shared with his wife, Morgan, gradually acquired shelves of Stone Age treasures.

During breakfast at my B&B up the road, a fellow guest who'd grown up on South Ronaldsay remembers playing with Kathleen and Freda's younger sister. 'Ronnie Simison had all these skulls on top of a cabinet in their living room and it used to freak me out,' she says. But Ronnie also received professional assistance. A professor of archaeology visited the tomb, but was more interested in excavating the Burnt Mound, a Bronze Age tumescence on Ronnie's land. An archaeologist, John Hedges, took charge of this excavation and then began examining the artefacts that Ronnie had dug up from the tomb, which was formally called Isbister Chambered Cairn. Everyone preferred 'the Tomb of the Eagles'.

I first heard of the Tomb of the Eagles while watching a sea eagle on the Hebridean island of Mull. *Iolaire sùil na grèine*, 'the eagle with the sunlit eye', is the most awe-inspiring bird I've ever seen, meat cleaver for a beak, spanned wings like a plank of scaffolding. The last British sea eagle was a small-islander, an albino female who built a raggedy nest on Shetland cliffs at the turn of the twentieth century. She paired with a male but he disappeared in 1908. As white as a gull in flight, she lived in spinsterdom for ten years before vanishing. Island rumour said she was shot.

Repentant conservationists began making amends in the 1970s and, over a decade, eighty-two young eagles were airlifted from Norway to the island of Rum. Never biddable creatures, the eagles flew south to Mull instead, and in 1985 successfully fledged chicks there for the first time. Despite incurring the hostility of many crofters, who blamed the eagles for taking lambs, the birds thrived, as did Mull, whose cash registers ring to sea eagle tourism. This big predator is the closest beast to the wolf in Britain. Thirty years on from the first British-born chicks, the hundredth pair of Scottish sea eagles returned to build a nest on Orkney. This couple didn't fledge any chicks, and their nest failed again in 2016, but it was fitting that the eagles had recolonised their ancestral land, a few wingbeats from the Tomb of the Eagles.

I knew I was unlikely to spot any eagles during my visit to Orkney, but I had still scanned the skies hopefully when we set sail from the scruffy jetty at Gills Bay, where the mainland slumps to unspectacular defeat before the treacherous Pentland Firth. 'Time of passage will be approximately one hour,' boomed the tannoy on the bulky catamaran, which had tears of rust weeping down its red-and-white hull. The ferry heaved itself surprisingly nimbly into a cold blue sea ripped with white crests. The waters that sloosh around the northern end of Britain are some of the fastest tidal currents in the world. At times, disconcerting circles of surface water as smooth as oil appeared, looking as if they might suck seafarers down.

Past a salmon-coloured container ship I got my first glimpse of the low, grey cliffs of Orkney, and above them the skeletal gun emplacements, slender concrete buildings, one, two, three storeys high, dotted around every entrance to Scapa Flow. They remind us that this northern edge was at the centre of events in both First and Second World Wars.

The breeze carries a strong whiff of cowpat to greet us before we dock at St Margaret's of Hope on South Ronaldsay, a peaceful town of swallows and big stone houses with stepped gables from the Victorian fishing boom. Slate tiles are smudged with lichen the colour of sunflowers. Beyond is an open, treeless, hedgeless, fertile and gently undulating terrain of large rectangular pastures fenced with barbed wire. Parallel lines of telephone wires and roads cross the country. Every half-mile or so stands a low grey farmhouse with low grey barns over which a small wind turbine whizzes.

South Ronaldsay is austere, even in summer, but when I reach the Tomb of the Eagles and park by the chalet-bungalow-turned-museum that had once been home to Kathleen and Freda's brother, I see verges rippled with clover, buttercups, meadowsweet, purple vetch and pink ragged robin. The wind smells of nectar.

Now, once again, I find myself looking towards the skies. Kathleen and Freda say they've had one credible sea eagle sighting above the tomb, but rather more *in*credible ones. Visitors mistake the great skua, a big, piratical brown gull also known as a bonxie, for a sea eagle. Another pair of eagles reported by one woman turned out to be microlights – a plausible misapprehension given that these birds are so huge. I ask Kathleen and Freda if they will welcome the eagles back, and I'm surprised that Kathleen is cautious. 'It's fine as long as they don't get a taste for sheep. I can understand people's feelings if they lose some lambs.' Then there's a glint in her eye. 'Eagles would be an added attraction.'

I pay my £7.50 in the small hallway of the chalet-museum, squeeze down a corridor and join a handful of mostly German tourists for a personal tour of the Mesolithic, Neolithic and Bronze Age rooms and their artefacts given by Kathleen, Freda and their helpers. It's far more intimate than any conventional museum and I love Kathleen and Freda's interest in visitors' reactions. 'A whole lot of clever people come and tell us things,' says Kathleen. 'We've had so many experts and they all say different things and they all think they are right,' adds Freda. As if on cue, Betty, a student helper, rushes up to tell them a holidaying osteologist has just diagnosed a skull called Old Granny as having a 'rodent ulcer', a tumour of the bone, often caused by osteomyelitis, an infection usually caused by a bacterium which enters the bone via a cut and eats it away. Granny has a conspicuous hole in her palate but was probably saved by the sea air, which cauterised the wound and stopped the tumour spreading.

The tomb is on the cliffs, half a mile from the chalet-museum, and is entered via a very low tunnel. Kathleen asks me if I do a lot of crawling. I'm not sure what to say. Usually, she says, men answer: 'Just enough to get by.' She reassures me that if I don't fancy crawling into the tomb, they provide a trolley called the Pensioners' Skateboard.

I take the long straight track east, through fields where a curlew is calling in extravagant warbles, its magnificent cutlass rising above the long grass. By a damp hollow stands a peppermint-coloured former German ambulance turned camper van that came to rest in this field. It was formerly headquarters for Ronnie, while he interpreted the Burnt Mound. This site of low stones reveals a Bronze Age heating system which some imagine was a kind of Neolithic sauna. Ronnie loved sitting here and discussing his finds with visitors, until he 'joined the ancestors', as Kathleen and Freda put it, in 2012. By one of South Ronaldsay's many clefts in its cliffs, known as 'geos', is a standing stone three metres high, in memory of Ronnie and Morgan.

I walk on through the wind, the gurgle of a fulmar echoing from the rocks. The tomb is set into the cliff beneath a head of thick hair-like turf. In front of a rectangular stone entrance a metre high rests the Pensioners' Skateboard, a square trolley that runs on tracks of lino into the gloom. A young boy slides in with effortless economy, pulling himself on a rope attached to the entrance ceiling; older visitors heave themselves onto the skateboard with a grunt and a shuffle.

We trundle along for three metres or so, then the tomb opens into a space about half the size of a London Underground carriage. Sea and wind are snuffed out by a cool, quiet twilight. Orkney Islands Council re-roofed the tomb with concrete for protection, and its drystone walls are immaculate. Three skylights cast a dim illumination. At each end are altar-like structures made with flat stones. There are also three womb-like cells off the central passageway, into which I can just about squeeze. It is soothing to curl up inside.

Was the sea eagle a special totem for Neolithic islanders? In some mythology, birds mediate between people and gods, carrying the souls of the dead into a spirit realm. Sea eagles may have played a direct role in excarnation. 'I don't like that word very much,' says Kathleen, 'I prefer sky burial.' A body would be placed above the cliffside tomb, its bones picked clean by the eagles, incorrigible scavengers. Inside the tomb, bones are buried, separated, grouped together and tidied. 'Spring cleaning began at least five thousand years ago,' says Kathleen.

I'm puzzled by the chamber's lack of symmetry – two cells on the landward side of the tomb and just one on the seaward side – but when I return to chat further with Kathleen and Freda in their kitchen-cum-office I bump into Babette Barthelmess, who has a different perspective on this lopsided structure. Babette is a German geneticist turned artist who made it her mission to understand more about the ancient uses of the tomb by discovering whether sunbeams ever pierce its velvety blackness. Her abstract paintings, inspired by the Isbister Chambered Cairn, hang on the museum walls, and she is a gale of energy and ideas. 'She's as high as a kite, she's floating,' say Freda and Kathleen, laughing, as Babette immediately thrusts a copy of her book into my hands and signs it, writing the nicest thing anyone has put into words about me for a long time.

Babette settled on a neighbouring farm in the 1970s, and when Ronnie began excavating the tomb she felt it was 'a disturbance'. It took her a while to accept Ronnie's dig. Then, when the chamber was still open to the elements, she looked down on it and saw the shape formed by the cell that faced the sea. 'I just stared and stared, time and again. The shape! I kept thinking of an apple core where the pips sit so neatly, perfect little homes. It was very moving, that shape, the cosiness of this little nest.' She was inspired, and the cell's outline became a recurring motif in her art.

Babette challenges my puzzlement over the tomb's asymmetry. 'These were people who didn't oblige our sense of beauty.' The Neolithic islanders who built the tomb did have an awareness of symmetry and followed a pattern, she says, but they allowed for variations as well. She questions whether we are flexible enough today to think like they did; she worries that contemporary society is far too rigid, in all sorts of ways. 'As a geneticist, I know that allowing for variants allows for mutation so things can evolve. If you get too stuck in a pattern, you've had it – evolution stops.'

The tomb 'is a place that reminds me how deeply rooted in the past every present moment of Orkney life is', writes Babette in her book *A Celebration of Sunrise at the Tomb of the Eagles*. Discovering whether the rising sun ever penetrates the chamber's low entrance is not easy, given Orkney's variable weather, but Babette dedicated a lot of early mornings to finding out. At 5.12 a.m. one 2nd of May, she finally saw the sun shining into the passage. It is calculated that the rising sun aligns with the entrance most precisely on 26 April and 17 August. On the August alignment, Babette found a crowd of seals snorting and singing on the rocks below this enchanted place.

A large number of deliberately broken pots were excavated by Ronnie from the sunlit spot inside the tomb. Were sun ceremonies once held here? They are today. On the tomb's northern altar I found scattered some sea pinks the colour of the sky at sunrise. I wonder about the spiritual meaning of this tomb's location on the eastern periphery of a small island on the edge of an archipelago, but the archaeologist John Hedges reveals a more prosaic reason for its situation. Chambered tombs are mostly found on Orkney's North Sea and Atlantic seaboards. During a Neolithic period of 'population stress', as early farming communities grew quickly, the tombs were as much 'territorial markers' as places of worship, argues Hedges in his *Tomb of the Eagles: Death and Life in a Stone Age Tribe*. Containing the remains of a community's ancestors, these magnificent buildings spoke of ownership in this world as well as of a journey to the next.

Contemporary fascination with the tomb seems focused on its spiritual rather than its more earthly qualities. I read a breathless account of a visit by a group of spiritualists published online which mentions that Kathleen is now the tomb's spiritual guardian. It is, says Kathleen, 'a very busy place'. She means in terms of the spiritual presence perceived by visitors. Worshippers bring drums and crystals and metal bowls. One sunrise, she and Freda were invited to a ceremony. The spiritualists carried a crystal bowl coated with gold into the tomb, and the rising sun refracted light like rainbows onto the tomb's walls. 'It was a beautiful, beautiful morning,' says Kathleen.

She and Freda are as interested in the spiritualists' interpretations as the archaeologists'. One psychic told them that Tamson was angry about a natural disaster that befell his people. Another said that Old Granny was a very feisty little lady. 'Someone was drumming out at the tomb and Granny got very annoyed because she wasn't drumming fast enough,' says Kathleen. One visitor suggested to the sisters that the Neolithic ancestors wanted them to take their museum artefacts into the sunshine once a year, so they followed that advice. They are free with the tomb, allowing people to conduct ceremonies. 'We've only had one person here who had a bad experience, and I think she was dabbling in something dark,' says Kathleen. 'She felt her finger-nails were being pulled out – I didn't have a good feeling about that person.'

I am struck by Kathleen and Freda's verve as tour guides, and also by their listening ears, their openness to visitors both ancient and modern. One person they attend to particularly closely is their mother, who died some years before they converted their brother's old place into the museum. They run it as she would have wanted: personal, hands-on tours for their 12,000 annual visitors, who thankfully don't all arrive by coach at the same time. 'This would've been mum's dream,' says Freda of their museum. Mum is not so far away, and they are guided by her. 'She keeps us right,' adds Freda. 'She's in the corner of the Tomb Room with her finger like this.' She wags it.

On a small island, writes D.H. Lawrence in 'The Man Who Loved Islands', 'the past is vastly alive, and the future is not separated off'. On the Isle of Man, the persistence of old beliefs is called superstition and marketed to visitors via stories about fairy bridges. But if historical artefacts can survive unusually well preserved, as on Orkney, then it seems plausible that ancient feelings, presences – or as rationalists would have it, ghost stories – could endure more strongly on small islands as well. When I first read Lawrence's story, I was unconvinced by Mr Cathcart's troubles with ghosts. Our island-loving hero begins to feel afraid of his first island. In winter he detects a resentful spirit, 'like a wet dog coiled in gloom'. At night, he feels exposed and his 'slippery, naked dark soul' finds itself in a timeless world, surrounded by the souls of the dead. What at first sounds like a bizarre fiction to mock Cathcart, or Compton, is actually based on real life.

D.H. Lawrence and Compton Mackenzie became friends shortly before the First World War. Monty was drawn towards the 'elfish' way Lawrence made the tea and swept the floor and 'delighted by Lawrence's habit of giving himself up to emotion', according to Monty's

biographer Andro Linklater. Years afterwards, Monty would imper-
sonate Lawrence's high-pitched voice forbidding his German wife
Frieda to mention the war. For his part Lawrence liked Monty, but
privately thought his acclaimed novel *Sinister Street* a 'frippery'. The
friends were separated by the Great War when Lawrence retreated to
the village of Zennor in Cornwall, where he and Frieda, a cousin of
the German fighter pilot the Red Baron, were wrongly suspected of
signalling to German U-boats. Meanwhile, Monty lived with Faith
in Capri, before becoming head of Britain's counter-espionage in
Athens and possibly the least discreet spy ever. He called himself 'Z'
and drove around in an open-topped Sunbeam, in a white suit and
white felt hat and with a bodyguard who wore a matching white kilt.
Later, he moved his HQ to the Greek island of Syra, from where on
a clear day he could admire ten other islands in the 'dark and flashing
blue Aegean'. Bizarrely for a man who later detested bureaucracy,
Monty can be credited with the invention of the travel visa, which he
helped devise in 1915 as a way of gathering information on spies and
agitators moving between Greece and Egypt. The following year, this
innovation was approved by the Foreign Office for use in embassies
all over the world.

After the war, Lawrence's literary reputation grew as Monty's diminished. Postwar critics sneered at Compton Mackenzie's sentimen-
tality. '[His] candle is out,' declared one. 'You get no sense from him
that he feels his work has gone to pieces,' noted his former admirer F.
Scott Fitzgerald. 'I think he's just tired. The war wrecked him as it did
Wells and many of that generation.'

The 1920s may be more often remembered for the Bloomsbury
set, but there was also a significant exodus of writers escaping Britain:
Lawrence Durrell to Corfu, Robert Graves to Majorca, Katherine
Mansfield to the Riviera, Aldous Huxley to California. Monty was
desperate to flee London literary bitching and found in Lawrence a
willing accomplice in this escapist fantasy. Monty returned to Capri

to live with Faith, and in 1920 D.H. Lawrence and Frieda came to stay. The writers talked about sex, read *Ulysses* – Monty claimed that Lawrence pronounced it 'more disgusting than Casanova' – and dreamed, together, of making a voyage to the South Seas. Their dreams became serious. They placed an advert in *The Times* for a secretary with a spirit of adventure. Monty decided they should buy a boat and recolonise the Kermadec Islands, 400 miles north of New Zealand. He wrote to the New Zealand High Commissioner about it. Next, he tried to persuade one of England's new cinematic companies to fund him and a boatful of actors to sail to the South Pacific to make a film of *Treasure Island*. (It is just as well he failed, for Pacific cinematography and island-lovers make for a troubling combination: after Marlon Brando filmed *Mutiny on the Bounty* in French Polynesia, he bought a coral atoll, Tetiaroa near Tahiti, which was his 'Zen heaven' until his son Christian killed one of the native islanders.)

While Lawrence lost interest in Monty's schemes and skipped to another island, Sicily, Monty's craving for a Pacific retreat was astutely redirected by his publisher, Martin Secker, to something more proximate to Western civilisation. Secker alerted Monty to a newspaper advert for a sixty-six-year lease on the Channel Isles of Herm and Jethou. Enchanted by the chance to actually possess two islands, Monty applied to the Treasury without even inspecting them and in August 1920 was promptly made tenant of the Crown, paying £1,000 for the lease of both islands. Hearing of Monty's impulsive decision, Lawrence wrote from Italy: 'What is this I hear about the Channel Isles? The Lord of the Isles. I shall write a skit on you one day.'

Compton Mackenzie had found his first proper island home, and during that autumn an envious-sounding Lawrence bombarded him with questions about it. 'Are you going to farm Herm?' he asked on 7 October. 'Who is going to farm it? How many houses? Are you letting or having a farm bailiff? News!' he demanded two weeks later.

Monty, the thirty-seven-year-old master of Herm (two years older than his fictional counterpart Mr Cathcart, who Lawrence described as a blue-eyed 'young Hermes' – surely a mischievous nod to Monty's island), began his first and last attempt at island farming in 1921. It was not simply an escape from the London critics, thought Faith, but a chance to regain his wartime importance and 'organise something out of nothing'. This time, instead of commandeering spies it was pedigree cattle, shire horses, and making Herm 'a prosperous community of contented people'. Her words are precisely echoed in D.H. Lawrence's fiction, where the man who loved islands is 'a delicate, sensitive, handsome Master, who wanted everything perfect and everybody happy'.

The summer of 1921 got off to a glorious start. Monty read forty-three books about farming and played at Lord of the Isles. His dependants included a farmer, alongside a carpenter, an engineer, a valet and two secretaries, a Great Dane called Hamlet, and a parson who helpfully cut more bracken than any individual had ever cut before. Monty and Faith mingled with their landlords, the King and Queen, when they visited Guernsey. Later, Hamlet killed a duck and spent the rest of the day with it tied around his neck in punishment, recorded Faith. 'He also bit a visitor, but not seriously.'

There was such a splendid heatwave that Monty's crops were ruined by drought. Trippers ran wild, and Hamlet had to be permanently silenced with a shotgun after he tried to savage another visitor. Monty was also haemorrhaging cash. A new motorboat to service Herm, *Aphrodite*, cost £2,000. Two shire mares, £100 each. Several horses fought, and had to be shot. The valet was a drunk, the housekeeper pocketed tips left for the maids, and female guests squabbled over Monty. Islands may be treasured by artists for awarding them the gift of detachment, but Monty's island-love was to the detriment of his art. He kept Herm afloat by churning out two potboilers each year, managing his tiny kingdom by day and writing in twelve-hour night shifts to music from the gramophone. (One of his two secretaries stayed up all night changing his records.) After farming failed, he decided to turn Herm into a tourist attraction and in 1922 set about converting the grand Manor House into a pub he named the Mermaid Tavern. A landlady, a cook and a parlour-maid were employed. But the islanders were turning against their idealistic, cash-strapped lord. And so, it seemed, was the island.

The Compton Mackenzies became convinced they were being plagued by malevolent spirits. Faith recorded that Herm was once home to pagan sacrifices and then a place of penance for unruly Norman monks. When in the sixteenth century a slaughter of Catholics took place on the island, pirates caught off Guernsey were hanged conspicuously on Herm and Jethou as a deterrent. During the First World War sentries patrolled in pairs because of the ghosts, said Faith. 'It was an island full of tricks.' She and Monty were badly spooked one evening walking across the common, where island chieftains were buried, and had to hurry home. 'There is not much doubt that Herm was one of those islands that hate to be visited,' concluded Faith.

Monty's island sanctuary was a chimera and, as his infatuation faded, he wished he'd joined Lawrence, who had reached the South Seas, alone, in 1922. But Lawrence was also falling out of love with islands. He sent Monty a series of postcards. The Cook Islands were 'very lovely'. Tahiti, less so. 'If you are thinking of coming here don't. The people are brown and soft. DHL.' To another friend he wrote: 'These are supposed to be the earthly paradises: these South Sea Isles. You can have 'em.'

Perhaps Lawrence and Mackenzie should have looked north to realise their vision of liberation through small-island life. Orkney feels like the land's last laugh, broken free, slipped off north. There is a lightness about this rolling country, surrendering to the water and then rising again. I feel untethered as I drive along empty roads, crossing the wind-buffeted causeways that link South Ronaldsay via Burray, Glimps Holm and Lamb Holm to Mainland, the prosaically named principal island of Orkney. One causeway is backed by such a large dune system that I don't immediately realise it is a human creation, the Churchill Barriers. In the first year of the Second World War, Churchill reluctantly cut loose the Channel Islands – including Monty's former homes – but the prime minister was not about to countenance the loss of more strategically important fragments of the archipelago. His barriers were built by Italian PoWs during the war to block Scapa Flow's eastern approaches to German U-boats.

As I drive across the archipelago I scan the verges for a glimpse of a cute, blunt-nosed rodent with a short tail. Near the turning for Windwick, a herring gull picks at the flesh of a roadkill oystercatcher but there's no trace of any voles, dead or alive. 'Tomb of the Voles' may not possess the same romantic cadence as Tomb of the Eagles, but the Orkney vole's presence and participation in Neolithic society is a mystery more perplexing than the eagles'.

Small islands are vivid laboratories for the study of evolution, extinction and the relationship between species. The island-hopping of Charles Darwin in the Galapagos and Alfred Russel Wallace in the Malay Archipelago gave rise to the theory of evolution. When he journeyed to the Galapagos, Darwin wondered why each island had its own versions of things – giant tortoises with saddle- or dome-shaped shells, different kinds of mockingbird, and finches, famously, with differently shaped beaks; and distinct ecological niches. The creatures of the Galapagos may have appeared strange, but their weirdness was utterly typical of island life. The strangeness of animals on small British isles – supersized St Kildan wrens, shrinking Soay sheep, stumpy-tailed Manx cats – is trumped by glamorous oddities around the globe. Madagascar has the smallest chameleon on the planet; Komodo has its dragon; Tasmania its devils. Until recently, St Helena had a three-inch-long earwig.

Insularity is not simply a characteristic of human life on islands; these island creatures are strange because they are isolated, develop their own quirks and evolve into unique species. Small islands are great inventors of species – speciation. The Orkney vole was wrongly declared a new species in 1904, causing the world's first and only vole tourist boom as naturalists trekked north to see it. The fact that chromosomal genetic studies in the 1950s established that the Orkney vole was only a subspecies of the common vole is no less thrillingly strange because the common vole does not exist on the British mainland. Its absence from Britain's fossil record suggests it never did. The nearest vole colonies to Orkney are found in continental Europe. This small-island rodent poses two big questions: where did it come from and when did it get here?

The fossil record shows that the Orkney vole was the only rodent on the islands in Neolithic times. Like many small residents of small islands, it has grown larger during its comfortable confinement and is 50 per cent bigger than the continental common vole. Island species may rapidly become different, but they become different in similar ways: birds incline towards flightlessness while other islanders embrace gigantism or dwarfism. In a curious evolutionary symmetry, small rodents tend to become bigger, while large mammals become smaller. Prehistoric elephants marooned on Mediterranean islands lost 98 per cent of their body mass during their slow transformation into one-metre-high pygmy elephants. There's a theory that every mammal is seeking to evolve into a body of about one kilogram, said to be the most efficient size if freed from pressures such as predation or competition.

The Orkney vole has thrived on rough grassland in a land unstalked by mammalian predators such as rats or foxes. Despite declining because of more intensive farming, the island population was still estimated to number in seven figures by the end of the twentieth century. There was a vole boom in 2011, after an unusual blanket of snow in successive cold winters protected them from aerial predation. Orkney still has good populations of short-eared owls and hen harriers, which feast on them.

The question of the Orkney vole's origin has long puzzled scientists. And answering the Where? question also leads to a How? and then a Why? Closer to Bergen than London, Orkney is strongly Norse-influenced – indeed, the vole was assumed to be a Viking until radiocarbon-dating proved that vole bones in sites such as the Tomb of the Eagles were up to 5,500 years old. In the 1970s, the characteristics of vole skulls led scientists to conclude, surprisingly, that its closest relatives came from the Balkans. This was challenged by 1980s research, which established that the voles hailed from Spain and France, fitting the prevalent idea that Neolithic civilisation spread to Orkney up the west coast. But the latest DNA studies found the closest match to Orkney's voles among the vole populations of the Low Countries, around Bruges. The Orkney vole is Belgian.

To learn more about the how and the why, I drive to Kirkwall airport to catch up with Julian Branscombe, an ecologist who co-wrote a fascinating paper on the Orkney vole. Julian is about to take a tiny plane called the *Islander* back to his home on Papa Westray. (The fact about Orkney repeated by every visitor is that the two-minute flight from the small island of Westray to the smaller island of Papa Westray is the shortest scheduled flight in the world. A second fact, I come to realise, is that airports are important social hubs on small islands.) Julian first pops to the inter-island flight desk, which is staffed by a man from the Czech Republic. The sign reads: Czech In. And if he takes a break: Czech Out.

No land bridge has linked Orkney to mainland Scotland since the last ice age, so the Orkney vole must have come by sea. Julian sketches out one theory, which suggests it could have arrived naturally, on rafts of vegetation swept down European rivers that were much bigger and closer to Orkney eight thousand years ago. Usually, island subspecies have a limited genetic diversity but the latest DNA studies show that Orkney voles have an unusually large one. This makes a chancy natural colonisation by river raft unlikely: there must have been a massive single influx of voles, or lots of voles arriving from many different places.

'My collaborator, the archaeologist Keith Dobney, thinks they may have been brought here accidentally,' says Julian. He's not convinced. 'I think it was deliberate.'

Humans are the usual vector for introducing pestilent rodents to small islands. But voles are less likely candidates for such accidental landings because they don't set up home in grain stores like rats or mice. If Orkney voles arrived by boat as stowaways, large numbers must have hidden inside bundles of freshly cut animal feed, which Neolithic farmers transported direct from the Low Countries. Most early traders worked their way up the east coast, stopping at ports – Hull, Edinburgh, Inverness – on their journey. Why, then, were there not common voles in mainland Britain? Is it possible there were some, but they were so swiftly wiped out by foxes and other predators that there is no fossil record?

Julian is more persuaded by the theory of deliberate Neolithic introduction, particularly as the Orkney vole's genetic diversity is so wide. 'I think they came here either because they are quite cute and domesticated – they look like a hamster and they don't bite – or they were a Neolithic snack,' he says. Polynesian people transported the Pacific rat across the South Seas for a similar purpose; Romans ate dormice.

If they were brought deliberately, in large earthenware pots, perhaps they had a ritual significance. Many animals on Orkney seem to have had totemic status. Neolithic tombs contain a wide range of animals, from red deer to songbirds. A ritual purpose sounds solemn, but the apparently intimate relationships between animals and people in Neolithic Orkney may be analogous to our own. The fact that people loved keeping pets two hundred generations ago should not surprise an era in which we pore over pictures of kittens on the Internet. Assuming that the Orkney vole was transported here by humans, this also suggests that Neolithic Orkney was not a peripheral place but central to civilisation, enjoying connections with a continental Europe that may have been closer than what we now consider to be the mainland.

Islands may be the last refuge for some rare species, but island rarities are also uniquely vulnerable. They are often ecologically naive – the Falkland fox was observed to be 'incurably unsuspicious of man' and was quickly exterminated – or lose their ability to disperse. Flightless birds are particularly susceptible to the ravages of humans and their companionable rodents. The last flightless great auk in Britain was probably killed on St Kilda in 1840, four years before it became extinct worldwide. Island species are also readily imperilled because islands are small territories, easily conquered by disease, people or other predators. And now, the position of island animals is similar worldwide: humans have destroyed so much habitat that endangered species are isolated on island-like fragments of habitat or 'reserves' for nature. 'Island biogeography is no longer an offshore enterprise,' writes David Quammen in *Song of the Dodo*. 'The mainlands are going, going, gone, the world is in pieces, and reality conforms to a new model.' Every animal is an islander now.

Before he jumps back on the *Islander*, Julian tells me that the Orkney vole is newly in jeopardy. In 2010, stoats were spotted on the archipelago for the first time ever. Conservationists organised trapping, but animal welfare groups insisted this couldn't be done during the stoat breeding season; Julian thinks the trapping effort wasn't ruthless enough. The stoats have spread. He fears they will decimate the vole population, which will also hit the short-eared owl. Voles are hard to count, but short-eared owl numbers are already falling. Every island, from South Ronaldsay to Australia, ends up with rats, cats and stoats – generic, human-transported predators which wipe out the animals that have evolved there uniquely. Julian calls it a 'McDonaldsisation' of wildlife. 'I'm very sad that we're getting such homogenisation in ecosystems,' he says.

The stoats appeared simultaneously in two locations on Orkney, which points to a deliberate introduction. 'It could have been people thinking, "This bloody conservation lot!" or "We've got a plague of rabbits, let's get a rabbit predator in here",' thinks Julian. Then again, he's heard no boasting about bringing stoats here and it's hard to imagine such an act staying secret on a small island. The stoats could have arrived accidentally in hay from the mainland. 'We can't be certain about what happened with the stoats, and that was just six years ago,' says Julian. 'How the hell can we be sure what happened with the Orkney vole six thousand years ago?'

Certain animals take on special significance for islanders, so it is perhaps not surprising that Compton Mackenzie identified his own spiritual protector. When he lived on Capri, Monty admired two kingfishers flying over the blue Aegean, where the ancient Greeks supposed they must nest. After he moved to Herm, he saw another two fly out to Jethou. They were a kind of lucky totem, he believed, and it was to this little island-calf that he retreated when Herm's money-swallowing might and restless spirits overwhelmed him. He had lavished £23,000 on his schemes for Herm, but by 1923 he had admitted defeat: the best way out of 'a veritable spider's web of complications', as Faith put it, was to sell up. Herm was bought by Sir Percival Perry, a self-made businessman from Birmingham who didn't seem like the sort of person to be easily spooked. Sir Percival wanted Jethou too, to grow poisonous plants for the chemical indus-try, but Monty resisted and moved there himself. Herm's lease cost £900 per year, but Jethou was a bargain at £100.

At first, Faith was underwhelmed by their drastic downsizing to a

44-acre rock with an air of dereliction. Thistles were seeding in the fields below a heathery hill with a flat top and a solitary pine tree. The place was overrun with rabbits and pheasants and its only house was 'a dreary little hole' with a rickety balcony. But the kingfishers helped convince Monty that this island held 'welcoming spirits'.

Despite his fading literary fortunes, his own spirits were irrepressible: he had a new island, a little world, to bend to his will. He obtained an old army hut and installed a carpenter and a gardener; shipped over his secretary, her parents, a maid and an Old English sheepdog called Bob. Faith recalled him gesturing grandly at Jethou's little house and pledging to build a new wing. 'Perhaps a dance-hall. Perhaps a library. I'm not sure yet. There must be a big room for gramophones and records,' he declared. Although these grand schemes didn't come to fruition on this particular island, Monty was in his element. Faith felt that Herm's 'curse' followed them, but she had seemingly unquenchable faith in Monty and was won round when she returned to Jethou early the next summer: 'White campion was like snow on the cliffs, foxgloves stood in noble groups against granite boulders. Sea-pinks clustered, the bracken was still pale-green and young. Jethou in June!'

The time Monty spent on Jethou was perhaps the most industrious of his career, as he wrote through the night to clear his debts, churning out fourteen books and numerous newspaper articles to stave off bankruptcy.

After seven years on Jethou, he reinvented himself again by taking up residence in a luxurious rented house on another island – on the River Beauly in the Highlands of Scotland. As he left Jethou, he saw two kingfishers fly across the water. Even though he felt a 'deserter' he convinced himself that this was a good omen. Jethou's kindly spirits, he later claimed, 'foresaw the German occupation of the Channel Islands', ushered him away, and so saved his life.

*

The Orkney vole leads me to a low isthmus between two lochs on Orkney's Mainland: the Ness of Brodgar, where the sheer number of vole bones found in an alcove could point to their ritual significance. We can't be certain, because it remains a possibility that these vole bones come from owl pellets discarded by prehistoric barn owls living in the ruined buildings, but archaeologists are on firmer ground when they declare that the Ness of Brodgar, one of the earliest stone building complexes unearthed in Europe, signals the significance of Orkney's Neolithic civilisation. Orcadians are excited too. Babette Barthelmess has already told me that the Ness of Brodgar is 'absolutely mind-blowing', and Kathleen at the Tomb of the Eagles believes they will have to rewrite the history books when they are finished. 'That will take a few lifetimes,' she says. 'It's absolutely huge.'

Situated between the mighty Stones of Stenness and the Ring of Brodgar, which even in torrential rain looks more impressive than any mainland stone circle, the Ness of Brodgar does not exactly catch the eye. On a ragged patch of land the size of a couple of football pitches between a bungalow and a stone cottage stands a scaffold platform, a white trailer and dozens of car tyres beside a large excavation, not much more than a metre deep, which reveals a maze of drystone walls. A line of young archaeologists, bent over on their dirty kneepads, look like the bedraggled members of a cult, praying to the god of discovery. It is cold, grey, and pouring with rain, but the soil is still hard and dry and the archaeologists' trowels make an urgent chink-chinking.

A volunteer in a yellow sou'wester tells me I'm just in time for a free tour led by Keith Brown, an experienced Historic Scotland ranger, who is excited. 'What we're about to see is absolutely extraordinary,' he says. 'This site is of world importance.' Archaeologists sometimes overstate their finds, but the Ness of Brodgar has been hailed as the most significant Neolithic discovery in the northern hemisphere. Students pay their own way from North America to volunteer here, desperate to put it on their CVs.

In 1925, two archaeologists furtling in this field extracted a spectacular stone, the Brodgar Stone, which is now sitting in the National Museum of Scotland in Edinburgh. The land then lay undisturbed until 2003, when the owners of the cottage, who also owned the field, decided to turn it into a wildflower meadow. A neighbour ploughed it for them and discovered a stone with four distinct notches on it. The owners thought the stone looked like it had been made by hand and called their neighbour, Nick Card, a roofer turned archaeologist. He called in another archaeologist, who did a little digging and discovered a Neolithic wall with a beautiful right-angle in it (archaeologists find beauty in such things). Geophysical surveys showed a confusing mass of 'activity' below ground. Test pits were dug into the 'quiet bits'. In almost every single one, whispered Keith, they found 'archaeology'.

Led by Nick Card, a coordinated excavation began and is still going on, slowly revealing a group of buildings of monumental scale. A wall at the western end is thicker than Hadrian's. One stone building is 80 feet long by 60 wide. Keith takes us to the edge of the excavations. 'Here is a complex of buildings the like of which you have never seen before. None of them are domestic. People were not living here. They weren't cooking or sleeping here either.' We peer at an immaculate drystone wall with a surface almost as smooth as plaster. It looks like a reconstruction, but it's 5,300 years old. 'Everything is exactly as it was found,' says Keith. 'What you're looking at is drystone walling supreme.'

Grooved-ware pottery, intricately decorated pots which archaeologists believe originated on Orkney around 3100 BC, has been found right across the site alongside polished axes, maceheads, carved stone balls, stones decorated with butterfly motifs and stone spatulas. If people weren't living in these buildings, what were they used for? Much of what has been dug up so far appears to be ritual and ceremonial, 'which is archaeological speak for "I don't know",' says Keith. He cautions against using modern words, but the Ness of Brodgar is likely to have been a Neolithic temple or meeting hall.

These excavations are adding nuance to our crude portraits of Neolithic society. Many materials have come some distance – pitchstone from the Isle of Arran 250 miles away, which shows that Neolithic Orcadians were a mobile, outward-looking trading people. Keith pulls out a photograph of a jumble of flat rectangular stones, which Nick, as a former roofer, instantly recognises: tiles. This confirms that these Neolithic buildings were built with stone roofs, as opposed to the usual thatch. Reconstructions typically depict Stone Age people in drab greys, but the Ness of Brodgar shows them in colour: reds and yellows, in stripes and chevrons, have been found on stones. 'They were painting and decorating in their buildings,' says Keith. They were playing music and making jewellery. Life may not have been nasty and brutish, but it was still short: life expectancy was thirty-five, and the high incidence of arthritis suggests Neolithic people were used to carrying very heavy weights.

Perhaps the most mysterious feature of the Ness of Brodgar is its destruction some four thousand years ago. The buildings were covered in rubbish and surrounded by complete skeletons of red deer and wigwams of cow shin bones – 400 to 600 cows were slaughtered for the purpose. The equivalent today, according to Keith's back-of-an-envelope calculation, would be Orkney farmers donating half a million quid to throw a party. 'Our local farmers cannot come to terms with that,' he says. 'Why do you bury buildings? This is a huge effort. The whole thing put to sleep and lost to collective memory. We have no stories, nothing associated with this place at all. We'd have expected something. We have folk tales associated with the stone circles, but something as significant and monumental as this has been completely lost to memory. That's very strange.'

*

As I drive fast along empty roads back to South Ronaldsay, I feel keenly conscious of my elevated latitude, which may be a common geographical recalibration. In *The Outrun*, the Orcadian-Londoner Amy Liptrot describes how her centre of gravity shifts further north when she returns home; as she started to think about Shetland, the Faroes and Iceland, London came to seem a distant bubble by comparison. Small islands are often far from insular for human beings; they can be open places that enhance our awareness of the world beyond. That evening, racing through the Orkney twilight, I feel I can perceive the Outer Hebrides over the glowing westerly horizon, even though the northern tip of Lewis is more than a hundred miles away.

The Scottish writer Eric Linklater, great friend of Compton Mackenzie, took a grand house on Mainland, but Protestant, English-speaking Orkney didn't fire Monty's imagination like the Outer Hebrides did. 'The difference between them is the difference between prose and poetry,' wrote Linklater, who visited Mackenzie many times in the Hebrides. 'Orkney is prose – the best of prose, with its variations of rhythm and sturdy utility – but Barra lives in perpetual music and breathes a magic air.'

Barra will be my next stop, but before I leave Orkney, I am drawn once again to the Tomb of the Eagles. I find Kathleen and Freda in their kitchen. We talk more about the skulls of their ancestors. The architecture and the artefacts within the tomb tell us so little about these Neolithic people that they invite imaginative speculation. An unusual number possess physical deformities. The fact that they lived to be adults showed they were cared for; that they were buried in a tomb suggests they were spiritual leaders or imbued with special powers. One, 'Charlie Girl', was probably blind: was she a seer?

'Some visitors try to tell us they must've been a miserable people, but I don't believe that at all – I believe they were a happy people and played music, games on the sand, and told stories,' says Kathleen. 'We don't have any evidence either way, but I like to think their society was egalitarian.'

While they let visitors handle the trinkets and pottery, they don't pass the skulls around. Do they ever let anyone touch them? 'Just with special requests,' replies Kathleen cautiously. I assume she means academics and professionals, but Kathleen's face softens. 'It's usually little boys who are going through the skull stage, they get a photograph.' A boy in his forties recently returned to the tomb for the first time since childhood and was ecstatic when they granted his request to hold a skull. 'He was floating,' says Kathleen. 'Not quite as high as Babette, but he was floating.' But they keep a close eye. 'They would never leave our sight,' says Freda, 'they are very precious to us.' I can't resist. 'Can I hold Jock Tamson?' Kathleen smiles indulgently. We enter the Tomb Room. She asks me to sit down, opens her cabinet and carefully hands me his skull. It is surprisingly light, as if made from plastic. 'He's been drying out for so long,' murmurs Kathleen. Tamson's skull feels smooth and well made, with a fine bone structure: a delicate forehead, symmetrical eye sockets and a neat hole for his mouth containing seven teeth in good condition and an impacted wisdom tooth. Time stands still. I can't remember what I silently say to Tamson, but I become flustered when I realise I am handing him back to Kathleen upside down, and I worry about disrespecting him. I have forgotten to ask him all kinds of questions. Was your society a peaceful one? Did you dance and sing? Who was your god? What kind of relationship did you have with animals and eagles? Did your people really keep voles as pets? He's back in the cabinet before I hear a reply.

3

An Island Home

Barra, The Outer Hebrides, 23 square miles, population 1,300

'He wanted an island all of his own: not necessarily to be
alone on it, but to make it a world of his own'
'The Man Who Loved Islands'

'There's a small chance we won't be able to land, but we'll see what we can do,' says the First Officer, twisting around in his seat next to the pilot of the Twin Otter. There is a long pause. The half-dozen passengers chuckle nervously. Gale-force winds of 45 knots are sweeping over Barra. 'If we can't,' the First Officer explains in the phlegmatic manner of a Highlander, 'we'll just come back here to Glasgow.'

An hour later, we shudder through a thick layer of cloud and I catch my first sight of the ocean below, churning dark granite and angry white spittle. We bump in the air. I'm desperate to get down safely, but this small plane staggering through a big wind towards an empty island of rock and yellowing grass at the edge of the Outer Hebrides doesn't offer much comfort. Beyond the rocks is a bay of improbably jade-coloured water and a calming expanse of sand the hue of champagne. We fly low over the only beach in the world to take scheduled flights, and on its grassy fringe I spot a low white house, alone in the storm. I recognise it instantly from a photograph: Suidheachan, 'the sitting-down place', built in 1934 by Compton Mackenzie. This is the first island I'm visiting where a piece of it was created by Monty.

A year earlier, I'd chanced upon five volumes of his autobiography stacked in a second-hand bookshop in Northumberland. I hadn't bought them and on my way north this time, I call in again. All five are still on the shelf and, moved by their desolation, I buy a couple. Like a dead person's possessions left for the house-clearance van, these books contain far too much detail to interest any merely passing person. Their fate, Monty's fate, shows the futility of hoping to be remembered much beyond death. And right now my own mortality is a pressing concern as the Twin Otter is jostled in the gale above the thrashing blades of a solitary wind turbine at the north-western tip of Barra.

Monty experienced a similar rattling trying to reach Barra, but he wasn't scared. 'I must say that flying in a gale is a most exhilarating experience,' he wrote to Faith in 1936 when, typically at the centre of events, he took one of the first scheduled flights from Glasgow to Barra. There was hardly a bump, he said, until they turned into the wind to land.

Our plane shudders precisely when our pilot attempts this man-oeuvre. As we turn across the wind, we are suspended in the sky as precarious as a toy in the hand of a vexed toddler. Then the wind slams us towards the earth. Lower, lower – come on! – we bump through the air, but there's no reassuring beach and we are up again – above desolate rock and the wind turbine once more. Landing aborted, the side-wind too strong, we jolt across the wind for another buffeting. I can't help but look at the pilot's forearm. It is rigid, as his hand grips a shaking yoke. Then, mercifully, a lull, and suddenly we steeple down. Is this a crash landing or the beach runway? All is grey water and then we bottom out with a dinky splash, and the cockleshell sand of Tràigh Mhòr is smoother than any concrete and I exhale queasily and wipe my sweaty palms on my trousers as we taxi past Monty's old house to the terminal. I'm alive. I've been granted another few days at least to explore Compton Mackenzie's former home. My terror over a modestly bumpy arrival reminds me I must try harder to reach an acceptance of the day when my life will be another overlooked detail from the past.

*

'You're twenty minutes late,' says the driver of Barra's bus, a grey Mercedes in the small wet car park. I'd disembarked onto the sand, taken the obligatory photo of the small plane on the beach and followed my fellow passengers through someone's office and into a large shed that smelled of cake and hummed with the murmurs of people who know each other well.

'I'm sorry, the plane was late leaving Glasgow,' I stammer, paying £2.10 to be swept around the island's circular road, the single-track A888. 'A bus in Glasgow wouldn't have been waiting for you. You were dawdling, taking photos.' Two other tourists tap on the door a minute later and receive the same treatment: their photoshoot lasted longer than mine. 'We're sorry,' says one sharply. 'We won't come to Barra again.'

We take the western route, which wiggles between low rocky fells and the machair, the flowery grassland lying at the back of the sand dunes that is characteristic of these islands and looks as smooth as a golf course, grazed by sheep and cattle. Surf is swept back by the wind, and after ten minutes we reach the centre of Castlebay, whose sheltered waters housed six hundred herring boats in the late 1800s when people came from all over to chase these silver darlings. Now its harbour is home to just one sizeable boat, a handsome black-and-white ferry with twin red funnels. Beyond, the grey oblong of Kisimul Castle is cast adrift on a rock like a miniature container ship. The ferry, the *Isle of Lewis*, isn't much good, complain locals: a hand-me-down from the larger island of Lewis, it's too big and tall for this section of the Minch, the notoriously treacherous waters between the Outer Hebrides and the mainland, and gales have stranded it on Barra for three days now.

Castlebay is built on the slopes that gaze south-west towards Barra's companion island of Vatersay. This is my first experience of the Hebrides and of crofting culture, and it is markedly different from the bits of Britain I know. It is not twee or cosy like an English village. Apart from a short street leading to the ferry terminal, most of Castlebay, home to about half the island's 1,300 population, is scattered wherever a flat rectangle of land can be chiselled from the granite. There are several corrugated-tin shacks which were once houses. Some have been superseded by peppermint-coloured static caravans; others by bungalows or chalets, mostly in grey pebbledash, with an occasional lurid red-tiled roof. A few dwarf red-hot pokers aside, most houses have rough grass for gardens, where the daggered leaves of yellow flag iris sprout and sheep – and one colossal white rabbit – graze. There is a wealth of interesting sheds: a curvaceous 1950s caravan, filled with junk; a VW Transporter with surfboards inside and no back windows; an old white summer house. Boats and lobster pots and Mitsubishi pickups are parked on neat tiled-brick driveways. A child's bright-orange plastic swing is pushed by the wind. A trampoline is wedged on the hillside, looking like it might flip away at any moment even though its metal foundations are weighed down by big stones. Two young girls wrestle each other in the gale, long hair flying. It feels a spirited place.

The light comes and goes, capriciously, as the weather blows from the west and I totter about like a geriatric in the wind along a well equipped stretch of municipal main road that features a school, community hall, gym and swimming pool. I duck into the library, where there is reassuring evidence that the man who loved islands has not been totally forgotten: there's a volume of Barra essays edited by Monty and a copy of his light comic novel *Whisky Galore*.

The next day is auspicious: it's Ascension Day and my landlady announces she's heard the first cuckoo of the year. A couple of cuckoos call across the valley on the fifteen-minute walk from my B&B into Castlebay. During this short stroll, I encounter two mysteries. The first is a strange sound. From some unseen spot, wherever the little road crosses a boggy crevice by a thicket of low willow, comes a piercing scratch-scritch mechanical-frog craziness. It sounds like construction work, metal on serrated metal, but must be some kind of cicada-like creature. It's impossible to pinpoint precisely where the noise comes from but it always ceases when I draw near. I try creeping up. The noise halts. I walk over the tufts of grass from where it arises but nothing hops, springs or flies off. I'm baffled.

The second puzzle is virtually Castlebay's only garden, a profusion of bluebells, tulips, daffodils, hydrangeas and a weeping pussy willow. It doesn't have a house attached but lies beneath a thicket of stunted sycamores, not yet in leaf, by a noisy stream. Signs say *Coille Na Sithe*, 'the Wood of Peace', and 'Welcome', so I step through a green gate. Inside is a Celtic cross on a low memorial of round grey stones collected from an island beach. This small garden is stuffed with things: a swing chair, benches, several pergolas, two honeysuckle arches (one wooden, one plastic), an ornamental well, a summer house, a shed and a pebble-dashed outhouse with a green door below a corrugated-tin roof. Inside the summer house is a miniature gypsy caravan, a rocking horse and an ornamental plaster lighthouse-and-rowing-boat. By the shed are plastic fish-boxes stacked with gnomes, toadstools, fairies bearing flowers, a Tigger, a cockerel, and a hedgehog couple standing upright on two legs, the mother offering the benediction of a cup of tea. Inside the outhouse are tea-making facilities and a family of large teddies. There are also ornamental swans, cats, ashtrays, vases, ducks, owls, robins and blue tits. Every square centimetre of wall space carries framed pictures: castles, teapots, dogs, beaches, puppies and horses. 'Came up to see your garden, brought you a present,' reads the latest message in a visitors' book. What is this marvellous place, and who is its creator?

I continue on my morning's mission, which is to visit the island's Heritage Centre, a small museum where tourists from America, Australia and Canada search for relatives in box-files full of old photographs. Folk music plays in the background as I read the Centre's wittily written displays that record Barra's history.

Barra is one of 270 Hebridean islands, of which forty-one are permanently inhabited, situated towards the southern end of the great line of the Outer Hebrides. For many generations of charmed and rather colonial-English-speaking trippers and writers, this archipelago has been 'the faraway nearby', as Madeleine Bunting puts it in her recent history of the isles – 'accessible but still "other", with a foreign language and a distinctive culture on the point of disappearing. This was the past, still present.'

Settled by Irish missionaries and the Scots, a Gaelic people from Ireland, in the sixth century, Barra was virtually untouched by the Reformation, unlike Lewis and Harris to the north. So while these islands became staunchly Presbyterian, priests from Ireland continued to visit Barra during its 'spiritual starvation' and preserved its Catholic, Gaelic character. As Bunting points out, the basic building blocks of the British nation over the last half-millennium – faith and language – were never established on the Outer Hebrides. Its rural culture 'survived the powerfully centralizing history of the British imperial state until well into the twentieth century'.

Barra did not escape the Clearances, however, where the Gaidheil, Gaelic-speaking Highlanders, were forcibly replaced with sheep by landowners from lowland Scotland and England. Owned for a period by the famously brutal John Gordon of Cluny, Barra islanders were chased down with dogs, tied up, and loaded onto ships for the New World.

Such evictions were finally outlawed by the Crofters Holdings Act of 1886. The sheep began disappearing from the Highlands when Australia and New Zealand flooded the market with cheap wool towards the end of the century, but the people, mostly, never came back. On the periphery, however, the Gaidheil clung on. Ruled by an absentee landlord as the twentieth century began, Barra islanders began retrieving their lost land by seizing a large farm at Northbay. In 1901 the Congested Districts Board purchased 3,000 acres on the island and offered it as fifty-eight smallholdings, which were snapped up. Crofting was re-established, fishing for herring helped provide relative prosperity and five hundred migrants in summer, and this egalitarian community of 2,250 islanders enjoyed a golden age.

Barra was buoyant in the early decades of the twentieth century, but by the time Compton Mackenzie made it his home he was almost sunk. No longer a vivacious and prosperous young talent, Monty turned fifty in 1933 and finished the year in the dock of the Old Bailey, disgraced, in agony, and virtually bankrupt.

Years of extravagance had caught up with him. In 1933, the man who loved islands was lumbered with three: a riverine island on the Beauly in the Highlands which cost an eye-watering £450 a year in rent; Jethou, for which he still couldn't find a buyer; and the uninhabited Shiants, the three Hebridean islands he had bought at auction in 1926 and which closely resembled the place where Lawrence's Mr Cathcart went mad and died. Book sales had slumped and Monty was now required to pay income tax, having left the haven of Jethou. His overdraft – £3,000 – was as large as his annual income.

Worst of all, he was prosecuted under the Official Secrets Act for *Greek Memories*, his account of his wartime spying in Greece. Advised that the authorities were keen to make an example of him – *pour décourager les autres*, specifically Winston Churchill and Lloyd George, then feared to be writing memoirs – Monty pleaded guilty and was spared jail. He was fined, forced to return his advance for the book and pursued by the taxman. He scavenged money from friends and was compelled to auction off, too cheaply, his collection of rare books and his own manuscripts. Faith couldn't bear to live with him. He suffered debilitating episodes of chronic sciatica. In the midst of this mess, Monty, seemingly destined to fulfil Lawrence's narrative and constantly repeat his mistakes, sought salvation in Barra.

Monty first visited Barra during a grand tour of the Western Isles in the summer of 1929, because he was rushing out a money-spinning biography of Bonnie Prince Charlie. This project spoke to his bizarre new obsession: Scottish nationalism. For much of the 1920s, he had enjoyed parading over his Channel Islands in the theatrical regalia of a Scottish gentleman: a kilt made from Mackenzie tartan with sporran, flat cap, pipe in mouth and shotgun over his arm. Despite being born and raised in England, he'd long considered himself a 'perfervid Gael'. He claimed he insisted, as a three-year-old, on being called 'Mackenzie' (his father's surname was Compton). As a young man, he cleaved to the romance of Bonnie Prince Charlie's doomed attempt to win the crown of Scotland in 1745, joining secret societies that venerated the Young Pretender. In 1914, he converted to Catholicism.

During his research trip to the Hebrides, Monty became entranced by the tiny island of Eriskay in the Sound of Barra, where the prince first set foot on Scottish soil in July 1745 for his quixotic tilt at the British Crown. Prince Charles, the grandson of the former King of England James II who had been exiled in France, did not immediately win support from sceptical Catholic clans, but the Gaidheil eventually recognised a chance to recapture power and rallied around the prince after he reached the mainland.

By September, the Young Pretender had taken Edinburgh; within five months of landing on Eriskay, he'd swept through Carlisle, Manchester and Derby, less than 125 miles from London. The thirty-eight-year-old union of England and Scotland was looking decidedly disunited but Charles, fatally, was advised to turn back and consolidate, and his Jacobite forces were massacred the following spring at Culloden. Miraculously, the prince was spirited out of Scotland, but in subsequent decades the Highlanders who had supported him were terrorised. The teenage Monty had treasured a gold locket containing a hair from the prince's head and joined late Victorian 'Legitimist' societies who believed that the Stuarts possessed a more authentic claim to the crown than the Hanoverian interlopers. This was an eccentric cause but, as Madeleine Bunting argues in her history of the islands, the apparent improbability of the Young Pretender's tilt at the Crown may be the creation of a history written by the victor, the Hanoverian British state.

By the time Monty reached Eriskay, he was participating directly in the nascent campaign for an independent Scotland. He had been recently elected to the council of the new National Party of Scotland and his visit to the island reinforced his desire to embrace Charlie's spirit. Unable to quell his extravagance, he bought the only property he could find for sale, a wooden coastguard hut, for £60. He later fancied that a BBC broadcast in which he hailed the intense greyness of Eriskay's rocks must have been approved by 'the genius loci' – the spirit of the place – for he was ultimately rewarded with the inspiration to write his bestselling novel *Whisky Galore*.

It took four more years for Monty to make Barra his home. Nearly bankrupt, he finally broke the lease on Beauly and arrived in Barra in the spring of 1933. Compton Mackenzie's eighth island infatuation was perhaps his most pragmatic yet, a sensible place to live cheaply and write quickly, without distraction. But Monty was always more governed by romance. 'When at last he assumed the identity of a Scot,' wrote Andro Linklater, 'it was with the excitement of discovering what he felt to be his true self.'

Barra was beautiful. On sunny days, Monty could rest his gaze on the distant mountains of the mainland 'riding along the horizon like snowy galleons' and the Hebridean island of Canna 'like a great whale'. On summer nights, 'the pearly shimmer of the Hebridean midnight simply cannot be wasted in sleep'. The sound between South Uist and Barra could turn 'a richer ultramarine than any stretch of water on this side of the Mediterranean', and he declared the seascape unequalled beyond the Aegean. Such comparisons were not hyperbole, based as they were on his direct experience of wartime Greece. I'm puzzled why Monty never settled on an Aegean island, but perhaps they were a place of war for him, or maybe he shared the view of Jean Cocteau, who cruised around them in 1952 and decided: 'The Greek islands are nothing but an idea one creates for oneself.'

Barra was not an island idea; it was a strong and vital community. Like every other visitor, proclaimed Monty, what he loved most were the islanders. 'Barra is an extraordinarily happy place. Laughter is the keynote. There is always a good story going the rounds,' he said in a rather smug 1936 broadcast about his newish life, called 'Living Off the Map'. He had been encouraged to Barra in the first place by John MacPherson, an islander he befriended at a Gaelic music festival in 1928. MacPherson was postmaster and a kind of unofficial king of the island. Like many residents, he was known by his nickname, the Coddy, and was an inexhaustible source of Gaelic stories and songs. Like many Hebrideans, the Coddy was the very opposite of insular – outward-looking, well travelled, sophisticated. 'I say that The Coddy was the outstanding character, but when I look back at them all the characters in Barra were outstanding in one way or another,' Monty wrote later. Another character he met was the Crookle, to whom he paid £3 a week to lodge in a corrugated-tin cottage on the north-east shores. Like many on Barra, the Crookle had gone to sea in his youth; he had been held prisoner by the Turks during the First World War; he had seen the world, and read widely. Compton's cronies were fellow Catholics: Sundays on Barra, dominated by Mass, were more like Italy than Scotland, observed his wife Faith, approvingly.

Monty celebrated his permanent arrival on Barra with an expedition to Mingulay, an uninhabited island to the south, home to thousands of seabirds on spectacular cliffs to rival St Kilda's. He was joined on this adventure by friends including the Coddy, the Crookle; and Neil Sinclair, the Red Scholar, headmaster of the Northbay school. The Crookle was appointed ship's steward, drams from two bottles of whisky were served on departure at 8 a.m., and 'that long June day remains in my memory as one of the supreme days of my life,' Monty remembered. Landing on the white beaches of Sandray, Pabbay and then Mingulay, they prayed among the stony ruins of a community that had been abandoned in 1912, then at dusk returned to Barra.

Barra was known then, as it is now, for its conviviality. I get chatting to a Glaswegian builder in a lane. He married a Barra woman, loves it here but, he exclaims, there are 'some heavy sessions'. When the summer days are long, the parties can go on for days. Monty attended local weddings with ceilidhs that lasted until dawn; and the *Luagh*, the 'shrinking of the cloth' ceremony where women tightened tweed by vigorously thumping it on tables of rough boards, accompanied by songs. Monty did plenty of entertaining too. After he laid on fireworks one evening he saw an elderly lady walking bent over, he recalled, searching for something: the gold that had fallen from the sky the evening before.

Monty had a store of similarly patronising anecdotes, but he genuinely admired the Barra islanders' gift for freedom. He too felt liberated. His irrepressible romanticism had been stimulated by something else during his first summer exploring the Outer Hebrides: 'a sloe-eyed young beauty from the Outer Hebrides', as Veronica Maclean, a lifelong friend of Monty's, described Christina MacSween. The twenty-two-year-old daughter of Malcolm MacSween, Monty's grazing tenant on the Shiant Isles, Chrissie had dark eyes, dark hair and rosy cheeks. She was a newly qualified teacher who could type, speak Gaelic, sing and dance. When Monty first met her, he said he 'knew that this girl must become a part of my life', and she became Monty's secretary, housekeeper, fixer, crutch and translator – for all his fondness for the language, Monty never learned much Gaelic – and then his lover and de facto wife on Barra. 'Chrissie Chompton' (Chrissie of Compton), as the locals called her, was probably the reason he was so swiftly made to feel at home on the island he came to love more than any other.

Monty's partaking in island pleasures, and multiple wives, looks at first glance like the fatuous behaviour of 'the playboy of the Western World', as one newspaper described him. Another, the *Daily Record*, likened him to Robert Louis Stevenson in Samoa who built an island home and 'fashioned a "golden circle" with servants and retainers around him and became a benignant island chieftain'. The paper wondered whether Monty's exile was 'a spiritual adventure, an evasion of life's problems or merely a glorified holiday'. In his 1936 broadcast Monty protested that his life on Barra was no escape, then in the next breath mentioned that the post arriving only three times a week was a blessed relief. Fair enough, for letters must have been the same obstacle to productive work as today's oppressive Inboxes, but this latest island crush certainly seemed like an act of escapology by a man seeking to flee professional and financial failures.

On Barra, Monty wrote as efficiently as ever to clear his debts. He was also possessed of a book column in the *Daily Mail* in which he could avenge D.H. Lawrence, who had died of tuberculosis in 1930 aged forty-four. Lawrence 'can enshrine the whole Mediterranean in one charmed sentence', wrote Monty of his friend's posthumously published *The Man Who Died*, but 'he cannot infuse with the breath of life one solitary human figure of those he tries so arrogantly and so ineffectually to create. Lawrence understood flowers, birds and animals . . . but some bad fairy saw to it that he must nearly always misunderstand human beings.'

For all Monty's self-centred life of writing, his time on Barra was a repudiation of the caricature Lawrence had created in 'The Man Who Loved Islands'. Lawrence's fictional Monty treated islands as 'I-lands', as the writer and present-day owner of the Shiants, Adam Nicolson, puts it: an ultimately barren place where the nesomane's inflated sense of self smothers all other life. In his short story, Lawrence argued that the healthy state for an individual is to live socially, not alone, and a small-island home represents a withdrawal from the mainstream, where it is our duty to remain. Was Monty haunted by Lawrence's accusation? His transmogrification into Compton, the activist of the Western Isles, looks like a concerted attempt to prove, if only to himself, that Lawrence too had misunderstood him.

Monty's reinvention began with the arrival on Barra of a young Gaelic scholar, John Lorne Campbell, a shy, sensible, meticulous man. He and Monty were temperamental opposites but shared a love of Lepidoptera and a desire to reconnect with Gaelic Scotland. They wanted to preserve Gaelic and the crofting tradition, both of which needed economic support. That is a common aim on the periphery of Scotland today, but this was the 1930s, when Gaelic was forbidden in many schools and the islands began haemorrhaging jobs and people. They made prescient calls to limit the amount of land owned by one person and for a development board for northern Scotland; for the nationalisation of ferry services and the local control of hydro power; and for civil servants to be required to learn Gaelic.

After Monty had watched a large steam-powered English trawler flagrantly ignoring the law that banned them within three miles of the shores of islands such as Barra, he and Campbell formed the Sea League, a union that grew to include six hundred fishermen across the Hebrides. The islands were poor because their greatest source of wealth, the sea, was sacrificed to outside trawlers, and Monty and Campbell called on the authorities to close the Minch to such vessels in the way that coastal seas around Norway had been protected for the local people.

To raise funds for the Sea League, he and Campbell produced *The Book of Barra*, a collection of the island's traditions that was also a rebuke to the sentimental image of the Hebrides peddled by touring writers such as Alasdair Alpin MacGregor. 'We are tired of being put to sleep by Gaelic lullabies to dream sentimental dreams,' wrote Monty. Perhaps assisted by Chrissie, he was a more shrewd observer of Hebridean culture than most outsiders. When he received well-meaning letters suggesting Barra required an 'organised uplift' via new facilities such as a library, a choir or evening lectures, he wrote: 'Now, if there is one place in Scotland which knows how to amuse itself that place is Barra and if there is one place on which organised uplift would be completely wasted that place is Barra.' He was particularly effective when fighting for the individuality of his island against the authorities, which wanted to treat it like any other patch of Scotland. He lobbied the Department of Agriculture to plant grasses to protect its dunes from erosion, and presciently protested against the Forestry Commission despoiling Barra's uplands with desolate blocks of non-native conifers. And in 1937, he led an uprising on behalf of individual islanders against the universality of mainland rules.

Barra highways were unmetalled, and the road vanished when it met the huge beach of Tràigh Mhòr, requiring islanders to drive across salty wet sand. Nevertheless, the mainland authorities demanded that they pay road tax. The 'Barra Eleven', all but one of the island's twelve car and lorry owners, including Monty, decided not to pay. They went on strike. They were arraigned before the sheriff on the island of North Uist, who imposed fines and costs of more than £142. Monty spoke out, and the national papers pronounced it a vindictive verdict. At appeal, a judge rebuked the sheriff, the fine was reduced to £50 and the eleven motorists were awarded expenses.

Despite Monty's efforts with the Sea League over five years, local fishing all but died out around Barra. In 1964, John Lorne Campbell wrote to Monty to note that their call for the Hebrides to be protected from foreign trawlers had finally become law – 'one if not two generations too late'. After Monty's death, the generous Campbell praised his friend's farsightedness and credited him with providing 'a vivid, imaginative and inspiring intellectual leadership of the kind which the Highlands and Islands then needed badly.'

*

When I ask the receptionist in the Heritage Centre whether she knows of a local historian who can tell me more about Compton Mackenzie's time on Barra, she unhesitatingly replies: Mairi Ceit MacKinnon. I'm poring over old newspaper cuttings when I find a yellowing picture of primary school pupils from the early 1970s with their teacher, Mairi Ceit MacKinnon: a pretty young woman with straight dark hair, cut short around her face. As if by magic, Mairi Ceit materialises in the Centre shortly afterwards, with exactly the same straight hair and fringe, only grey now. She seems a little tentative but agrees to meet me at her home the following day, which conveniently (as ever, on islands) happens to be next to my B&B.

Within minutes of inviting me into her traditional stone house, Mairi Ceit has solved the mystery of the scritchy soundtrack to my strolls around Castlebay and the puzzle of the fairytale garden. I ask her about the noise. 'Corncrakes,' she replies. Corncrakes! The male of this funny, scaredy species, which resembles a miniature partridge and hides in overgrown grassland, makes a mating call that is alien to me. It was a commonplace sound to earlier generations, an ordinary part of a mainland spring. Now, like so many other once common species, it has been pushed to the margins, thriving only on small islands such as Barra. Then I compliment Mairi Ceit, genuinely, on the striking pink gnomette by her backdoor. Someone has donated it for her memorial garden, she explains. I glance around her living room, crammed with ornaments, paintings and pictures, and realise that she is the architect of the special garden under the grove of sycamores. 'People go in and just sit,' she says of the garden. English is her second language and she speaks it perfectly, with a singsong pronunciation that sounds almost Russian to my ears. She works hard at the garden, she says, tending flowers, putting out the boxes of gnomes each summer and serving cakes there to raise money for charity.

The garden is on the site of her parents' house, where she lived too and which burned down in a fire on 21 November 1994, a night of a wild storm. Her dad died in the blaze, and her mum not long afterwards. Mairi Ceit suffered brain damage so the right side of her body couldn't function, as well as damage to her lungs. The wind was so fierce that 'the helicopter had difficulty getting me away, but I'm alive and there's people worse off than me and I live on a beautiful island and I'm safe,' she says.

It's brave, I say, to live in a cottage overlooking the site of the place that killed her parents and nearly killed her. 'Life's got to go on. I had many happy childhood memories down there and tragedies happen and there's nothing we can do about it,' she said. We talk about Adam Nicolson's *Sea Room*, and the enduring presence of the past. 'You can't really have a present without a past here. It's very important. They go together. When you're on a place like this you can't forget the past.'

Just like the corncrake, forgotten on the mainland but still audible on a small island, so Compton Mackenzie is remembered with more clarity on Barra than elsewhere. Mairi Ceit is too young to have known him personally but remembers many people who did; he was respected for his writing, accepted for his eccentricities – his mainland wife and his island lover – but most of all he was welcomed as an equal. 'People have always said that Barra is a very classless island, more so than the other islands,' says Mairi Ceit. 'Nobody is better than anybody else.' And why did Monty like it so much? 'At the time it was quite a cosmopolitan place. There were all kinds of people and I think he liked people,' suggests Mairi Ceit. 'The bay was full of fishing boats, shops were open until ten o'clock at night, big boats came in from Russia and Germany to buy fish, there were gutting women from the east coast, Lowestoft and Yarmouth, it was full of life and it was a Mecca for poets and literary people – Louis MacNeice, Halliday Sutherland, John Lorne Campbell, Eric Linklater, Lord and Lady Londonderry – and there was a wealth of song and music. The ceilidhs were still going on. It was a Catholic island and music and poetry – these were God-given gifts.'

Barra's Catholicism and the romance of the place inspired Compton Mackenzie to fall for it, and both are part of Mairi Ceit's deep attachment to her home too. The daughter of a merchant seaman, she passed her eleven-plus and in those days had to board at Inverness. 'It did us no harm. It made us independent and no way could we leave after buying the school uniforms,' she says: her generation's parents spent what little they had on those uniforms. The 1960s were a time of crisis on Barra. The yellowed newspapers in the Heritage Centre tell of the declining population across the Highlands, but Mairi Ceit did not join the exodus.

In her last year at school, she decided she needed a job that would take her back to her island. She trained as a primary school teacher and returned to Barra, aged twenty-one, in 1970, to teach in Gaelic as well as English. 'It's more poetic, it's more beautiful, it's more magical,' she says, comparing it to English. 'The words are so descriptive they practically speak.'

I'm acutely aware of being yet another visitor to the Outer Hebrides who lacks this most vital piece of linguistic equipment to make a perceptive interpretation of the place. The Irish poet Louis MacNeice wrote a book called *I Crossed the Minch* about his visit to the island in 1937, in which he confessed to his own shortcomings: 'Owing to my ignorance of their language I was unable to become intimate with the lives of the people. This book is consequently a tripper's book written by someone who was disappointed and tantalised by the islands and seduced by them only to be reminded that on that soil he will always be an outsider.'

Mairi Ceit's return home in the 1970s embodies the revival of Gaelic and the upturn in Barra's fortunes that decade. The Highlands and Islands Development Board had been founded in 1965 to halt the loss of humans from this landscape by creating new jobs. It helped revive fishing on Barra; a fish-processing factory opened in 1976 and is still going; and a (less successful) luxury hotel was built. Families began returning, encouraged by grants to rebuild houses and a realisation that the island offered a good life. Barra's population is steady now, but the flash cars I notice around the place – an Audi RS5, a VW Amarok – are not a sign of great wealth earned on the island. These are bought by islanders who work offshore – in shipping or on oil-rigs – and come home to labour on their family crofts during their time off. What does a small island need to survive today? 'Work and commitment,' says Mairi Ceit.

We discuss the confident character of the children on Barra, where life is 'not too regimented', and the fact that they tend to reject both Gaelic and the Church when they are teenagers, but later return to it. We talk about the statue of the Madonna and Child erected halfway up Barra's biggest hill by the island's seamen in 1954. 'The people here have always had a great devotion to Our Lady,' says Mairi Ceit. Our conversation flows, subjects ranging from the bright-orange flowers of montbretia that turn Barra into a painting at summer's end, to the TV series *An Island Parish*, which inspired thousands of visitors to descend on Barra in search of their relatives. 'The following summer, you could've sold grannies in the Heritage Centre,' says Mairi Ceit. Then there's Barra in winter. 'The shores change with the movement of the sea in winter and the sound changes too,' she says. 'The surge of the sea, the rocks glistening, in the wintertime it's got a beauty of its own.'

The following morning brings bright sunshine and a gentle breeze, dispatching puffy white clouds across an illimitable horizon. Compton Mackenzie wrote of gales followed by halcyon interludes, 'days of such surpassing loveliness and clarity that the islands seem to float suspended between earth and heaven in a crystal globe, nights when the shafts of the Aurora Borealis dance across the sky above the curlews fluting in greedy triumph by the ebb'.

I hire a bike and cycle north to Monty's house. Cuckoos and corncrakes sound, a mile beyond. I've never before seen so many little birds as well: wheatears, linnets, stonechats, wrens. Gorse-filled glens smell of coconut, and on the far eastern horizon the battlements of Rum and Skye reach up, godlike, to the clouds.

Where Barra's miniature Highlands give way to a flat spit of sand dunes and machair behind the airport beach of Tràigh Mhòr, Compton Mackenzie put down roots. On a rare occasion when his official wife, Faith, visited him on Barra, he drove her to this place between two beaches with magnificent views east across the Sound of Barra towards Eriskay, and proclaimed he would build a house here. A house on sand, miles from anywhere, without any running water, scoffed Faith. But – typical Monty – it turned out that there was a fresh-water spring. When he finally sold Jethou in 1934, with the Coddy's approval he bought an acre of land and built his home on the spot called Suidheachan, 'the sitting-down place', where the chieftain MacNeil of Barra once ate lunch when shooting snipe. Two hundred residents joined Monty for the laying of the foundation for Suidheachan, which in positioning and style resembles an old coastguard bungalow, a single-storey white-painted stone building with sash windows and a grey slate roof. According to local legend, the builder erected it the wrong way round, so the bedrooms face the dunes and only the kitchen and the billiard-room-cum-library enjoy the fine views.

The house is not lived in these days – islanders say it stands empty for most of the year, boards protecting the windows of the billiard room. After Monty left Barra it was converted into a small factory that crushed cockle shells from the beach into a kind of pebble-dash, but was bought and renovated in the 1990s by Mackenzie's great-nephew, the late actor Alan Howard, and his wife the novelist Sally Beauman.

Monty would have approved of his house now, I think, when I rest my bike on the gate and go for a nose around. It is beautifully furnished for holidays, and in the kitchen stands a sand-coloured Aga just like the one Monty – always in need of some quick cash

– promoted in *Good Housekeeping* in 1938. 'The Aga which was installed in my house on the island of Barra two years ago has burnt steadily night and day ever since,' he wrote. 'The economy of it is incredible. The luxury of it is exquisite. My Siamese cats consider the top, covered with a blanket, provides them with the finest lodging outside Siam.'

As I peer through the windowpanes, it is easy to imagine the life he created here 'under the hospitable management' of Chrissie, as John Lorne Campbell put it. Suidheachan became the social and literary centre of Barra, the Bloomsbury of the Hebrides. As well as his glamorous literary guests, each Sunday Compton invited the Coddy, the Crookle, local ministers and schoolteachers for whisky, conversation and a game of pool, which became so popular they had to invent a 'quickfire' version.

His friends were in thrall to his theatrical stories and perfect impersonations, and only the visiting Louis MacNeice was unimpressed by what he perceived as Monty's self-importance. John Lorne Campbell insisted that although Monty was 'a magnificent raconteur' he was also 'completely unspoiled', and did not impose himself. 'He was always willing to listen to the other man's point of view,' he remembered. Monty's gift for positioning himself on the periphery but then finding himself at the centre of things continued with his new home: within a year of building it, flights began on the sands outside after the Coddy chose the eye-catching location for Barra's airport. In the summer of 1936, Monty bragged that it took eight minutes to fly from the gate of Suidheachan to the Gaelic Games on the neighbouring island of South Uist.

A green-veined white butterfly sails through the warm shelter of Suidheachan's front garden and I walk round the back to where a tiny room faces out onto blank pasture of little distraction. An old-fashioned desk stands in the study, as if waiting for Compton to return from one of the afternoon walks that turned him 'very brown', according to Chrissie in a letter to Faith – his Barra wife and his mainland wife were in regular communication over how best to mother their husband. It was here that Monty perfected his fanatical nocturnal writing regimen. Rising well after midday, he would retreat to this gold-papered room, settle back into a dramatically reclined chair that resembled a dentist's and write, longhand, to the sound of Brahms, Mozart and, shortly before dawn, Sibelius. Chrissie stayed up to play these records from an adjoining room until Monty stopped at 6.30 a.m. His scrawl was typed up by his loyal second secretary and former mistress, Nelly Boyte, the next day. In this way, he wrote a novel of more than 100,000 words in thirty-one days.

Compton Mackenzie finally felt at home on an island. He did not try to buy it, possess it or shape it. His commitment was of an enthusiast, not a dilettante, and he was loyally embraced by the locals. 'He was very unconventional. People thought it was odd that he stayed up all night, but they accepted him,' says Mairi Ceit. 'People here accept all kinds of people. It doesn't matter. If they can prove their worth, so what? We've had a lot of strange people over the years.'

Despite the contentment he found on Barra, Compton left Suid-heachan barely a decade after he had arrived. In 1938, while living there, he had toyed with buying another island along with his great friend John Lorne Campbell, but in the end it was Campbell who spent £13,000 on the Hebridean island of Canna while Monty bought a cottage in London's 'Vale of Health', by Hampstead Heath. He retreated again to Barra during the Second World War and had tremendous fun leading the island's Home Guard in war games against South Uist. 'Wild sea-horses would not drag me away from the Hebridean island where I live unless my journey was more than necessary,' he claimed in 1943, but his fading interest in Scottish nationalism – where the romantics had been supplanted by professional politicians – and a growing desire to involve himself in London film projects prompted him to move to the capital permanently in 1945, taking Chrissie with him. When she was dispatched back to Barra to tell Monty's friends he was selling Suidheachan, the Coddy barely concealed his sense of betrayal. 'I am very sorry to hear you are winding up at Suidheachan and unfortunately cutting out Barra from your map,' he wrote to Monty. 'The fact that you were staying on it attracted a big percentage of the visitors to the Island.'

Lawrence's Mr Cathcart pursued island life as an egotistical mission and, from an islander's point of view, Monty's transient passions appear no less selfish. His islands were muses or creative conquests, inhabited and brusquely cast aside when books had been written and inspiration dwindled. Small islands offer artists 'the gift of detachment', as the literary critic Peter Conrad puts it. 'Islands are aesthetic refuges from the confused, congested public realm.' Monty clearly relished being a big fish on Barra, and openly admitted it stroked his ego and sustained his creative output. 'Life on a small island restores human dignity: the individual is not overwhelmed by his own unimportance,' he wrote. 'This is particularly beneficent for the artist.' He was not alone. Robert Louis Stevenson (*Treasure Island*), Barrie (*Peter Pan*) and Arthur Ransome (*Swallows and Amazons*) all had dalliances with the Hebrides. In 1940, Monty urged George Orwell to retreat there and Orwell, long-fascinated by Robinson Crusoe, admitted in his diary that he was 'thinking always of my island in the Hebrides, which I suppose I shall never possess nor even see'. But Orwell did get to live – to the detriment of his health – on damp Jura, which afforded him the vantage point to write *Nineteen Eighty-Four*. 'I like islands,' wrote Will Self more recently, 'because they're discrete and legible, just like stories.'

In the 1870s, Rimbaud fled France to hop onto islands, where he reinvented himself: on Java, he served as a soldier; in Cyprus, he worked in a quarry. Monty took what he needed from each of the islands he lived on, and then moved on, seeing the next one as a chance to jump-start his creativity. After he installed himself on Jethou, he popped back to Capri for a few months with Faith and declared: 'Those weeks of spring and earliest summer in Capri are not as vivid as earlier days.' Faith was sad when they sold their house on the Italian island, 'but Capri had given all it could give to me and was already seeming something in the past,' said Monty. Once he left Herm, and again with Jethou, he never looked back, and never returned. 'The places I have loved best I have always tried to avoid revisiting after I have left them,' he wrote as an old man, 'because I like to keep the picture of them in my mind's eye as they were once upon a time so that in evoking them I evoke simultaneously myself once upon a time.' To use an island merely as a mirror for the self is precisely D.H. Lawrence's charge in 'The Man Who Loved Islands'.

Monty's love of Barra was not quite so self-centred, however. The island was defined by its people. When the Coddy died some years after Monty departed, he betrayed uncharacteristic emotion. 'I felt as if the island itself had floated away like St Brendan's isle,' he wrote. Unlike his other island loves, Barra was tethered in his memory. Perhaps because of his uncharacteristic commitment to it, Barra gave Monty his most successful creative work.

In 1941, the SS *Politician* ran aground on rocks off Eriskay, the island that was visible from his Barra home. On board were cotton, machetes, bicycles, biscuits and other essential items for the colonies of the West Indies. But it was the contents of hold no. 5 that made it famous: 264,000 bottles of King's Ransom, McCallum's Perfection, Haig's Pinch, White Horse and Mountain Dew – whisky, destined for America, to help pay for the war. A salvage firm rescued the cotton and bicycles but oily water in the hold prevented them from extracting the whisky, and the first salvage effort was abandoned. Word spread among the islanders, who looked askance at this waste, and a group of locals including Kenny MacCormick, Monty's chauffeur, sneaked away to where the salvagemen didn't dare, slithering around 'the *Polly's*' oily hold to liberate the unexpected *gu leoir*, Gaelic for 'abundance'. MacCormick 'came back in the morning as black as a crow and exhausted by the night's work down among the cases of whisky in the hold', noted Monty, who particularly enjoyed a brand called Grant's Standfast among the six dozen bottles liberated for him.

Customs and Excise got wind of the looting and made some vindictive arrests, but about 24,000 bottles were spirited away and, during an era of war-induced abstinence, a minor epidemic of revelry and drunkenness enveloped Barra. The liquid gold that became known as 'Polly' was medicinal too: the Coddy told stories of old ladies bathing their feet in it to cure their rheumatism.

The war years passed with Monty aspiring to write great literature, labouring over *The Four Winds of Love*, an epic quartet in six volumes he hoped would be his lasting legacy. Then, once he had left Barra for good, he knocked out *Whisky Galore*, inspired by the sinking of the *Polly*. An irresistible setup – an island starved of whisky during the war and two individuals requiring its lubrication for successful proposals of marriage – and a series of affectionate caricatures, *Whisky Galore* is a celebration of Monty's favourite island home, its amiable satire targeted not at the idealised islanders but at the bureaucratic state they so successfully subvert. It was Compton Mackenzie's smash hit and, unlike almost every other volume of his hundred-plus books, is still in print.

When the film quickly followed, Monty finally achieved his South Pacific dream – filming on an island location. Unusually, the Ealing Studios comedy was shot in Barra rather than on a set in London. Monty returned to the island for the occasion and, with characteristic chutzpah, wangled himself a cameo as the captain of his fictional wreck, SS *Cabinet Minister*. 'The film helped define post-war notions of Britishness with its plucky humour and gentle satire of the class system and officious bureaucracy,' judges Madeleine Bunting. As she recognises, for all its conventional stereotyping, the novel also posits a subtle challenge to mainland culture and religion. It is replete with Gaelic sayings at a time when the language was outlawed in many Hebridean schools, and the sole Englishman is a figure of ridicule. At the centre of the novel is a Catholic priest, and the hero converts to Catholicism. Monty, who understood what it meant to convert to Catholicism, regularly received letters 'denouncing my Popery. All were anonymous and most of them obscene.'

For three decades or more, the novel came to define Barra for the outside world. No newspaper stories or travel features could avoid mentioning it, and by the 1970s the islanders had begun to weary of being known as '*Whisky Galore!* Island'. 'Because of the film, we got branded a bit like alcoholics,' says Mairi Ceit. 'But it was just good fun and the argument was, the whisky was just going to the bottom of the ocean anyway. There wasn't any harm in it.'

I suddenly realise that Mairi Ceit is talking not about the fiction but the fact, and she isn't voicing her own opinion, but the views of many others on Barra whose histories and stories she has absorbed over the years. It is a magical moment: voices of the past are speaking through her.

A lark sings as I cycle beside the sand dunes north of Suidheachan and onto the Eoligarry Peninsula, a spellbinding place of humongous bumblebees and crofts of grey stone scattered among meadows parted by reedbeds the colour of sand. The sea beyond is shallow and the palest of blues, but within the Sound of Barra is a thread of vividly coloured current, the green of the Northern Lights.

'Ah! Eoligarry! The very name is mellifluous,' wrote Alasdair Alpin MacGregor, the writer whose maudlin view of the Western Isles was criticised by Monty. Eoligarry is still a working place. Its sandy-grey soil is more fertile than the rocky fells of central Barra, and the paddocks here are grazed not by sheep but by cattle, who drink from discarded baths reused as water troughs. I wonder if any are from the *Polly*: several of the baths salvaged from the wreck were proudly installed in houses without running water.

There are grey sandy fields where potatoes have been planted, a few incongruous bungalows, a large field of rusting metal where four generations of Barra buses have gone to die, and the ruins of the island's oldest church on a hummock of land filled with graves, cuckooflower, celandines and primroses. A corncrake grates in a ditch and a lapwing flounces overhead, peewitting noisily.

I follow the road to the land's end, by the solitary wind turbine I saw on my arrival. Great slabs of granite slope away to meet a treacherous-looking tidal current. The rocks are fringed with kelp swishing back and forth, deliberately, like the tail of an angry cat. The water pours into the Minch, speeding flotillas of froth to the east. To the west, the horizon is the sharpest I've ever seen. As the sun lowers in the sky, the hills of Barra glow like skin in firelight.

The human world going by on Barra looks pretty much like everywhere else: it mostly consists of people bustling about in their cars. But the grandeur of this space, its light, and the way the days shuttle between wild wind and calm peace must change people's internal lives. On Eoligarry, I stop to chat to a man with a London accent who is rebuilding a two-storey cottage. He hadn't planned on becoming an islander, but he met a Barra girl thirty-five years ago and here he was. We talk about the prohibitive cost of raw materials. Small-island sorcery turns ordinary stuff into expensive stuff: he shipped concrete over from South Uist, which added a third to its price. It's a familiar kind of grumbly conversation, so I'm surprised when he abruptly changes tack and declares he loves his stress-free life on Barra. What about everything being expensive and wages being low, and having no money? 'I never go to a shop. I don't spend money. I grow my own vegetables, keep some sheep. I'm sixty-six, I'm fit and healthy and I'm still working,' he says. His two daughters are on the mainland, working as a nurse and a veterinary assistant, carefully chosen jobs that will allow them to return to work on Barra. 'The young people have to go away but they come back. It's self-sustaining,' he says. He detects a real work ethic among the young islanders. 'There's peer pressure to work hard. You don't want to let your family down.'

Compton Mackenzie shared that work ethic. His fondness for the limelight might have led to a long retirement holding court in the clubs of London, but in 1953 the newly ennobled Sir Compton abandoned the south and returned to his Scottish heartland. He took Chrissie MacSween to live in an elegant terrace in Edinburgh and continued his relentless regime, writing his voluminous autobiography through the night, sleeping until afternoon, then holding court to assorted visitors, his godson Magnus Linklater remembers, while reclining in his single four-poster bed. These included school parties from Barra, who visited the city in 1960 to compete in its Gaelic music festival and were photographed awkwardly clustered around the bedside of 'the man who made their island famous'. Through all these years, Monty remained officially married to Faith; she and Chrissie even colluded to drag him down to London, where he was surprised with an episode of *This Is Your Life*. After Faith died in 1960, he finally married Chrissie. She passed away just a year later and Monty wasted no time in marrying her younger sister Lily, whom he'd first met in 1925, when she was eight. Lily, a beautiful and spirited woman who was very protective of Monty as his sight faded in his final years, opened a hair salon in the basement of their home.

In 1972, when Monty died aged eighty-nine, his body was flown to Barra on a specially chartered plane which barely made it through a gale to bump down onto the sands at Tràigh Mhòr, by his old home. A large crowd was waiting in the rain. 'It was a wild day, the wind was howling but we were all down,' remembers Mairi Ceit. An old friend of Monty's, Calum Johnston, who was in his eighties, wore his

Highland uniform and played the pipes. With a touch of the kind of drama that had cascaded through Monty's life, as Johnston followed the coffin up the slope into the graveyard he collapsed and died. He was buried close to Monty.

I circle the graveyard's three small fields twice before I find Monty's grave. Among all the MacNeils – Roderick, Peggie, Marion, Mary, Donald, Iain, Murdoch, Fr Calum, John, Malcolm, Archibald – is a modest stone cross mounted on a roughly shaped lump of granite with the words: 'Compton Mackenzie 1883–1972'. This man of four million words is enshrined in unobtrusive minimalism. He was a high-profile champion of Barra and its causes but he has been laid to rest in the island's democratic tradition. 'There was just a space for him,' says Mairi Ceit. 'It's with the people. He's not in an elevated position. When it is adorned with the primroses, the same carpet goes over him as everyone else. He's got a beautiful resting place.'

The next day, I fly home. The airport café is bustling once again but there's no call for the plane, only a few people quietly disappearing onto the beach, and I hurry out, heartened that the airport's shop – one shelf of souvenirs – stocks copies of *Whisky Galore*. Compton Mackenzie may not be much more than a footnote in the rich present of Barra, but there are still little tremors of him all over.

The Twin Otter's two women pilots – the matriarchy at Barra's airport is an object of fascination in many yellowed old newspaper stories about the island – flick switches and we taxi onto the asphalt-smooth sand. Water splashes around the wheels, tiny flecks of sand splatter onto the windows and we steeple upwards over jade waters. I glance outside and catch a final glimpse of Suidheachan, Monty's house, a large white exclamation mark on a blank page, alone on a small island.

4

The Island for Idealists

Eigg, The Inner Hebrides, 11.8 square miles, population 100

'The Master himself began to be a little afraid of his island.
He knew quite well now that his people didn't love him at all.
He knew that their spirits were secretly against him'
'The Man Who Loved Islands'

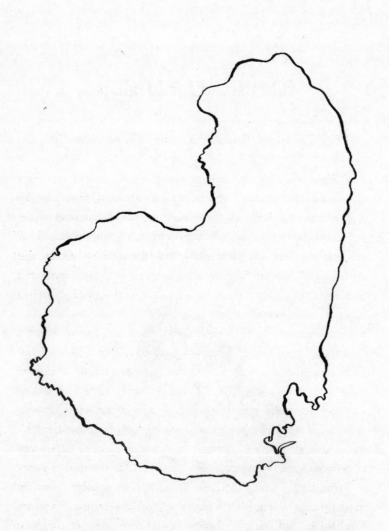

The *Sheerwater* bounces over the waves past trim great northern divers and seals as fat as slugs. Ahead is a green island with a rocky peak sticking up like a quiff. We pull onto an old concrete ramp beside a small shop and a café with a couple of benches outside. A group of islanders cast an expert eye over the arrivals – visitors and provisions – which are variously bundled into an old black taxi with a bent door, a Post Office van and a pea-pod of an electric car. 'Doubles up as a hoover,' says someone.

Locals come and go but an ever-changing constellation of half a dozen people chat by the benches in the sunny shelter of the buildings. There's an artistic-looking woman with a French accent, a bloke in high-vis, a young lad with a flick of dark hair, a mum with a baby, and an assortment of men of late middle age with florid complexions.

It's midday, I buy a fizzy drink from the shop and join the milling. A sheepdog with psychedelic eyes drops a piece of frayed rope at everyone's feet, expectantly, for a throw. After the treeless purity of Barra, Eigg – from old Gaelic for 'notch', or possibly Norse for its 'sharp edge' – is a shock, a fecund riot of bracken, meadowsweet, hazel woods and waterfalls beneath two rising ridges of columnar basalt. The trees have wild beards of lichen, the residents just have wild beards.

'What, are you boys on the drink?' says the man with the electric car, catching sight of a pint glass.

'It's Friday afternoon,' says one of the men, checking his watch to make sure.

The young lad returns from the cafe which, it transpires, is also a bar, and sinks down on the bench, by a map of the island. 'Magners,' he explains. 'I had too much coffee.'

Pausing to pass the time of day, the locals turn their faces to the sunshine, gazing south over a solitary sailing boat in the harbour. Above us to the west rises the rocky quiff, An Sgùrr. The water is a perfect blue, the light is so strikingly sharp it renders everything in high definition, and the most miraculous thing is the air – not a fresh salty blast but a complex, constantly changing infusion of sweet, peaty bracken, flowers, kelp and mud.

I comment on this idyllic scene. 'Quite a lot of people come in the summer and think it's a Caribbean island. Try it in the winter,' says the lad, Ruairidh Kirk. He's actually a boyish mid-twenties, his father from Eigg, his mother from Hemel Hempstead. He turned seven the day the islanders bought out its owner, Keith Schellenberg, and the Republic of Eigg came into being. This triumph of David versus Goliath has created an apparently marvellous sustainable community that seems at once industriously creative and lackadaisical, with its colourful houses, gardens filled with strawberry patches, hammocks made from old fishing nets and swings from old pink buoys.

Ruairidh works in rope access. In the old days, young islanders would join the Merchant Navy. Now they go off to climb – fixing netting on cliffs above roads to stop falling rocks, for instance. On a good day he can earn £250. Highlanders are in demand.

'We've got a different work ethic to the southern softies. We're quite happy to do fifteen hours without a stop. Most Glaswegians want to stop every half-hour for a water break.'

'Who would've thought the Eigg boys were tougher than the boys in Glasgow,' says the woman with the French accent.

Ruairidh isn't bothered by the gentle mockery.

Interesting work, I say politely. 'Not really,' says Ruairidh, miming holding a drill for fourteen hours.

He comes home when he can. 'I couldn't stay here all the time, no way, not at my age. But most of the younger folk will be drawn back.' He gives me an ironic look. 'We try to make it as interesting as possible.'

I don't know the swirl of personalities by the shop and the café – known as the tea-room – but I can believe it: there's an abundance of charisma in this small island gathering. Everyone seems to be a storyteller, and to have the time to tell their stories. A few visitors like me mill around too, but it's difficult to identify them because they've been so rapidly welcomed into island life by the locals. I'm soon hearing about one arrival a few years back who pitched up after midnight in a kayak and ended up settling on Eigg. There's one islander known as the Exorcist because after he visits there's never any spirits left; another, a regular visitor from the mainland, is called the Moth because if someone leaves a light on late at night, he'll find it, invite himself in and start a party. I'm captivated. It reminds me of Compton Mackenzie's description of the 'outstanding' characters on Barra in the 1930s – the Coddy, the Crookle, the Red Scholar – and his perceptive comment that this surfeit of personality was set within a very equal sort of place rather than a rampantly individualistic society. These islanders, thought Monty, 'were all aristocrats of the democracy'.

The shop and the tea-room at the southern tip of Eigg are the modern centre of the island, where tourists get their bearings and hire bikes. I look at the map on the shop wall and realise it's at least three miles up and over the moor to the wooden camping pod at the north-western corner of the island, Cleadale, where I'm staying.

'Ah, the rebel stronghold,' says a handsome bearded man of late middle age called Brian Greene, in a crisp English accent, when he learns that I'm heading for Cleadale. And then he quickly offers me a lift up Eigg's main road, a tiny lane wiggling over its middle.

Every car on Eigg looks decrepit and sounds sick, emitting gravelly bass notes, wheezes and death rattles. Most are island-only cars, and don't require the MOTs and tax of the mainland. Brian's ancient Peugeot 406 possesses a random patchwork of green and grey body panels and the voice of a tractor. We chug up the hill past a young couple. Brian waves cheerily and they wave back. Locals? 'They are definitely tourists,' he says. 'I don't recognise their walk.'

Everyone waves on Eigg. We pass another man and his son. Brian waves again. The man gives a flinch-cum-nod. 'You've got to fucking move your wrist,' mutters Brian in a good-natured way as we sweep by. 'I've been past him five times today and he still can't wave.' Perhaps he's shy, I say, understanding a fellow visitor struggling to shake off his mainland reserve. 'Women always wave back,' says Brian.

That's a nice house. I point to a large Victorian stone building with solar panels and a massive woodshed, alone on the moor.

'It's the school,' says Brian.

I ask him how he came to Eigg and he tells me about *Man Alive*, the slightly sensational BBC documentary series that featured Eigg in 1979. His mum watched it, saw an advert for a job on Eigg, and answered it for him. That was how he came to work for Keith Schellenberg, the former laird of Eigg. He was given a six-month contract that came with accommodation. 'I was supposed to do fifteen hours a week and it was sixty hours with this monster on my back.' Brian issues a couple of expletives about his ex-boss. Schellenberg 'wanted to retain it as a 1930s paradise,' he thinks. 'The Republic of Eigg is far better.'

Eigg is perhaps second to St Kilda as the most famous small island in Britain. St Kilda is renowned for its extinction as a place of human settlement; Eigg is celebrated for its rebirth, triggered by its unusual answer to the perennial small-island question of ownership.

The Isle of Man, Orkney and the Outer Hebrides do not have such a vexed history of capricious landlords. Perhaps their remoteness, their bleakness and the strength of their local culture militate against individual possession but, in modern times, the ownership of islands is often simply related to their size. Those islands are mostly too large to be owned by an individual. The industrialist William Lever, 1st Viscount Leverhulme, overreached himself when he bought the whole of Lewis, the British Isles' largest island after Britain and Ireland, in 1917. His plan to revitalise its fishing industry failed, and he sold up in 1923.

With Eigg, my fourth destination, I've reached an island of a size that can be owned by one person. Eigg is part of a quartet with Muck, Rum and Canna: the Small Isles are small, perfectly formed and eminently possessable. For the last two centuries, these striking islands have been an object of desire for wealthy men – and it has always been men – who love islands, with disastrous consequences for both sides. Fredrik Sjöberg, whom I visited on Runmäro, believes small islands possess 'a peculiar attraction for men with a need for control and security' because 'nothing is so enclosed and concrete as an island'. Peter Conrad offers a more Freudian interpretation, suggesting that an island is a 'uterine shelter' surrounded, like the foetus, by fluid, and attracting men in search of a mother or a primal source of safety. This sounds like glib literary theorising, but in the case of Compton Mackenzie, denied any maternal affection as a child, it makes sense: islands may have fulfilled his nagging need for a mother figure and the comfort of home.

Islands have also been viewed as eggs, unspoilt but eminently spoilable. One of Eigg's old Gaelic names is 'the Island of the Powerful Women', which it was respectfully called by male islanders at sea, to avoid bad luck. But its matriarchy was despoiled by a succession of men whose craving for Eigg outdid their means. The English Runciman family were reasonably enlightened – Lord Runciman's wife became one of the first women MPs – but they sold Eigg as a 'perfectly secluded island of the Old World' in 1966. It was bought by an elderly Welsh farmer whose Herefordshire cattle promptly died of bracken poisoning. Disheartened, he got rid of Eigg for £110,000 in 1971 to Bernard Farnham-Smith, head of an English charity that wanted to run the island as a school for handicapped boys. By 1973, Eigg's own school was down to one pupil and so islanders welcomed the charismatic 'Commander' with his stories of his Navy days in China. Farnham-Smith's ingenious ideas were a bit vague, however, and he was soon cutting costs. The island doctor described his regime as 'living under enemy occupation, without the satisfaction of being able to shoot the bugger'. It turned out that the most Farnham-Smith had commanded was a fire brigade, and Eigg was back on the market in 1974.

On 1 April 1975 Keith Schellenberg, a dashing Yorkshire-born businessman and former Olympic bobsleigher, acquired Eigg. He was a charming, persuasive adventurer who, over the next twenty years, fulfilled the narrative of 'The Man Who Loved Islands' more faithfully than any other real nesomane. Legend has it that Schellenberg found himself locked in his home at Udny Castle, a grand pile belonging to his second wife, with the deadline for a blind auction for Eigg approaching. Unfazed, he abseiled down the walls to offer Farnham-Smith £274,000, seventy-four thousand more than the state-run Highlands and Islands Development Board was prepared to pay.

The thirty-nine remaining islanders – an all-time population low – were initially pleased. They didn't want a takeover by the government, which had shown little interest in renovating their pier or reforming the high freight charges on the ferry. At first, Schellenberg promoted a prescient modern vision of self-sufficiency through tourism, the miracle industry then hailed by the authorities as the solution to the

Highland 'problem'. Farnham-Smith had kept the wooden community hall locked, but in a popular early move Schellenberg gave it back to the islanders so there could be badminton in winter and dances in summer. Dozens of ceilidhs took place during that first golden year. Unlike other Highland lairds, Schellenberg was a vegetarian who objected to shooting, and he quickly involved the Scottish Wildlife Trust in creating three nature reserves. Buildings were renovated for holiday homes, and flashy boats, including a motor cruiser called the *Golden Eye*, brought tourists to the island. Job ads in national newspapers brought an influx of new residents to work for the new owner.

Maggie and Wes Fyffe were running a craft workshop on the east coast of Scotland when Schellenberg turned up and invited them to start a similar project on Eigg. Maggie has keen, twinkly eyes, a Lancastrian accent and an excellent smokers' chuckle. She and Wes loved Eigg and felt an immediate sense of belonging. 'Apart from the fact that it is beautiful, I just liked being part of a small community,' she says as we drink tea in her croft (her mug, dating from the Scottish referendum, reads 'Dependence Is for Kids' with an image of a spaced-out child). Maggie and Wes had two children and, on Eigg, they no longer felt excluded from things. 'Kids go to everything here because if there's something happening everybody goes,' says Maggie. 'It just felt right.'

As on Barra, the Gaelic-speaking Eigg natives were far from insular. 'It's a real misconception that folk have about Hebridean crofter types,' says Maggie. She mentions an old islander who has travelled the globe and fought in Palestine. 'People in general here are very hospitable, it's part of the culture. They were really happy to see young people and kids arriving,' she says. That outward-facing mentality is still a feature of the island.

By the summer of 1979, Eigg was open for business. The population jumped to sixty and the school, that crucial barometer of small-island health, suddenly had twelve pupils. There was a new tea-room and craft centre; moped hire, day cruises, sea-angling, lobster fishing and pony trekking were on offer. Visitors could even help with haymaking or shearing sheep. Unfortunately, when the tourists arrived, these activities were rarely available. Staff turnover was worryingly high. New employees were housed in run-down buildings with polythene for windowpanes. Schellenberg's grand Lodge was open house for his High Society friends in high summer. One likened him to Mr Toad: 'Keith actually wears those round goggles and he's always arriving in places with a lot of noise and clouds of dust.' His prized possession was a 1927 Rolls-Royce. Guests would perch on the running board as he drove them to beach picnics or moonlit games of hockey. 'We spent our days as if we were Somerset Maugham characters, sunbathing or playing croquet on the manicured lawn,' said another friend. In the village shop I meet Sarah Boden, one of Eigg's two farmers. She remembers a German playboy landing in the Lodge gardens in a helicopter. Two models dressed in catsuits brandishing toy guns stepped out first. 'Schellenberg was very charismatic, a real showman,' says Sarah, who recalls him driving around in an eight-wheeled ArgoCat, an amphibious all-terrain vehicle. 'He'd drive it to the boat and park it in the most ridiculous place possible at the pier, just so the visitors would watch.'

Schellenberg revived the inter-island games that traditionally took place between residents of the Small Isles, and for his guests devised war games with yellow tennis balls, which were insensitively billed as Jacobites versus Hanoverians. During the 1988 games the island ceilidh band, who had agreed to play for his wealthy guests, decided there would be a small entrance fee to raise money for a new hall. When Schellenberg discovered his American friends had been charged, he demanded that their money be returned. The band walked off stage and many islanders left the concert in protest, pursued by one of the laird's aristocratic Scottish guests who shouted: 'Scum of the earth, half-baked socialists!'

Behind the comedy was genuine suffering. In 1980, Schellenberg had divorced his wealthy second wife and, suddenly much poorer, was running Eigg on a shoestring. The farm manager quit, labourers were made redundant and the tractors ran out of diesel. His regime was propped up by the generous government tax breaks for new, environmentally damaging, plantations of non-native Sitka spruce. The rain came in through the nursery roof; old islanders' homes were by now particularly dilapidated. Life 'was quite grim', remembers Sarah, who spent the first six years of her life on the island in the 1980s. 'We lived in five different houses and two caravans. Schellenberg would employ and sack people on a total whim, so there was no security.'

Inadvertently, though, he created an island community that would ultimately depose him. Many of the outsiders he hired and fired, such as Maggie and Wes Fyffe, liked Eigg so much that they stayed, and scratched out a self-sufficient life on crofts in Cleadale, the fertile valley that had been the island's traditional centre. Older inhabitants were welcoming, if perplexed to see newcomers adopt the life they urged their children to escape. Old and new bonded over house ceilidhs while Schellenberg fretted about Eigg's 'hippy' population. He characterised them as misfits fleeing the mainstream, 'wandering itinerants who found the island a nice refuge but were not mentally strong enough to cope with the life and earn a living'.

The laird was struggling to earn one too. Planned golf courses and tennis courts never materialised and tourism petered to a halt. 'I've kept its style slightly run down – the Hebrides feel,' he claimed in later years. Eventually, Schellenberg's ex-wife, who still jointly owned Eigg, took him to court, accusing him of mismanaging their declining asset. Across the Highlands, by the 1990s, there were growing calls for land reform. Tom Forsyth, an unsung hero of Scottish land reform who had helped regenerate crofting on an isolated peninsula north of Ullapool, imagined that Eigg could become a new Iona. Together with Alastair McIntosh, a Lewis academic, Robert Harris, a Borders farmer, and Liz Lyon, an artist, he would found the Isle of Eigg Heritage Trust. In 1991 they launched a public appeal: to buy the island for £3 million.

The following May, Schellenberg was forced by his ex-wife to put Eigg up for sale. In July 1992, it was bought by the highest bidder: Schellenberg. He planned to take his Rolls-Royce on a 'triumphant tour' of the island, reported the *Scotsman*, 'once it was rendered roadworthy'. The car's days were numbered, however: early in January 1994 the sheds on Eigg's pier burned down, with Schellenberg's Roller inside. The police arrived to investigate but the culprits were never identified. 'It was once the laird's factor who went about burning people out. Now it seems OK to burn out the laird himself,' fumed Schellenberg, blaming 'hippies and drop-outs' for subverting island traditions with 'acid-rock parties'. Eigg's indigenous population responded with an open letter refuting his 'ludicrous allegations'.

Schellenberg was determined not to let the islanders take over, and in 1995, needing money for an acrimonious split from his third wife, he abruptly sold Eigg to a fire-worshipping German artist and self-styled 'professor' who went by the name of Maruma – Gotthilf Christian Eckhard Oesterle had read his new name in a pool of water in Geneva. Schellenberg returned to Eigg one last time to requisition an 1805 map of the island from the craft shop. Islanders heard he was on his way and parked a disused community bus against the shop's door to block it. Then they took the day off to see what would happen next. A local police officer told the furious ex-landlord that if no one claimed ownership of the bus within thirty days he could remove it. Schellenberg stormed off, by boat. 'You never understood me,' was his anguished parting shot to the islanders. 'I always wanted to be one of you.' Brian almost felt sorry for him. 'He was like an alien. The Scots can be pretty hard on their thousand-year-old oppressor sometimes,' he says. 'Everyone has good points, but he refused to show his.'

Maruma arrived with grand plans. He declared it was impossible to own Eigg and vowed to improve opportunities for the community, build a swimming pool and replace the dirty diesel generators that provided electricity with an integrated system of wind and solar power. Unfortunately, the press discovered that Maruma was not quite what he seemed: he was unknown in the art world, he wasn't a proper professor, and he had used Eigg as security for a £300,000 loan at a punitive 20 per cent interest rate. He promised to remove the island's rusty old cars, but a pile of wrecks soon accumulated by the pier: locals dubbed it 'the Maruma Centre'. In July 1996, the island was up for sale again, at the inflated price of £2 million.

The Trust redoubled its fundraising efforts. The story of the islanders who wanted to buy their own island was portrayed as a jolly romp in the style of Compton Mackenzie's *Whisky Galore*. Eigg folk didn't particularly relish this stereotype, but it captured imaginations and raised money.

Maggie Fyffe, who became the Trust's administrator, sorted through the mail from wellwishers: donations began flowing in at the rate of £1,000 per post bag; soon it was £30,000 per bag. Concerts took place in Edinburgh, Glasgow, Tyrone – even Detroit – to raise funds. A mystery benefactor, a woman from northern England whose identity Maggie still won't reveal, gave £900,000. According to Alastair McIntosh, most donations came from England. Outsiders were shocked by the feudalism that the islanders endured – the owners even decided which of them, if any, could eat Eigg's seaweed – and worried about the possible fate of its pristine environment. The wildlife trusts, including the Scottish Wildlife Trust, were particularly effective at mobilising their members to help Eigg.

Meanwhile, the island's Trust feared that Maruma's German estate agent would sell Eigg to another international client. The agent described the Scottish islands on his books as 'the Van Goghs' of 120 personally inspected paradises: 'There is a sense of romance in buying islands. It is the ultimate purchase you can make, a complete miniature world of which you can be king.' Maruma's creditor, a German clothing exporter, finally put the islanders out of their misery. After Maruma defaulted on his £300,000 loan, the creditor used the Scottish courts to force Eigg's sale. His solicitors accepted the islanders' offer of £1.6 million on 4 April 1997, Ruairidh Kirk's birthday. Finally, the people of Eigg owned their island.

'It's the difference between black-and-white TV and colour,' says Brian. 'That's what it was like after the revolution.' I get a sense of what he means after three days on Eigg during which the rain does not relent for thirty hours. Low cloud smothers every tone but green and grey. I lie in my wooden cabin and read the excellent history of Eigg written by Camille Dressler, Brian's partner, to the sound of water tumbling down the great basalt cliffs by God's Finger, a pinnacle pointing up into the gloom above Cleadale. Finally, I wake on the third morning to the kind of explosive Highland summer's day that English visitors – Compton Mackenzie's boat trip to Mingulay springs to mind – remember for the rest of their lives. In a humid frenzy, lawnmowers rev in croft gardens, washing flutters on the lines that run up the hillside, and butterflies jink out of the steaming greenery.

To the west, finally, is revealed the island of Rum, six jagged peaks in a sea of glass. Rum shares the fate of many small islands in the second half of the twentieth century: it was emptied of people and turned into a nature reserve. Even today, on the brightest of mornings, it possesses a personal cloud, which slowly thins and flattens and dissipates like the desire to work as the day warms up.

The modern centre of Eigg may be its pier-side shop and café, but Cleadale is its traditional capital. Crofts are dotted over the valley, tending strips of land running westerly down from the cliffs of Beinn Bhuidhe to the beach, where a flotsam of unmatchable wellies are artfully arranged on fence posts. Some crofts are a picture of dereliction, swallows darting from broken roofs. Others are pretty working smallholdings, with tractors and 4x4s or tea-rooms or B&Bs. 'The landscapes of the Small Isles are a bit like the people,' islander Karen Helliwell tells me when she gives me a lift down the road. She describes the island of Muck as 'intensively farmed and well organised'; Eigg is 'a bit more complicated, with all the good things and bad things that brings'. Muck has a single landowner, unlike Eigg with its numerous small crofts.

I've found the human story of Eigg's last century so compelling that I'm caught out by its natural beauty. The naturalist Seton Gordon described it as 'the island of flowers', and now everything is flowering simultaneously. Wet meadows are piled high with hogweed, bramble, thistle, buttercup, meadowsweet, yellow flag iris and pink clover. There are foxgloves, which bloom in May down south, flowering alongside August perennials montbretia and fuchsia. I pick tiny tart raspberries from tangled banks and abandon my research for a lone walk, striking out across the moors. In a sheltered hollow I find a dead cow, reduced to a skeleton. Beyond are lichens as white as bone, pale cotton grass, greasy to touch, and beneath my feet sphagnum moss the colour of a sunshine-faded Afghan rug.

I climb to the broad mile-long ridge of Beinn Bhuidhe, Cleadale laid out like an aerial photograph far below. A pallid shape hugs the contours of the moor on long thin wings, a hen harrier, banking, threatening to land, violently, on a hidden vole. Its owl-like head swivels, it knows I'm here, and then it's gone, over the edge. There are no grouse moors on Eigg and, unlike on the mainland, no people persecuting predators such as this beautiful bird.

A profusion of cotton-coloured magpie moths crash-land in the perfumed purple heather. Grayling butterflies gather on the tops, snapping their wings shut whenever they alight on the ground. For a small spot at the northern edge of Europe encircled by water, Eigg is unexpectedly rich in butterflies and moths. I admire the powerful dark-green fritillaries that glide over the flowery meadows, and remember that the same insects soared through Compton Mackenzie's life during his happy retreat at Jethou. A small island, he thought, endowed people with a more intimate relationship with its fellow inhabitants: birds, flowers and butterflies. 'One seems to recognise them as individuals,' he wrote. 'I recall the graylings sunning themselves with their folded wings tilted over almost flat on the ground (does any other butterfly do this?) and seeing a female brimstone with folded wings who looked so much like a leaf that a fly had alighted on her under the impression that she really was a leaf.'

When I first read 'The Man Who Loved Islands', I didn't realise that Monty loved butterflies as I did. And there is something of the butterfly about Monty too. The hero of his epic *Four Winds of Love* is generally accepted to be Monty himself, and he is accused of being a butterfly. His Faith-like wife defends him: 'He may be. But even butterflies have their uses. They fertilise many flowers during their beautiful existence.'

The butterfly effect of Compton Mackenzie is revealed to me by Magnus Linklater, who tells me about the time he rang up Monty's third wife Lily in 1988 to tell her that he and his wife had found the house of their dreams on the same Edinburgh street as Monty's last home. 'Well, I can tell you something,' Lily replied. 'We were married in that house.' It had been a Catholic seminary, Monty had married the woman he first met as an eight-year-old there, and now it had been unwittingly bought by his godson. Mackenzie's life was replete with striking symbolism and serendipity. His obsessions were so wide-ranging that they seemed to spirit fortuitous coincidences into being, or at least that is what he chose to believe with his lucky pair of kingfishers on Jethou, ushering him away from the island before it was invaded during the war. Monty wove around himself a protective cocoon of anecdotes, stories and connections, real and imagined. His biographer Andro Linklater argues that he was at heart an actor, that the world was his stage, and that his greatest artistic creation was his own existence.

High at the north end of Eigg, I discover the outline of a zigzag path down the saddle and descend towards a strip of white beach called the Singing Sands. On my way down, I'm stopped by a large furry fox moth caterpillar, marching across the path in a proprietorial fashion, searching for a place to pupate. Its shiny brown fur resembles an acrylic sofa from the 1970s and it possesses the fearlessness of a big insect, curious about my outstretched hand, its feet gently tacky as they tramp across it. As I admire it, I sense that the butterfly effect of Compton Mackenzie will follow me to every island I visit.

Community-owned Eigg is twenty years old now. Like a celebrity, it must handle fame, fans, negative publicity and hangers-on. A constant stream of filmmakers, journalists, anthropologists and scientists pitch up to study the place, so I sense a certain weariness when I pull my notebook from my pocket. Sarah Boden moved back to Eigg in 2010, after years as a music journalist in London. She's amazed by how many members of her former tribe arrive on storytelling business each summer and expect her to delightedly drop everything. 'A lot of them come with a script that they expect you to conform to – "As a community we are forging forwards and revolutionising X, Y and Z" – but usually the reality is a lot more complicated than that. They don't really listen to what you say and go away none the wiser.' Or, as her partner Johnny Lynch puts it: 'I find it quite embarrassing because there's folk here who say, "I saw you on the TV, you fanny."'

At the time of the buyout, Simon Fraser, then chairman of the Trust, called it 'a triumph for all that is good in humanity and certainly one in the eye for everything that is mean spirited and self-seeking'. The islanders celebrated independence day on 12 June 1997 with ninety bottles of malt donated by Skye's Talisker distillery, originally founded by brothers from Eigg. The hangover, an eruption of mean-spiritedness, came six years later. A Scottish-German journalist, a critic of land reform, visited Eigg and penned an unflattering portrayal of the new island rulers for *Die Zeit* in Germany, which British tabloids were only too happy to echo. Islanders were quoted speaking of a 'clash of cultures' – between Hebridean residents and incomers – and Keith Schellenberg chipped in, claiming Eigg had been despoiled 'by people who had lived in Tibet and had "Make Love, Not War" painted on the sides of their vans'.

This little storm was a perfect tale for the moralising media because critics felt it so neatly echoed the narrative of Jura's most celebrated islander, George Orwell:

'The creatures outside looked from pig to man, and from man to pig, and from pig to man again; but already it was impossible to say which was which.'

Fables seep into our consciousness, and the newspapers' cautionary tales about Eigg appear to have lodged in the minds of many who briefly visit the islands. I met two tourists on Barra who passed on gossip they'd heard about Eigg politics, claiming it was a cliquey, 'clannish' place. I encountered an ex-resident of Rum who declared that Eigg was 'a bit too full of scandals and growers and dropouts', and suggested residents needed to grow up. Robert Louis Stevenson, who adventured through the isles of the South Pacific in the 1880s, described the drifters in the Marquesas as 'people "on the beach"' – beached like driftwood – and more than once before I reached Eigg, I heard that familiar accusation: it's full of people who flee to a small island because they can't hack it in the mainstream.

There was another charge too: its residents were grant-junkies, sustaining their laidback lifestyles with mainland subsidies. I chat to the owner-captain of the *Sheerwater* on my way to Eigg and he criticises his larger rival, the government-subsidised CalMac ferry. I assume he'll attack Eigg's subsidised existence too but he unexpectedly defends the island: everyone talks about Eigg's grant money, he argues, but no one on the mainland describes the National Grid or roads or hospitals as state handouts, whereas Eigg built its own electricity grid and doesn't have hospitals or proper roads. Subsidies are hoovered up by whoever owns land in Britain, so Eigg's former owner, Keith Schellenberg, benefited from tax breaks on his forestry. It does seem unfair, then, to criticise the islanders for applying for the subsidies enjoyed by wealthier landowners. As islanders point out, taxpayers' funds provided just £17,517 towards Eigg's community buyout.

Plenty of outsiders look more positively upon Eigg. On my way home from the island, I stopped for supper in Glasgow with Alastair McIntosh. I found the author and activist who invigorated Eigg's independence movement volunteering at GalGael, a charity based in an old workshop in the redbrick terraced streets around Rangers' Ibrox Stadium. Young people were carving wood and learning how to build boats. We shared a creamy communal lasagne.

Alastair's beard is turning white and he controls a hearing aid with his mobile phone, but he still possesses an aura of both vitality and peace, and is as inspiring as the best kind of preacher. To my surprise, this man of Lewis is only a little bit more Scottish than Compton Mackenzie, who was born in Hartlepool. Alastair was born in Doncaster to an English mother and a Scottish father. When Alastair was four years old his father took the family to Lewis, which remains his son's heartland, and worked there as a GP. The island is the foundation for Alastair's belief in the importance of communities rooted in a local culture that can transcend the spiritual paucity of global capitalism and its veneration of consumption.

Activists, he told me, must get used to the notion of many more defeats than victories, and so he cherishes Eigg, a rare win. 'When we set up the first Eigg Trust, the original vision was about renewable energy, cultural renewal and renewal of the spirit. Not only has all of it been fulfilled, but it's been considerably surpassed.' He's not claiming the credit, it's the islanders who've exceeded the Trust's hopes. He recently returned to Eigg. 'The ones who were heavy on the drink were still heavy on the drink, but the thing that impressed me was the number of young people who were back, balancing babies with a rich matrix of economic activities by which they held their lives together and built their homes, unfettered by an absentee landlord.'

The old divide between indigenous people and newcomers has disappeared on Eigg with a younger generation who are a melange of both. The supposed Hebridean/hippy divide was never so stark or so simple, thinks Alastair, and many islanders working quietly at the heart of the community – such as Ruairidh Kirk's dad and uncle – are from indigenous families. Eigg's success has come from a genuine fusion of Hebridean culture and mainland counterculture. Incomers who have fitted in with island life, and not just come to buy the view, have taken on the best Hebridean traditions of spirituality, cooperation, hospitality and music, believes Alastair, and Eigg has attracted people wanting to participate in a nurturing, less materialistic community. 'It's infectious. Eigg has drawn people who feel that need, and we need to serve that need.' But to create a community less focused on money and personal profit, people need a platform to share it, he argues, and that platform is 'the land'.

The fact that the community owns the island of Eigg makes it different from alternative-minded communities in, say, Totnes or Hebden Bridge, or almost any place in England where daily life, and most possibilities, are mediated through the landownership of private individuals.

The community-owning Eigg is 'not a selfish endeavour. It's not about just wanting to be landowners, it's about the community having life and individuals having life within that community,' said Alastair. 'In Scotland, we spit the word out – "property". You can't own the land, the land owns you. What I found in England is there's such a lack of physical space and it's usually upper-class-controlled. England has never recovered from the Norman conquest. That deeply embedded class system is so divisive.' In contrast, community ownership enables Eigg to be its own housing association and to provide cheap rents – currently about half the market level of 'affordable housing' in this region of Scotland. Low-rent societies where residents are liberated from the grind of earning a lot to pay for a house are likely to be more radical, creative places: people have the freedom, and time, to pursue less money-oriented goals.

I spend several days walking across Eigg to meet different islanders who have helped run the Isle of Eigg Heritage Trust. Contrary to the critique of Eigg, the Trust looks rather grown-up. It is scrupulously democratic: four islanders are directors and serve four-year terms, with one elected each year. The Trust's work is scrutinised by the Eigg Residents' Association, which represents every adult member of the community. Newcomers must have eighteen months' residency before they can vote. The Trust's directors are augmented by a representative from the local council, another from the Scottish Wildlife Trust and a chairperson from outside the island. 'It's good to have an independent chair,' says Maggie Fyffe. 'Small communities can be a little bit interesting sometimes.'

Apart from replacing feudalism with democracy, the Trust's first priority after buying the island was to ensure that the islanders, who mostly lease their properties, had one basic right they never enjoyed under previous individual owners: security of tenure. They established longer leases and renovated dilapidated homes. Then the Trust built the shop and the tea-room, with toilets and showers for visitors.

The early years of the Trust were not riven with conflict, but the historian Camille Dressler reveals some tensions in her island history. The directors of the Trust realised, to their 'bafflement and frustration', that 'the suspicion towards power-holders, which was once directed at the landowner, now found itself directed at the Trust'. The Schellen-berg/Maruma era was, at best, a negligent one, and the islanders were used to quietly sorting things out themselves. Many had enjoyed this feeling of liberty from bureaucratic conventions, and were not sure they liked the box-ticking new regime. As Karen Helliwell told Dressler: 'The more efficient we try to make this organisation, the more we end up like the mainland.' Those early years were a steep learning curve, admits Maggie Fyffe, but Camille says any unease about the self-governing regime has disappeared now. A high proportion of residents volunteer for the Trust or for various committees and teams that manage everything from the island's rubbish to its culture and history, but there are some refuseniks. Sarah Boden is currently serving as a Trust director. 'The same people tend to complain and the same people have to step up. If you're semi-sensible you get roped into quite a lot,' she tells me. 'We still struggle with an us-v-them mentality. Sometimes decisions get made and people moan about 'the Trust this' or 'the Trust that'. You have to remind them that they *are* the Trust.'

The people who've volunteered for the Trust over the years are open about their disagreements, but Maggie Fyffe believes that almost every decision is reached by consensus. Over twenty years, she can remember only one community-wide vote being taken, which was to determine who would be awarded the multi-million-pound contract to build their expensive new pier.

Eigg has thrived, thinks Alastair McIntosh, because the community has developed a way to manage disputes. 'That's of such importance. In my view, the main inhibitor of community landownership is that people are afraid of themselves, they are afraid of what might be set loose if they don't have a controlling figure above them.' Many portraits of island dystopias are driven by this fear. On his tour of Scotland, Samuel Johnson wrote of the dangers of brooding brought on by small islands: 'The evils of dereliction rush upon the thoughts; man is made unwillingly acquainted with his own weakness.' Mr Cathcart is confronted by precisely this in 'The Man Who Loved Islands'. Was D.H. Lawrence scared of small islands too? William

Golding brooded much upon this danger, and this shows not only in *Lord of the Flies*, where the schoolboy inhabitants of a small island rapidly turn feral, but in *Pincher Martin* too, where a wrecked sailor's small island is revealed to be a hallucination of his own ruined mind, or perhaps even purgatory. The residents of Eigg have faced down their inner demons and won, thinks Alastair.

As I sit in Maggie's croft, which smells of roll-ups and woodsmoke and where fairy lights twinkle over the mantelpiece, I ask if Eigg is a utopia. 'Utopia is a bit strong.' She cackles wildly at my silly question and then pauses. 'I think it is. I love it here.'

The Eigg Trust's ability to manage discord and provide secure tenancies for affordable housing is not particularly visible to outsiders, but it has won round doubters with its most feted achievement: its green electricity grid. Like many small islands, Eigg has never been connected to the National Grid, and power used to be provided by expensive, unreliable and dirty diesel generators. Businesses such as the shop couldn't run without reliable electricity, and the island even had a communal freezer because no householders could run a fridge or freezer themselves. So the Trust created a subsidiary, Eigg Electric Ltd, and built its own renewable grid, harnessing the power of the island's bountiful winds and streams with solar to generate twenty-four-hour power for all. The grid opened in 2008. 'The electricity is the biggest thing that's happened here,' says Maggie. 'It was a big scary project, £1.5 million, and it's been life-changing. It really has made a huge difference to everything.'

This renewable power is so discreet that I don't see any turbines during my stay, and only realise when I'm leaving that the small noisy shed by one of the rushing streams is a hydro plant. Some power is stored, but it is also limited. The islanders agreed to a 5-kilowatt cap per household, with 10 kilowatts for business. If she were to put on the washing machine, immersion heater and kettle simultaneously,

Maggie explains, her electricity would trip. This would require a visit from a maintenance man, for which Eigg Electric charge. 'It hardly ever happens,' she says.

Islanders are very aware of their electricity use, perhaps because it costs 23p per unit (I pay 12p on the mainland). This is still cheaper than diesel generators. Almost all repairs and maintenance are undertaken by the islanders themselves, and extra solar was added to the grid when they realised they could make use of the fine, dry spells when wind and hydro go quiet. In a time of rising uncertainty over energy prices and production, the people of Eigg enjoy energy security. This is practical and inspirational: visitors travel from all over to learn about Eigg energy – groups from Malawi and Italy are shown round during my time here.

On my penultimate evening on Eigg, I walk three miles across the moor to the tea-room hoping to enjoy the island's legendary hospital-ity, only to find it shut. A few people are sitting on the bench outside creating their own entertainment, with drinks and 'proper prawns' – southerners like me would call them 'langoustines' – on the barbie. Several of the blokes have spent the day fishing. It's 9 p.m., and the sun still lights the fells above Arisaig on the mainland.

I've got no drinks to offer, but I'm invited to join the group and handed a bottle of ale and a giant prawn. The crowd is a mix of locals and tourists and everyone has an interesting story. Dean is a trim, bearded middle-aged Midlander who is the fabled kayaker I'd heard about earlier. A keen adventurer, he was paddling up the Scottish coast when he stopped for the night at Arisaig. He reached his campsite at 10 p.m., heard there was a ceilidh on Eigg and thought What the hell, and kayaked over. He arrived gone midnight, the bar was still open and he ended up dancing on the tables. That was thirteen years ago and he's never left, volunteering on a crofting farm, doing building work, living in a caravan.

Donna is a slim but strong-looking Highlander in her early forties who works in the shop and lives in a shed. Her mum taught her Highland dancing aged two, and she toured, performing, as a tiddler. She'd leap in the air five thousand times, practising before breakfast; no wonder she was high at school – totally adrenalised, she says. Later she learned to play the pipes. When I tell her I'm only here until Thursday, she disappears and returns with her Highland pipes, the big daddy of the pipe world. She tunes up, and her dog, a plump OAP terrier, howls. He knows a tune, she says, he's been listening to them for eleven years. When she pipes up properly he pipes down, and the sound fills the harbour and drifts on the water like a battle-cry.

Half an hour after I arrive, a battered Land Cruiser Intercooler 2800 pulls up carefully, right by our table. The driver falls elegantly out of the door and sits down at the table, eyes hardly open. I've never seen someone so drunk behind a wheel; I've hardly ever seen anyone so drunk since my student days. The passengers clamber out too: Ruairidh, the young man I met when I first arrived on the island, and a couple of older, slightly wild-eyed holidaymakers. It's easy to see why mainlanders are drawn to Eigg, as an escape from their everyday lives. Here is a perfect blend of Hebridean traditions and alternative lifestyles: generous, democratic, open and hedonistic.

'The Only Way is Eigg! Baby! For you and me now,' sings Ruairidh in his deep, stately tones – he would be great for voice-overs. Generous vodka measures are topped up with Cawston Press rhubarb juice. A joint or two is rolled. Ruairidh's driver passes out, still at our table.

Another of our group disappears then reappears with his accordion, which makes a lovely noise. We talk about how to make a woodburner from old gas canisters, about beavers v badgers, and the news of an old islander who was busted for having some marijuana plants on his windowsill; a tourist was blamed for telling. The stories flow. When Dean worked as a fisherman he'd pull up creels of crab, and lobster, prawn and whitebait would jump out and swim away, and the shags would come in. A family of shags followed his boat and he called them Horatio, Henrietta, Horace and Hubert. He can't remember why. The birds got so tame, he could stick a whitebait in his mouth, lean over the side of the boat and the shag would leap from the water and neatly take the fish from his mouth.

Two young men are different from the others, both very pale, short and as lively as firecrackers. The others call them the Glaswegians and tell a funny story about them driving a moped into a bog the previous night. Tam Stevenson is twenty-five and has been coming to Eigg on holiday since he was a teenager: £50 on the train, £7 on the ferry, free camping, free fishing, long drinking. 'The people here are a different class,' he says. 'The fishing is out of this world.' Mackerel, mostly. He's a roofer, a Rangers fan, a Unionist and the kind of Glaswegian who, as he puts it, could sell sand to the Arabs. His mate, Michael, is of the same diminutive stature but quieter, beefier, tattooed and sunburned.

Donna plays another tune and thunder cracks in the western sky. 'There's a double whammy you know,' she tells me when I mention my book. 'There's what people tell you and the reality, and you will never hear the real story.'

The conversations bubble on around me, revealing a glimmer of this small island's unfathomable complexity to outsiders, especially those wielding notebooks, and I fear Donna's right. I'm not sure if I'm sitting here socialising for work purposes, or trying to enjoy myself, but as the music and the stories gather momentum I suddenly feel inescapably sober. It's nearly midnight, and I make my excuses: I must walk three miles home before the rain arrives.

I trot out onto the moor in the midsummer gloaming as enormous droplets descend from the sky, wondering why I'm unsettled by the heroic drinking I glimpse on Eigg. It must be because I'm an uptight Englishman, although of course a Saturday night in any English town reveals its own love of the drink. Eigg is no different from any other

Western Isle, although its song-loving incomers have probably made it even more musical. Back in my little wooden cabin, I open the pages of *Whisky Galore* again. It would be hard to make a more daring or amusing case for the liberating, lubricating and enlightening effects of alcohol, or more specifically, a dram or three of *uisge beatha*, the water of life. Compton Mackenzie has fun with his wartime Hebridean island shorn of alcoholic supplies, then unexpectedly blessed with a shipwreck-load of whisky. But his storytelling rings true, too: the drinking characters are more courageous, generous, funnier; qualities conspicuously lacking in the book's non-drinking figures, who include an emotionally stunted Englishman part-modelled on Monty himself. The book is a romantic, fulsome tribute to the hospitality he enjoyed for a decade as a Hebridean resident. Monty got it. The drinking islanders have poetry on their side. So do the drinks, for he invents many wonderful brand names, from Tartan Milk and Stalker's Joy to Fingal's Cave and Stag's Breath. Was it characteristic good fortune or a reward for his generosity that saw Monty handsomely rewarded, not just via book sales and the film spin-off but when he fronted a lavish advertising campaign for Grant's Stand Fast in the 1950s. This was a real brand of whisky he had particularly enjoyed when it was smuggled by his chauffeur from the wreck of the SS *Politician* off Barra.

I think Eigg's existence is amply justified by the freedom and support it gives the hundred souls who live there, but Alastair McIntosh echoed an earlier writer of the Highlands – and great friend of Compton Mackenzie – Hugh MacDiarmid, by raising the question of what a small island might bring to a bigger one. MacDiarmid, like Monty a founding father of the National Party of Scotland, criticised the 'fake glamour of the Hebrides' during their fashionable 1930s, and argued that the islands still had a serious purpose, worth preserving as their extinction as human societies beckoned. 'They have contributed far more to the spiritual wealth of mankind than the great cities have done or seem at all likely to do,' he wrote. Alive to the criticism that places such as Eigg are an indulgence, sustained by mainland subsidies, Alastair argued in a gentler way for their gifts. 'What does an island culture give back to the mainland culture by way of renewing people, refreshing people, inspiring people? I think Eigg pays its debts quite well like that.' Samsø, a small Danish island, also generates its own power, and Peter Conrad writes that such 'principled housekeeping' can 'only happen on a small, insular scale, and is unlikely to halt the liquefying of the poles'. I'm not so sure. Eigg is a cultural wellspring, a rich source of music and other creative work, for such a small place, but the currents that it stirs on the periphery may just invigorate the mainstream.

Alastair McIntosh's great hope twenty years ago was that Eigg would be 'a pattern and an example unto one another', to quote George Fox, the founder of the Quakers, and so it has proved. Of 19 million acres in Scotland, 500,000 are now under community land tenure. Land reform activists in Scotland such as Andy Wightman, currently a Green MSP, say progress has been painfully slow and legislation has done little to help it. A 2014 report for the Scottish government found that 432 individuals own half the land in rural Scotland – 0.008 per cent of the population, a striking level of inequality for a democracy. Alastair is more positive. 'Because we're starting from such a low base of understanding about how to be a fully functioning community, the progress needs to be slow so people learn in a solid way, they create patterns and examples that others can learn from. It's real, authentic community learning.'

He likes to repeat a saying of uncertain provenance: when the centre collapses, the periphery becomes central. Western societies seem to be witnessing a collapse in the centralised order of the recent century or so. Global capitalism appears increasingly dysfunctional and unsustainable. Its servants, the mainstream political classes, are conspicuously failing to engage or inspire citizens. In the West, at least, communities are riven with divisions of all kinds; particularly stark is rising economic inequality. Do the 'aristocrats of the democracy', small-islanders on a tiny spot such as Eigg, offer practical answers for much bigger places? Renewable community energy as practised on Eigg could certainly be more widely applied. 'Can the small-scale answers add up to the scale that's needed? We have to be careful with the optimism we kindle, that we don't breed false hope,' says Alastair.

As Scotland increasingly goes its own way, perhaps what's really needed is a pattern and an example for the troubled people of England. It may be wistful thinking to hope that Eigg can have an impact here. Cultural streams are flowing positively in Scotland, thinks Alastair, where 'we've reclaimed a strong Scottish identity and bent over backwards to ensure it's an inclusive identity. But it's important we don't over-glamorise our own case – hence I always emphasise the importance of conflict resolution and a spiritual underpinning, or else you get dropped in materialism.'

He considers Eigg to be a deeply spiritual place. It does not have a resident priest, but Alastair attended 'deeply moving' lay services at the Roman Catholic Church of St Donnán's in Cleadale. There are no services when I visit, but the church is a gorgeous little building, possessed of a deep peace.

What does the future hold for Eigg? The school – its barometer of good health – currently has just four primary-age children, but there are newborns, and plenty of teenagers attending secondary school on the mainland. Eigg's population has risen by 40 per cent over twenty years, to hover at one hundred. 'We need more children, more babies, more kids. Keeping the school open is the key to the future,' says Camille Dressler, the island historian and Brian's partner. Their two grown-up children currently live on the mainland. 'We need young people to prosper, as an island. Are we going to make it attractive enough for our youngsters to come back? If not, is it alive enough for young people to live here? Can we preserve the strong ethos of environmental stewardship and strike the balance between tourism and people, and make a living here?'

There are almost no Gaelic-speaking natives left now, but perhaps there's a new tension, which Camille touches upon: the differing approaches as between the revolutionaries who took over the island in 1997 and the more business-minded newcomers. The Trust has recently employed a business development manager to ensure it generates more income to fund the maintenance of the houses and facilities. When I climb the stairs above the shop to meet him, suddenly I'm transported into a little office full of spreadsheets that could be anywhere in the world, except that Ian Leaver is pleasingly plain-speaking.

His task is for the Trust 'to make money', he says. 'It boils down to: what's the best way to make money from tourists?' The rents charged by the Trust, he explains, are too low. Before it raises them – to levels more typical of housing associations in the region – the Trust must mend the properties, fix roofs, renew stoves. To fund this maintenance, it has bought three camping pods to rent to tourists, and is planning to build a bar that's separate from the tea-room and construct some light-industrial units for hire, particularly for Eigg's most thriving small business: its brewery.

Ian hopes the Trust can take advantage of the Scottish government's rural housing fund to build four new homes to rent. He aims to build a new visitor centre and make money from Eigg's forests, one happy legacy of Schellenberg's regime. The island currently has a forestry business, but Ian does not mince his words. 'It's very poorly run and needs to be done better,' he says: they need a shed to dry the wood, proper machines and fewer employees. Despite all the wood on Eigg, some islanders import briquettes for their burners from the mainland.

Older islanders such as Maggie Fyffe speak very positively of

Ian's work, and all agree the Trust needs to make money, but two recent developmental battles reveal a potential faultline between 'the revolutionaries' and a more pro-business younger generation. A phone company proposed to put a mobile phone mast in Cleadale, but the best site for a signal would have spoiled a glorious view. Conservation-minded islanders won, and Eigg is now looking to use an existing mast on Rum. Another company is also in talks with Eigg to place a new salmon farm in its waters. 'We had a slightly fraught meeting,' says Maggie. 'There was a most definite interest from some of the younger guys who wanted a job.' Older residents are worried about marine pollution.

Camille is concerned that the new generation is more conformist and too ready to accept a company's opening offer, to get things done. 'We have a history of having dug in. Through that resistance, we've managed to get a good deal. It's important that the governing body of the island continues with that challenging attitude,' she argues. 'With new people coming in all the time we must keep that strong ethos visible. Let's not forget that as an island you have to capitalise on your strengths. If we're aspiring to be like the mainland what's the point of people coming up here?'

On my last evening on Eigg I catch up with Sarah Boden. She and I worked in the same office for several years but – typical London – I hadn't ever met her until coming to Eigg. She spent her early childhood on Eigg, moved with her family to Devon and later worked as a music journalist on the *Observer*, a floor down from my desk at the *Guardian*. She took redundancy in 2010 to return to Eigg and become a sheep farmer with her father, who had also returned to the island. Sarah's partner Johnny Lynch is a musician who performs as the Pictish Trail, and runs an indie record label and a boutique festival called Howlin' Fling on the island. It all sounds so glamorous that, to be honest, I've been a little reluctant to interview

ISLANDER

them. Sarah's story is made for memoir, and the couple are plagued by everyone who wants to film Eigg for the wider world.

When I bump into her with her baby, Arlo, in the village shop, she invites me up to her place, which she's built herself. It looks like an episode of 'Grand Designs'. Triple-glazed glass between stout brown timbers of Douglas fir, their open-plan dream home faces south over the sea towards the most westerly point of the British mainland. There are piles of boxes, borrowed furniture and bits to finish, but they are warm and dry and have spectacular views over waters where schools of dolphins swim. 'I was wondering if I'd take the scenery for granted, but you don't at all because the sky and the sea change all the time,' she says. The seasons also change with a speed and drama not seen in the south: you wake up in the autumn and all the leaves have gone overnight. 'I still walk around taking pictures all the time. I'll still see cloud formations I've never seen before.'

Sarah has blue eyes and short hair; Johnny has even bluer eyes and a big beard, and apologises for turning up 6 Music when his new single comes on. What starts as a chat ends – typical Eigg – with them cooking me a delicious curry and telling great stories. Sarah talks so perceptively about life on Eigg, I feel I finally understand the island; I can see it in the round.

An outsider peeping in through Sarah and Johnny's curtainless windows would assume that their existence was blessed and comfortable, but it is not that simple. Their house is built using Eigg's unique shared-ownership scheme. The Trust provides a plot of land and holds that as a percentage of the house's value: if its price rises, so does the Trust's stake, which is a good disincentive to property speculation. Unfortunately, the tightening of bank lending after the financial crisis of 2008 made it almost impossible for Eigg residents to obtain a mortgage for such a jointly owned model; Sarah and Johnny struggled, but eventually found one lender who would support them.

130

Sarah farms four hundred north country Cheviot ewes and thirty-five Aberdeen Angus cows in partnership with her dad, along with Dan and Dave, their sheepdogs. Eigg's wind stunts the grass on the hills and the rain washes vital minerals from the soil so the lambs require supplementary feeding. Out in all weathers, Sarah wears a balaclava in winter to stop her face being ripped off by the wind; on rough days, Dan and Dave get blown off the quad. Grass growth may be poor but bracken growth is virulent, increasing across the island by 10 per cent each year. 'It's a nightmare, and clearing it is a lifetime's work,' she says. One of the things she's struggled with most is the fact that 'where there are sheep there's quite a lot of grisly death'. Ravens peck the tongues out of lambs when they are being born so they cannot feed and she has to shoot them. They'll also gang up with crows and black-backed gulls to peck holes into lambs' intestines, leaving them alive but doomed. Sarah, her dad and the other farmer on Eigg have a special dispensation to bury their livestock where they die because the terrain is so inaccessible.

Sarah has to sell her lambs 'unfinished' because there is such a short grass-growing season on Eigg, so other farmers fatten them up. 'We're at the absolute bottom rung of the ladder and the prices have gone down from when I started in 2010. Hill farming in the Highlands – nobody's going into it.' The disadvantages of small-island hill farms are even more pronounced: there's no vet on Eigg and it's expensive to get one over; they are forbidden to slaughter their own animals, so if they want to sell organic Eigg lamb locally, for instance, they must ship the animals off the island and then bring back the meat; long journeys are stressful for the animals and affect the meat's quality. Sarah will spend a week preparing her lambs for the journey off, then bad weather cancels the boat. She is also very alone. On larger islands, such as Mull, there are enough farmers to form a producers' group who can combine to get a better price for their lamb. But Sarah can't even bring her lambs back from the market if the prices aren't good that day: once she's booked her spot on the boat, she has to take them and sell them, whatever the price.

While Sarah battles the elements, Johnny cheerily admits he's 'unemployable' on Eigg.

'There's quite a 1950s machismo amongst the men here,' says Sarah. 'People have had fights about whose tractor can pull the most. Highland men have really got a thing about strength – who is the strongest. Johnny laughs off the fact that he's not practical.'

A Scot from the central belt, Johnny has found everyone on Eigg 'a lot more open-armed. Everyone is eating the same food, everyone here is experiencing life the same way, you can't really lord it over another person.' He can do most of his record-label work via Eigg's broadband. He has Skype meetings and finds the island has given him space for his songwriting. 'You can afford to live with the work you're creating a lot longer up here, and there's less distraction. On the mainland there's people to see and gigs to go to, so I've got more time to focus on what I'm creating.'

One in five of Eigg's population make some or all of their living from creative work, in comparison with 8 per cent in Scotland as a whole. As well as Johnny, there is Libby, a felt artist; Jenny who makes cobweb lace; Carl the knife-maker and a couple of willow-workers; there's also a graphic designer and filmmaker, a freelance journalist and a project manager called Lucy Conway who has worked remotely for years. 'I seem to be less frustrated with my broadband connection than people in Edinburgh,' she says. Suddenly, lots of people can do office jobs without making a daily commute to the city. There is no requirement for a century of centralisation to continue into the digital age.

I tell Sarah and Johnny about my awkwardness during the previous evening's raucous entertainment outside the shop. Sarah laughs and calls the drinking 'Celtic exuberance'. She remembers being taken to ceilidhs as a small child and being bedded down in the cloakroom, then getting trodden on by tipsy adults. She's done her share of staying up all night, but is not as keen as previous generations to take her baby to parties. Sarah recognises that Eigg does attract some hedonists and folk fleeing their responsibilities on the mainland. These extroverts tend to be the most conspicuous to visitors like me. 'Because people hear music and we have big independence day ceilidhs, people think it's a good place to come and party, but there's important stuff behind it all. We've had a few unbalanced people in the past and it really affects the collective mentality. In a small community like this, one person can wreak total havoc.' One or two incomers have caused trouble over the twenty years of independence but Camille Dressler tells me that's probably only because they were tolerated longer on Eigg than they would have been on the mainland. The hospitality of the Hebrides can be abused.

Eigg is changing, and Sarah recognises some of the tensions. Her uncle was a twelfth-generation farmer on Eigg. 'He finds it difficult to see Eigg as it is now. When he was a boy it was entirely Gaelic-speaking and there was still the ceilidh culture. It does suffer from people starting committees, and a lot of islanders don't enjoy going to meetings.' That would be true anywhere, but when the people taking part in those meetings are as smart and honest as Sarah, or Camille or Maggie, I feel sure that Eigg will not merely manage the potential conflicts that living apart from the mainstream creates, but will thrive on its own terms too. Perhaps because she straddles English and Hebridean culture, or perhaps because she has a gift for communicating the essential character of her home to outsiders, Sarah helps me understand the distinctive qualities of Eigg. I've felt inspired almost every hour I've been on Eigg; I've been made to feel very welcome wherever I've gone; but only now do I feel at home.

The following day is glorious, the start of a heatwave. People mingle by the shop again, dropping off, picking up, on the hunt for a diversion or something new, as the CalMac slides into place, ready for departure.

I trudge down the pier and meet Tam and Michael again, the Glaswegian boys. They are heading back to the mainland too. Donna comes out with us, and stands on the end of the pier with her little dog. We lean from the top deck of the ferry, and as the boat slides away from the promenade Donna holds up her loose black bag of pipes and plays a mournful tune. She's piping off the Glaswegian boys, and me too. Tam and Michael film her on their phones, and we shout goodbye and wave. Has Eigg shaken my stultifying Englishness a little? I give the Glaswegians a lift through the Highlands and back to their city, and we chat all the way home.

5

Isle of Seabirds, Isle of Stories

Rathlin, Northern Ireland, 5.4 square miles, population 130

'They were on an island in a little world of their own.
It depended on them all to make this world a world of true
happiness and content'
'The Man Who Loved Islands'

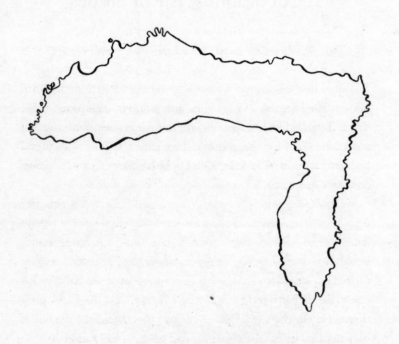

We stand in a sodden green field, grey clouds releasing rain, hurled horizontally into our faces by a westerly. I'm wearing a woollen hat that isn't thick enough to repel the wind and three pairs of trousers that aren't waterproof enough to repel the rain. My boss Liam McFaul and his assistant, Sean McFaul, are sporting heavy-duty green waterproofs and thick fleecy hats. The rain bounces off both of them.

We grab sixty new fence posts from a trailer three at a time and drop them at intervals on the squelchy turf. Liam fishes a pair of fencing pliers from somewhere and twists and tugs the rusted strands of old barbed wire from the rotten posts we're replacing. Sean rolls up the old barbed wire with bare hands, impervious to the chill. Trying not to be embarrassingly tentative, I join in, and the barbs prick through my thick gloves. I glance at Sean. Blood streams from one of his palms, a wire cut. He shrugs when I tell him, and carries on.

Liam had picked me up that morning in his exhausted black Land Rover, its bumper tied on with a piece of string, one electric window permanently open, broken, and the cabin crammed with useful objects: spare hats, leaflets, binoculars, a Neolithic axe-head. He is a handsome man in his fifties with a coppery beard and cheeks well beaten by what he pronounces as 'wund'. He is the RSPB's warden on Rathlin and – unusually for a small-island conservationist – a native islander.

We collect the trailer from Sean, who happens to be his nephew, and pause for a cup of tea. Our task that morning is to fence a field so that it can be grazed to create good habitat for the corncrake, the enigmatic bird I'd encountered on Barra.

Corncrakes have vanished from Rathlin but the RSPB hopes to entice them back. 'The fields here were alive with them in the 1970s and 80s,' says Liam, so common that their nocturnal 'crek-creks' were a nuisance. 'May the devil choke ye,' an old islander used to exclaim at the night-time song. Earlier this century, Liam became Rathlin's first nettle farmer, importing nettles from the mainland to create protective networks of green tangles which are ideal spring cover for the shy corncrakes. In 2014, Sean's dad rang and told him there was a corncrake in the field, hiding in the tall vegetation, just how they like it. Corncrakes fly north from Africa to nest on Barra and other Western Isles; Rathlin is on their flightpath. This male was calling for a mate. 'He was there for ten days. Everybody on the island was hearing him,' recalls Liam. 'Then some yuppies came in a helicopter and more or less landed on the bird's head.' The corncrake had hoped to attract a female but instead got an enormous metal bird. 'He must've thought, I'm not taking you on, lady,' says Liam. 'We never heard from him again.'

The day before, as we shuddered over the sea on Rathlin Island's petite catamaran, I immediately regretted my decision to join two foreign tourists in expensive cagoules on the violently tipping top deck. The wind was attempting to return waves like an angry tennis player, whacking spray from their crests, while half a dozen locals chatted downstairs, sensibly positioned in the calm centre of the boat alongside boxes of bananas, eggs and packs of bacon.

The diminutive size of Rathlin gives it an outline we can see in reality as well as on a map. Like clouds, the shapes of islands are given fantastical form by our imaginations. Jim Hawkins likens Treasure

Island to a fat dragon standing upright. Tasmania is a biscuit gnawed by rats according to Peter Conrad, who can write things like that because he grew up there. Alderney has been compared to a huge elongated skull, Bardsey to a sleeping otter and Rathlin to a boot or a pistol. I see none of these forms here. Rathlin is simply a back-to-front 'L' that has tripped over in an intimidating body of water known as Sloc na Mara, 'the swallow (or gulp) of the sea', which separates Northern Ireland's only inhabited island from its mighty north coast. 'Although less than nine miles from Ballycastle on the Irish coast, its inhabitants have very little traffic with the mainland; and they are accustomed to speak of both Ireland and Scotland as of foreign kingdoms,' marvelled Edwin Waugh in 1869. On his crossing, Waugh was excited by the agitated water. Long before reaching mid-channel 'we met with a glorious tossing,' he wrote.

Bouncing closer, Rathlin presents a cheerful face to the world. Church Bay is a pleasing cluster of stone houses containing a bar with 'McCuaig's' written on the roof in large white letters, and a ruined warehouse where – as across the Western Isles – harvested kelp was once stored, then burned for a bewildering array of uses including the manufacture of iodine, soap and glass. The island's cheerfulness comes from its two-tone geology. The dark layers of basalt which bequeath such character to the Antrim coast are deposited, on Rathlin, over white limestone. Stone walls are decorated with black basalt and white limestone rocks, and the stony beaches are bright white too.

It was a racing autumn day. Islay and the Mull of Kintyre were spotlighted between storms before disappearing behind them. Island-ers call it 'bruckle' – broken – weather. Liam met me and, before dark fell, drove me up the hill towards the lighthouse at Rathlin's western tip. The island is similar to Eigg in size, scale and population. Like Eigg, it is divided into two distinct regions: the Upper End of rocky, high heather uplands that finish in vertiginous cliffs, and the more populated Lower End with its softer though still impressively craggy landscape of fertile pasture. The perceptive German traveller Johann Georg Kohl noted in 1844 that even on tiny Rathlin, then home to 1,100 people, there were two distinct 'races': the fiercely independent cliff 'climbers' of the Upper End, also called 'furrins' after their local name for the seabirds favoured in their diet, and the more cosmopolitan Lower Enders, or 'cuddens' as they were known, after the small fish, abundant in the Bay. Liam is an Upper Ender, a climber.

The small wind-blasted rocks off Britain lack rich soils or climates conducive to rearing large quantities of livestock. Historically, their human populations have depended on fish to survive. They've also depended on birds. Rathlin escaped the ravages of Ireland's potato famine because islanders' diets were supplemented by seabirds and their eggs. Huge quantities of birds still cluster in screaming clans on its epic cliffs – 135,000 guillemots and 21,000 razorbills, the biggest colony in Europe, plus puffins and kittiwakes – and today seabirds sustain Rathlin in a more indirect way. Their presence brings bird-loving tourists whose seasonal largesse supports the local community; the birds also attract a big mainland charity, the RSPB. I anticipate that Rathlin will be an exemplar of small-island nature reserves but the reality is not nearly so simple.

A common fate for many small islands is to be emptied of humans and filled with other animals. The twentieth-century concept that transformed the Shiants more than any other was the idea that they should be 'conserved', writes their owner Adam Nicolson in *Sea Room*. Skomer, Skokholm, the Farne Islands, the Isle of May, Brownsea, Lundy, Rum, Fair Isle, Foula, St Kilda, Northey, Scolt Head Island: these small British isles are, if not exclusively reserved for nature, dominated by the conservation charities or government agencies that 'protect' them. Often, the only human inhabitants of these 'natural laboratories' are ecologists and wardens, who occupy the islands as seasonally as the birds, flying in on six-month contracts. Visiting bird-lovers are enraptured; travelling writers, siding with the one species that can tell them stuff, are often enraged.

Rum, the Small Isle next to Eigg, is the most extreme British example of an island reserve. In 1826, the laird shipped its human population of 400 Hebrideans to Nova Scotia and replaced them with less troublesome but more profitable sheep. In 1845 the Marquis of Salisbury, an Englishman, replaced the sheep with more entertaining and more profitable red deer.

Compton Mackenzie was scandalised by Rum, which became known as 'the forbidden isle'. In 1936, he wrote: 'The knowledge that there are still many who believe that it would serve the state to allow the Islands to become a wilderness for sportsmen like so much of the Highlands is always bitter with those of us who would rather see London a heap of ruins like Ur of the Chaldees than have one more abomination of desolation like Rum.'

Monty was equally critical of the conservation bodies that replaced sporting owners in places such as Rum. In 1957, the island was bought by the Nature Conservancy Council, a government organisation established for conservation in the postwar era and staffed by the first generation of professional wildlife scientists. Their radical plan was to return the island to nature. In an early iteration of rewilding, the Conservancy's head, Max Nicholson, insisted that the new science of ecology required an 'outdoor laboratory' to properly test how predator and prey interact, how populations reach an equilibrium, how species respond to environmental change. 'If we were serious we must have a larger tract of totally separate land on which visiting and living would be strictly controlled so as to minimise human impact,' he wrote nearly forty years later. 'And we must, by a blend of toughness and persuasion, show all concerned that this was how it must be.'

Ian Mitchell, a travel writer who visited Rum in the 1990s, was scathing about its 'bureaucratic paraphernalia'; shocked that the scientists did not seek to farm Rum or make a profit; and appalled at the absence of visitors and the amount of public money lavished on esoteric long-term studies of Rum's deer population. 'An underfunded Edinburgh bureaucracy flounders incompetently towards a half-remembered vision of something utterly ghastly, signally failing to get there,' he declared. But Rum's indigenous population had long gone, and Mitchell had no sense that an island might exist for anything other than human pleasure or profit. What about the rights of nonhuman islanders?

Twenty years on, after Scottish Natural Heritage acknowledged the role of humans on Rum and a community land trust was established to act for the people who had settled there, Madeleine Bunting remained critical of the conservation vision that still dominated Rum. The island may have a 'salvific role' in the looming environmental crisis, but its 'use', she argued, is another form of fantasy that privileges the wild, empty and remote.

Writing in *Sea Room* in 2001, Adam Nicolson was similarly withering about conservationists' ambitions for his Shiants. The islands' shoulders now sagged, he said, beneath 'a heavy load of modern conservation labels'. In the 1970s, the RSPB had unsuccessfully tried to acquire the Shiants from his father. Under RSPB management, more people would visit these uninhabited islands, and the charity suggested it might install hides, build a path and a nature trail to give visitors information. 'If the RSPB got involved with the Shiants, that might well be the most intrusive development the islands would ever have known,' wrote Nicolson. He quoted John Murdo Matheson, the tenant who managed the sheep that grazed on the three tiny islands: 'Promise me one thing, Adam. You will never, ever let one of those organisations get their hands on this place. It would be the end of it, the real death of it. It needs to belong to a person who loves it.'

In 2016, however, the RSPB did get their hands on the Shiants and I am amazed to discover that Adam Nicolson calls it 'a completely life-enhancing triumph'. I interrupted him finishing a book about seabirds to ask him about the fate of the islands which, true to his word in *Sea Room*, he has passed to his son Tom, who is in his twenties. Adam is still involved with the islands and so, now, are the RSPB.

One of the organisation's first recommendations for the Shiants was to get rid of their rat population. Ever since Polynesian sailors brought *Rattus exulans*, the Pacific rat, to New Zealand in the thirteenth century, rats have devastated indigenous bird populations on hitherto rodent-free islands. About a quarter of New Zealand's native birds, many of which evolved without requiring the power of flight on a virtually mammal-free island, are extinct. On the seabird-populous British isles, the living is easy for rats accidentally introduced by humans: they scurry into the burrows of puffins or Manx shearwaters and gobble their eggs or chicks. In recent decades, lengthy extermination programmes have removed rats from islands as diverse as Lundy in the Bristol Channel and South Georgia in the southern Atlantic. New Zealand is the world leader in extermination, dropping poison from aircraft to blitz possums, stoats and rats so as to fulfil a government pledge to remove all rats and other introduced predators by 2050.

In recent years, the RSPB undertook two scientific surveys to identify which British islands or nature reserves could most benefit from a rat-eradication programme. Both studies found that the Shiants would be most transformed if their large population of *Rattus rattus*, the black rat, could be removed. Adam Nicolson wondered if killing what in Britain is actually our rarest mammal (the brown rat is our ubiquitous rodent) in order to favour relatively common seabirds, was a kind of racism – or speciesism, as animal activists put it. But he was won round by the argument that *Rattus rattus*, globally, is far more successful than the struggling seabirds. More surprisingly, he was persuaded to allow RSPB-led exterminators onto his family's islands.

How did he come to accommodate those conservation forces he was once so suspicious of? 'With a very, very long spoon,' he says. 'Tom and I talked about this, weighing up the risks and rewards of getting into bed with the RSPB. The form of our long spoon was to be absolutely clear from the start: that the Shiants are not a bird reserve, they are a multivalent, multidimensional, deeply human landscape.' He insisted that the RSPB must not seek any publicity, nor erect any signs or change the island so they were anything other than 'naked' for the visitors who sail up to camp on their uninhabited shores. Putting informative signs on wild places 'just lays a skin of management all over them', thinks Adam. 'It's one of the modern world's most pernicious forms of pollution.'

He remained sceptical until he sailed to the Shiants in the summer of 2016, after the eradicators got to work on their rat population, which booms to 20,000 in the summer and shrinks to 3,000 in winter. He threw a little wobbly when he saw some signs, but these are a temporary condition of receiving EU funding for the 'unbelievably expensive' (nearly £1 million) cull. And then he saw that the islands were already transformed. 'The thing you get when you go to an island whose rats have been destroyed, it's not just the seabirds – everything feels more alive. There's an incredible sense of wellbeing. These little birds, wrens and wheatears and warblers, a fantastic buzz of life. It's an unequivocally good thing. I wake up at 3 a.m. and think, thank God for that. It's amazing.'

On Rathlin, the rats that have darted about on the island for centuries are still free to prey on seabirds. Liam McFaul's biggest problem is caused by another introduced islander: the ferret. They were let loose in the 1980s and have 'tipped the balance', he says. He finds them all over the cliffs, even scoffing shellfish inside lobster pots washed up on the beach. Puffin nests have been wiped out on inaccessible-looking cliffs. The only ferret-proof nesting sites are the great rock stacks off Rathlin's coast, surrounded by the frothing Atlantic.

No locals like the ferrets, and Liam, as RSPB warden, has taken part in discussions about a ferret and brown rat eradication project that would be funded by the RSPB and other conservation groups. An islander from rat-liberated Canna came over to discuss the benefits of extermination. Most Rathlin inhabitants favour a cull, says Liam, except for a few landowners, who are not objecting as animal-lovers – one traps ferrets and hangs their carcasses on his fence – but are deeply suspicious of 'outside' interference, and of the RSPB. They don't want conservation groups stepping onto their land. 'People say openly, "It's just the landlords back again",' says Liam. 'It just seems to be in islanders' genes, this resistance to anybody telling us what to do.'

As Liam explains, there is a deep-rooted fear on Rathlin that outside interference will jeopardise the islanders' precarious ability to make a living. For decades, residents have resisted 'experts' visiting their land to research rare plants or archaeological treasures, such as the Neolithic axe-head rattling around in Liam's Land Rover, because they fear it will disrupt their way of life. Discoveries bring problems. This suspicion of outsiders may be a universal characteristic of supposedly insular islands, but its close relation, secrecy, appears indigenous to Rathlin. This is revealed by Liam's mother Peggy, a shrewd woman in her eighties. 'You didn't tell your right hand what your left hand was going to do in case your neighbour got to know about it,' she tells me. 'It wasn't sinister. But you didn't voice your opinion in public because it would snowball or you'd probably be accused of saying something you didn't.' Rathlin's secrecy was created by the religious conflict in Northern Ireland, explains Peggy. Faith is still not much discussed on Rathlin. Nor is politics. No one flies a flag to demonstrate their allegiance to Britain, Ireland, Protestantism or Catholicism. The island is too small to tolerate a sectarian divide. 'I don't know who my family vote for in any election because we don't discuss it,' says Peggy. 'Catholic or Protestant or Muhammadan, they don't care on Rathlin.'

Liam calculates that if ferret eradication is 'led from within' then the objections will cease, and he hopes it will be taken up by the Rathlin Development & Community Association, a voluntary body that chiefly lobbies for better infrastructure but which recently drew up a 'biodiversity action plan' with the islanders. Liam points out that the presence of pest controllers will benefit the economy during the three-year eradication programme, while the longer-term boost for seabirds will attract more visitors. Liam's wife Alison, a kind-looking Englishwoman with a dry sense of humour, is hopeful. 'The community is beginning to take on board the benefits of the wildlife for themselves,' she says, 'rather than seeing it as being for the benefit of conservation organisations.'

The apparent hostility towards the RSPB on Rathlin surprises me because its behaviour here seems like an exemplar of how to conserve wild islander species in harmony with the human population. This is simply because Rathlin's warden is Liam, who is profoundly embedded in the island and its culture. In today's era of professional conservation, most small-island wardens are bright young graduates who breeze over from the mainland with an encyclopaedic knowledge of ornithology and rather less understanding of local tradition. The best wardens are always supreme diplomats, but the knowledge of an indigenous ranger is priceless. Liam offers a good example: if a mainlander is ever made warden of Rathlin, they will struggle with their annual survey of its six peregrine nests because they are hidden on its vast and inaccessible cliffs. Liam has known exactly where to find them since he was a boy; a peregrine nest is island intelligence as easily held as who makes the best cup of tea.

Liam is the reason why Rathlin is not like any other small-island reserve I've visited. Someone tells me an islander is like a penknife: open them up and they reveal all kinds of useful skills. If this is true, Liam must be a Swiss Army knife. He is not given to boasting and it is only gradually, over the next four days, that I discover this RSPB warden is also an organic farmer, a fisherman, a member of the Fire Service, and station officer in charge of the coastguard rescue team. He appears to know every field, rock, vehicle and, of course, every person. A drive over the hills with him is to see the island in ultra-high definition. The stunted sycamores are furry with peppermint-coloured lichen and the only sound is the urgency of small culverts dispatching water at speed towards the luminous Atlantic. We pass a curious iron gate by a stile: Liam explains it's a piece of railing from the deck of the *Hind*, one of many ships wrecked on Rathlin. Part of her cargo was potatoes; these were salvaged and 'Hind's potatoes' were grown over the island for many years. As an Upper Ender, Liam likes cattle but doesn't have time for sheep, which constantly get stuck on gorse, briars and rough ground. 'Sheep are vulnerable things,' he says. 'I always maintain that sheep were born with one mission – to die.' He has stories about every islander we pass. Most are nephews or cousins, and while eventually I grasp his fascinating family tree – his grandma was also his auntie because Liam's mother married her stepfather's younger brother – I sense that I haven't seen him reveal quite every one of his skills by the time I take the ferry home.

He shows me Rathlin's stupendous northern cliffs, tiered like a wedding cake. Columns of basalt are coloured grey by rare lichen, including one that is unique to Northern Ireland but more common in the Azores – a hint of the profoundly Atlantic quality of this island. Between the lichen are vertical grooves polished to a shiny black by the rainwater rivulets that incessantly dive oceanwards. These little streams show as white tracings, like veins, on the cliff's dark skin. Towards the bottom of the cliff spread skirts of lurid green grass. Below these is a final drop, perhaps forty metres of sheer black rock, pounded by a crinkled edge of white water and the rumble of the rolling Atlantic. A gannet rides the wind, low over the waves. It dives deep but doesn't penetrate the ocean: north of Rathlin the Atlantic shelves to a trench of 244 metres, where U-boats lay up during the war, haunting the Western Approaches.

The road finishes at the western end, by Rathlin West Light and a discreet new RSPB visitor centre serving posh coffee. It takes me a moment to figure out the full strangeness of the lighthouse. We take one hundred concrete steps down the cliff to a concrete courtyard and the lighthouse door. It is white and sturdy, and used to house the lighthouse keepers before its blood-red light was automated. The stairs to the light lead not up but down because there, at the bottom of the tower, shines the beacon of Rathlin's upside-down lighthouse, as if it was dropped to the base of the basalt cliffs.

This bizarre place was built in 1919 using a new high-tech material – precast concrete. Liam's grandfather was one of many islanders who hauled sand and stone to the construction site with his horse and cart. The light was placed at the bottom –halfway down the cliff – because at the top it would have been too high to help mariners. When they constructed the steps, the builders unwittingly created a brilliant bird-watching platform. From the clifftop, visitors can't see much, but during the nesting season they twist their way down the steps for a big reveal: thousands of seabirds screaming, chatting, flying, resting, nesting, shitting on the Stack of the Grey Man, a pillar of basalt and a fortress for the birds. 'You're not only halfway down the cliff, you're halfway out,' says Liam. 'It's so unique. People from all over the world enthuse about this.' I feel a twinge of regret that I'm missing this bombastic experience because it's autumn and the chicks have fledged, their acrid pong swept away by the bitter wind. Their only trace is a sandy-coloured dusting to the top of the stacks: crushed eggshells from hundreds of years of millions of eggs.

While Liam makes his living from protecting Rathlin's seabirds, his forebears scaled its cliffs to take their eggs. Liam's mother Peggy collected eggs from the seabirds; everyone did. As the sky deepens to navy and tails hang from clouds in the west – rain on its way – I call on Peggy to better understand the Rathlin that is slipping from view. We chat in her warm kitchen, below a collection of ninety mugs hanging from ceiling beams. One celebrates the Queen's coronation in 1953 and was given in a typically paternalistic gesture to every pupil at the school by Mrs Gage, the wife of the island's former owner.

Fought over by Scotland and Ireland, Rathlin began life under the rule of English landlords when the 1st Earl of Antrim was given the island by James I in the seventeenth century. The Earl deployed 'natural law' to successfully argue that it was part of Ireland: the sea was deeper between Scotland and Rathlin than between the island and Antrim; and both island and Ireland shared an absence of snakes, unlike Scotland. The Reverend John Gage, the son of a chaplain to Queen Anne, bought Rathlin from Antrim in 1746. For two hundred years the Gages governed the island, extracting rent from local people, shooting woodcock, recording its birds, writing its history. In the 1920s, the wife of an English vicar translocated from Sussex to Rathlin produced a revealing memoir. 'On Rathlin one is at the mercy not only of wind and sea, but of people on the island,' wrote Letitia Stevenson, a fervent member of the Anglo-Irish Protestant elite, who devoted her days to patronising the locals and arranging hilarious 'entertainments'. These included a game called False Leg, where a stocking was stuffed with tissue paper and all the ladies sat around while blindfolded men felt their feet. Oh my! The men got a frightful shock when the leg came away!

Aristocratic visitors to Rathlin dressed in plus-fours, went shooting and collected rare birds' eggs. In a curious way, they abused the locals' hospitality, deigning to visit those who would cook for them or hand out eggs or even lobsters. 'Some of the old people used to call them scroungers from the mainland,' says Peggy. Nevertheless, she judges the Gages to have been 'very reasonable' landlords. She knew of only one man who was evicted from Rathlin – for hiding sheaves of corn to cheat the landlord out of his hefty one-third tithe. Perhaps such punishment would have been considered reasonable in the light of Rathlin's bloody history.

In 1575 the Earl of Essex dispatched Francis Drake to confront Scottish settlers on Rathlin, and hundreds of men, women and children were believed to have been killed. (One revisionist history suggests that Drake embellished accounts of the massacre to impress his masters.) In 1642, soldiers led by Duncan Campbell attacked the MacDonalds on Rathlin, killing between a hundred and three thousand people by pushing them off the cliffs. The stories told about this massacre are particularly vivid. A woman who was among the last to be driven over the cliff only broke her leg because the pile of bodies was so high. She used some needles tucked in her dress to make hooks and catch fish, and survived at the base of the cliff until her leg healed.

Peggy's hair is hardly grey at all, although she is mostly confined to her chair near the Rayburn since a hip operation. She would feel guilty if she called herself an islander and prefers 'long-term resident'. Alongside her younger sister she arrived from County Derry in 1945, aged fourteen, when her mother, a widow, met and married Liam's uncle. 'What was my mother thinking of to come to a place like this? But a mother of six without a husband, it's needs must,' says Peggy. 'The island was about fifty years behind, in time. There was one car and a tractor with iron wheels. You had to work.' She tended vegetables, pulled wild heather for fires, and each day carried up to forty buckets of water from a well three hundred yards away, to fill the outdoor bathtub. 'People don't know they are alive now. I don't grudge it to them, I'm glad they don't have to live the way we had to live. But we were happy enough because it was just a way of life.'

Part of Peggy's work was collecting eggs. Around the Second World War, they were a cash crop because powdered egg was used in bakeries when making bread. Peggy got two and sixpence per dozen guillemot eggs, and the same for razorbills'. Paddy Morrison was the greatest of Rathlin's cliff-climbing egg collectors: strong, fearless and competitive. Peggy and Liam tell stories about 'Paddy the Climber' as if he's still alive today. He once wanted to salvage a large plank of wood washed up on a shore and, to beat the others going round in a boat, he tied a 'thirty-fathom' rope to the end of a mare's leg, in the dark, and scooted down the cliffs to take possession of it. If the mare had slipped, or bolted, Paddy would've been slung to his death, but he got away with it. Another story reveals islanders' attitudes towards their wealthy landlords. The Gages kept a pigeon loft, and one day fancied some wild rock doves for their cages. They asked Paddy to procure some rock dove eggs, which were to be found on the most precipitous cliffs. One morning, Paddy rose early, sneaked into the Gages' loft and collected some of their pigeon eggs before falling asleep on the doorstep, clutching his basket of eggs. The Gages were delighted that he had procured some rock doves' eggs and gave him cash and a handsome breakfast.

Liam's Aunt Rose was a brilliant climber too. 'She was like a cat,' says Peggy. 'But in her later years she wouldn't stand on a stool, she was so afraid of heights.' Rose lost her nerve. In fact, in 1945 the whole island did. The death of Joey McCurdy stopped the islanders climbing for eggs, and although it happened so long ago it is remarkably fresh in the minds of Peggy and Liam. Joey was a fine young man and an excellent climber. One morning his father warned him not to go out, because it had rained the night before; but young people know best, says Peggy, and Joey went to the cliffs to collect eggs. Halfway down, he was struck on the head by a dislodged stone and fell to his death. As a boy, Liam would mess about on the cliffs, but his father warned him and his brothers off. After the war there were safer ways to make a living, and regular visitors, ornithologists and experts from museums were preaching a message of conservation too.

As a teenager, Peggy didn't plan to stay on the island, she wanted to be a nurse; but, as she puts it, she 'got married instead'. As a young wife, she struggled for money – if a boat was going across to the mainland, her husband would rise early, gut fifty brace of rabbits and wheel them on his bike bars three miles to the boat so they could be sold in Ballycastle. But there was also a lot of fun. Just as on Barra, Eigg and other Western Isles, the ceilidh was the social engine of Rathlin. People went from house to house on an evening, telling stories, singing, playing music or tricks or cards to win a duck or a goose. Once, one young boy won the goose and took it home in a bag – ooh, it was a big heavy one, and when he opened it up he found a live seal pup instead.

This social life vanished, and 'that box there was to blame,' says Peggy, gesturing at the flat-screen television in the corner. (Even the box has gone now.) In the early days, though, TV remained a communal entertainment. Liam tells some good stories about gatherings at the house of his uncle, only the fourth person on the island to get a telly in the 1960s. One old man was convinced that the people on the TV were actually inside the box. During a Guinness advert, a young lad hid a Guinness behind the TV and then reached over to pull it out, confirming for the old man that he was right. Another time, the old man raced over to Liam's house, shouting that there was 'terrible trouble' at his uncle's. They found everyone watching a Western. The man believed its saloon bar brawls were real. Peggy's boys, and her boys' boys, are now key figures on Rathlin: ferrymen, fishermen, builders, coastguards, and Liam of course, who fulfils several of these roles and more.

Rathlin's population has risen from 100 to 130 in recent years; its community is growing in a way it hasn't for fifty years. Its mighty cliffs are in no danger of erosion, but an island shrinks existentially when it is remembered in less detail; Peggy and Liam both fear theirs is diminishing as stories and characters are lost to memory. Landlords, historians, anthropologists and bureaucrats have committed some of

Rathlin's oral history to paper, but this is a reductive process, as I realise when I spend an evening with Liam and his nephew Benji.

I first meet Benji in the harbour. An early-thirty-something who manages to look stylish in a grey hooded top and fishermen's breeches, he is repairing lobster pots with his bare hands in freezing conditions. He has been working away for seven years on a deep-sea trawler off Rockall, one of a crew of five, fishing for everything: cod, pollock, prawns. He's recently returned to live permanently on Rathlin as the island's only full-time fisherman, potting for lobster and crab on a small one-person boat (because Rathlin's harbour can't house a bigger one).

Liam is grateful that Benji is continuing the family tradition; fishing is still a fiercely territorial calling, and Benji's presence deters the mainland boys from putting their pots all around Rathlin. But Benji seems frustrated. 'The problem we always have is we are the only island off the north of Ireland. The islands of Scotland have the Highlands and Islands Council to represent them. You go to Scotland, all the islands have harbours. We only got electricity here in 1993. I grew up with an oil lamp and a car battery powering a black-and-white TV. That's how much the place was forgotten about. It never gets its fair dues compared to other places. It is improving. It's not "too little, too late", but it has been for a lot of people. They said, "Fuck this place" because they couldn't see a future. It's hard to make money over here.'

Young islanders are no different from young mainlanders in being unable to afford a house. But over in Donegal, says Benji, there's a special planning scheme to help local people build themselves a home. On Rathlin, farmers' children have the standard British planning right to build houses for themselves within the 'envelope' of the existing farm. The island's farms, however, are squeezed into nooks and crannies between hill and bog, so there isn't space for new houses. Such problems resurface on many small islands: policies designed in the centre don't suit the edge. 'Governments need a different approach when it comes to Rathlin because Rathlin doesn't fit their criteria,' says Benji. 'If you live in a city, opportunity is easy to come by. Over here, opportunity is limited. We're beaten with the weather. We're beaten with the location. We're beaten with the policy. We're just beaten every time.'

Benji is less downbeat later that evening when he comes over to the 'camping barn' where I'm lodging, a cottage bunkhouse with two dorms where RSPB volunteers sleep in the summer. An artist who is also staying here invites a couple of visitors she knows, and Liam and Alison come too. Everyone brings food and wine, and the tales flow – of shipwrecks, of snow and the great personalities of Rathlin island. Benji tells me about when he was a kid and, messing about on a bank of sand being excavated for a new sewage system, he accidentally kicked a skull. His mum sent it to archaeologists for testing. It was Bronze Age. The past on Rathlin is 'very close,' says Benji. 'You can touch it.'

Benji and Liam have a trove of funny stories. One hot day, a group of lads were tarring boats in the quay. An old man with a long white beard clambered onto one of the decks and fell asleep, head back, beard flopping over the side. So the boys tarred his beard to the side of the boat. When he woke he flailed around, shouting, 'Let go of me, let go of me.' The boys were in hysterics. One local man, Micky Joe, crops up in many tales. In the 1950s, when vets arrived on Rathlin to test its cattle for TB for the first time, the islanders were confused about how they intended to hold the cows still while they were injected. Micky Joe was a big man and so he got hold of a cow, wrestled it to the ground, and held it there for its injection. 'Right boys,' he called out to the vets, 'whatever you want to do with this cow, do it now.'

I can't do justice to their tales, for the act of writing down oral history, even word for word, seems to suck the vivacity from it. It dawns on me that all the old characters mentioned by Benji and

Liam are not only dead, but unknown to them. Just as Mairi Ceit MacKinnon had brought the past alive by sharing her memories of Barra, I realise that Benji and Liam know these old islanders intimately: they have been part of their lives since they were small, and when they speak they are hearing the voices of their mothers, fathers and grandfathers. 'You know the people who told you were telling it from the heart. You can picture them telling you the stories. And when I'm gone,' says Liam, pointing at Benji, 'he'll be telling you the stories that I'm telling.' Although Rathlin has lost its Gaelic language, its oral traditions endure, embodied in a few islanders.

John Lorne Campbell, Gaelic scholar and Compton Mackenzie's friend, believed that the 'Gaelic mind' existed in a vertical plane: an amazingly long history, stretching back to Viking times. This vertical thinking is infused with a sense of the reality of another world of spiritual experience, which brings up the phenomenon of 'second sight' – the ability of some Hebrideans to sense something was going to happen before it did, which so enthralled Victorian and Edwardian spiritualists. Campbell compared this way of thinking and remembering with the modern European mind, which is 'horizontal, possessing breadth' but so lacking depth in time that many of us forget the names of our grandparents. Campbell was writing in 1967 but his observations seem more relevant than ever in the broad shallows of the digital age.

The enduring power of Liam and Benji's stories makes me think, that night, about Compton Mackenzie, and the rapid vanishing from view of most of his written work. What makes these oral stories take root in the imagination and live again with each telling? And what was it about Monty's stories that lacked this vitality and staying power? Why is he no longer read like Lawrence? Monty's early novel *Sinister Street* is still highly regarded by the few critics who know it but, to be brutally honest, most of the others that I've tried to read are a cure for insomnia. *The Four Winds of Love*, an ambitious six volumes he hoped would be his great literary monument, has a hero, John Ogilvie, who, a bit like Monty, constantly opines on the great events of the twentieth century. It's exhausting, and even Monty's great friend Eric Linklater reckoned he was one of only a half-dozen people who ploughed through the whole thing.

Everywhere I journey within Monty's copious back catalogue, I encounter the same impulse: his refusal to admit or discuss any emotions. When he abandoned the island of Jethou, he also left behind Freud, Jung and Adler – more than thirty volumes of psychoanalysis – in his library. 'I had realised by now how much psychology was being administered to literature and did not want to swallow any more of it,' he proclaimed.

For all the books I've read by and about him, the island that is Monty somehow remains a silhouette only, a tracing on the map. We never really journey to its heartlands or meet the inhabitant within. Of course, he lived in a much less confessional age, but even by the standards of the day he permitted no emotion or self-reflection. In later volumes of his memoirs, he repeatedly justifies his failure to reveal his inner life as a spirited resistance to the mores of what he calls the 'sexy sixties'. 'I cannot escape from the conviction that a man does not kiss and tell,' he wrote, wilfully misunderstanding what critics were asking of him. In all those million words of autobiography, he never discusses his and Faith's stillborn son or his refusal to have another child; he never reflects upon the succession of mother figures he built his writing life upon; and never examines why he failed, where Lawrence succeeded, to write great literature. In his biography of Monty, Andro Linklater concludes that, unlike Lawrence's, his characters never really came alive, or gained psychological autonomy, because he so consciously banished introspection following his love-starved childhood, his rejection by his mother. Monty's most convincing characters were always versions of himself, but even these were one-dimensional. As Linklater argues, he was so often performing a role that when we look closely at his fictional selves it is 'like a mirror turned to face another mirror'. It cannot be a coincidence that the only two Compton Mackenzie novels to have stood the test of time, *Whisky Galore* and *The Monarch of the Glen*, are inspired by the oral entertainment he encountered in the Hebrides. Monty loved Barra for its storytellers, and their natural wit and style seeped into him during his decade on his best-loved island. His best fiction is infused with the Gaelic storytellers' comic style, as well as heavily borrowing their content. Monty's best writing was not simply inspired by island life, it was directly acquired from his fellow islanders.

After watching the sun rise over the sea as forty curlews swing their curved beaks like golfers over the dark moor, I find Liam enslaved to email just like any other white-collar worker, except that his office is his chilly garden shed with silver bubblewrap insulation taped to the ceiling, and papers are filed in polystyrene crates once used to transport broccoli. We talk some more and, that night, I wangle a spot in front of Liam and Alison's fire, eating pasta and bolognese off a plate on my lap. We talk, and I'm finally told the tale I most want to hear: the story of Liam and Alison themselves.

The McFauls came to Rathlin from western Scotland in the 1700s and many dispersed to the mainland, or Australia, which was where Liam had been planning to go in the 1980s. Something stopped him taking up the visa he'd obtained and, in the years since, he's never spent more than a month away from the island. Unlike other small-islanders, he doesn't take regular holidays either. 'I find it very hard to be satisfied with other places. I'm always looking for elevation and an edge.' He and Alison sometimes visit her sister in Oxfordshire. 'It's a nice place, but I just submit to the fact that I'm there,' says Liam. He spent a few days in the Lake District, 'and I quite enjoyed that'. He doesn't sound terribly enthusiastic. 'It gets a bit samey, there's never an edge to it.'

Alison is a lovely mixture of deeply romantic and rather wise, which gives her simultaneously the best bits of being both young and old. She grew up in southern England and, in the early 1980s, placed an advert in *The Lady* magazine, seeking domestic work. She received two offers: one to become a butler in Maidenhead, the other to work in the Manor House on Rathlin. She chose the island. 'It met every criterion I'd had since I was about five for the kind of place I'd live,' she says. 'I had this picture in my head, maybe it was from C.S. Lewis, of residing on a cliff in mouldering mossy dereliction. I also liked the idea of being with people who'd never been away from what they knew. Liam ticked all my boxes – he's wild and mossy.'

Alison worked on Rathlin for a bit, and adored it. When she returned to Britain to become a nurse, she continued to go back for holidays. She and Liam became friends, they say coyly, and in 1990 Alison finally gave up her job as a nurse and moved, to try full-time Rathlin life. It was autumn, and she found herself a caravan in which to live. Regulations prevented her from taking an island job until she had been unemployed for a year, so she bought a huge jar of dried peas and survived on £7 a week. Her first Rathlin job was to be paid £1 per walk to check on sheep giving birth on the moors. Then she did some labouring, helping build an extension on Peggy's house. She knew she couldn't return to southern England. 'It was far more interesting living here in a caravan,' she goes on. 'Everybody just did everything themselves. It was can-do, have-a-go, improvise – very creative and no health-and-safety laws or ticking boxes. You could relate to everybody on a really basic, no-nonsense, no-frills way, and that was enough.'

Finally, she got together with Liam. 'Some people get lucky, other people get unlucky and I'm not saying who is who,' says Liam, laughing loudly. Rathlin, unexpectedly perhaps, has also offered Alison advancement: she took courses in business management and computing via government schemes to provide residents of remote places with skills for the 'modern' world. 'There were loads of opportunities to do things I wouldn't have had in England,' she says. After volunteering herself, in recent years Alison has looked after hundreds of other volunteers who turn up on Rathlin for a few weeks, or a summer, to help run the RSPB's lighthouse visitor centre or to work with her and Liam on their organic farm. The farm volunteers are Wwoofers – World Wide opportunities on Organic Farms – who mostly come from Europe.

Alison generally finds the German girls best, the most practical and considerate; boys tend to wait to be fed in the evening, although one French guy from Lorraine baked delicious quiches. I leaf through a book of ecstatic comments from Wwoofers, who praise Liam and Alison's hospitality and allude to hard work, life-changing moments and romance. Virtually every male islander I meet seems to have married an idealistic young woman who first visited Rathlin as a volunteer. And the cliché that small islands attract eccentrics is upturned by a comment from a young Canadian oceanographer, who herself hails from an island: 'Islands are where you go if you want to meet the most sensible people.'

Alison identifies the essential psychological difference between the Rathlin of today and the Rathlin of the past: 'No one is here now who doesn't want to be here.' More precious than this small island's rising population is the fact that its people are islanders by choice. No one is stuck there any more, doomed to a lifetime of physical toil.

Rathlin is thriving. Its primary school has nine pupils, its highest number for years, and the previous year's baby boom – five babies born – is unprecedented in living memory. The West Light fully opened to the public in 2016 as part of the Great Lighthouses of Ireland trail, and the resident-run community association now employs a full-time member of staff and has reopened the Manor House as a guesthouse. While islanders still resist outside interference, most

praise Northern Ireland's devolved administration for taking a re-
newed interest in Rathlin. 'When I was growing up, there was no
big harbour and no official ferry service,' says Liam. 'It's changed so
dramatically. All these people who run this place wouldn't be here if
it wasn't for those changes.'

He welcomes newcomers – 'New life is breathed into it by the
people who come in, even though they don't have the old history.'
Children 'are growing up on the island but they don't have that
climbing around the cliffs that we had'. Liam believes the future of
fishing is safe in Benji's hands but is less sure about farming. Few
people want to labour like that today.

I see how much he cares, not simply about the success of one season
at the seabird colony but about the whole island – its past, present
and future. Liam is not the type to sell the brilliance of Rathlin by
gushing about his 'passion' but he is the truest custodian of a place
I have yet met, a man who feels an enormous responsibility for his
island and its inhabitants, from puffins to nephews.

On my last day, I enjoy the miniature rush-hour – five cars, a
dozen people – as the ferry comes in. An old man reverses his car
into the island nurse's Land Rover with a crunch, smashing her rear
light before driving off without appearing to notice. Liam turns up
in his battered black machine and I breathlessly relay the smash: less
than a week, and I'm an island gossip. Liam deduces that the hit-and-
run driver is more usually found behind the wheel of the 'puffin bus'
that takes tourists to the seabirds in summer. The characters, and the
stories, just keep coming.

I feel strangely reluctant to leave this small island, and the ferry
slips away, almost too quickly, with one of Liam's brothers at the
helm. The white beaches of Church Bay gleam and the boat murmurs
with chat as we bounce over Sloc na Mara to Ballycastle. I drive and
then fly home as if in a trance, oblivious to the mainland bustle, still
drawing deep from the stories and the vivacity of this small island.

6

Prison Island

Alderney, The Channel Islands, 3 square miles, population 2,000

'The island itself seemed malicious. It would go on being
hurtful and evil for weeks at a time. Then suddenly again one
morning it would be fair, lovely as a morning in Paradise,
everything beautiful and flowing.'
'The Man Who Loved Islands'

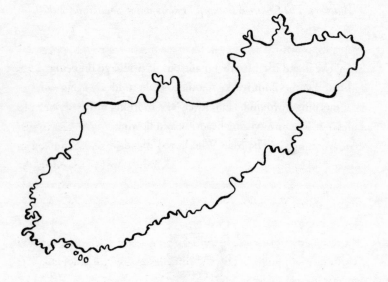

As I walk towards the sea, the fake headland resembles a conventional outcrop of granite laid down over five hundred million years ago. Struck methodically by waves that sound like distant detonations, Bibette Point thrusts into the English Channel beyond a crescent of white sand at Saye Bay. Closer up, it looks less robust than a natural promontory: a crazy-paving of small rocks fixed in concrete like those decorative stone chimney-breasts found in the living rooms of 1960s bungalows. In places, the sea has torn away this camouflaged cladding, revealing a concrete core of almost sensuous smoothness.

A rectangular black eye beckons me inside, an open doorway and a corridor leading into a bunker concealed inside the headland. The concrete floor is ankle-deep in sea spray. I take off my shoes and socks, flick on a dim torch and gingerly tiptoe into icy water, and the gloom beyond.

As when entering a cave, all natural light is extinguished surprisingly quickly. The corridor sloping gently upwards is similarly proportioned to a foot tunnel in one of London Underground's older stations. Doorless doorways open into spaces that could fit a dining table and eight chairs. Electric cables twist from broken casings, red with rust. Thin sheets of metal peel from the ceiling, but the walls are whitewashed and even now, nearly seventy-five years after they were painted, immaculate. I expect this labyrinthine warren to give me the creeps, but it actually feels domestic: calm, dry and quiet. The sea's rhythmic assault on the headland recedes as I step further into the gloom. The slave labourers did a fine job.

There is a glimmer of natural light. I turn off the main corridor, duck low and climb thirteen steep steps. A welcome waft of salty air comes from a small hexagonal space and a hole showing sky. I stick my head out: in the sky, an old-fashioned propeller-engined plane descends towards the airstrip; over the sea is the grey blur of France, casually close on the horizon.

A German gunner once stood where I am, pirouetting with his weapon, as if in a tank made of stone and rock. For five years of the twentieth century, Alderney was a fortress and island prison. In 1942, Bibette Point was renamed Strongpoint Biberkopf as this Channel Island was transformed from a feudal village to the most heavily defended component in Hitler's 'Atlantic Wall', bristling with heavy artillery, bunkers and searchlight stations.

This drastic change of character was given shape in concrete by Russians, Ukrainians, Poles and French Jews held in prison camps. During the Second World War, Alderney became the only slice of 'British' soil to house an SS concentration camp. Historians believe that a thousand slaves died on the island. Today, this dark past is everywhere and nowhere; visible and ignored; remembered solemnly but obliquely. It's someone else's history, a parallel universe, nothing to do with lovely Alderney or its charming people.

Alderney is twenty miles north-east of Herm and Jethou, the twin islands bestridden by Compton Mackenzie during the 1920s. All three islands met the same fate ten years after he had vacated them, abandoned by the British and invaded by the Germans during the war. The conquest of Herm and Jethou was uncomplicated because they had no human community. The war passed these islands by and I decide to bypass them too because Alderney's wartime history is much more compelling.

I journeyed to Alderney strapped to a bench seat behind an alarmingly youthful solo pilot hunched over the controls of the venerable Trislander, a fourteen-seater plane that is Alderney's only direct link with mainland Britain. We rose from Southampton Airport extremely noisily and extravagantly slowly, and darkness was falling over the Channel as I read the dials over the pilot's shoulder: 125 knots – 143 mph – airborne at a speed we could just about drive.

After an hour, we dived towards a rectangle and cross picked out in bright lights that hung in the foggy air ahead. The pilot gripped his yoke and forced the Trislander towards the ground as if it were a disobedient puppy. We flopped sideways into the lights, the runway's orange windsock fat with wind. Much windier, and we wouldn't have been yanked onto the island at all.

An after-dark arrival always paints a dreamy impression of a place. Beneath a cold mist suffused with woodsmoke, Alderney is particularly bewitching. Its airport looks like a farm, the entrance marked by an ornamental cattle trough. A popular means of transport along its lanes is the golf buggy: I first encountered one whizzing downhill past a tree stump sculpted into a giant puffin. Old tractors had been dumped in fields, and there were also the ghostly remains of a discarded threshing machine, as if someone only recently decided that this was a slightly outmoded piece of kit. When I walked into St Anne, the capital and only town, the first lit window revealed a taxidermied zebra in the corner of the living room. Was this a legacy of the old colonial when-Is who fled to the Isle of Man and the Channel Islands at the end of Empire?

There was a weirder sight. When I paused and glanced up from almost any corner of St Anne's pretty Georgian and Victorian stone houses, an ugly pebble-dashed tower, in slender concrete tiers, appeared on the horizon. 'The Water Tower,' shrugged the assistant in the visitor centre who gave me a lift to my B&B, directly under the tower's slitty black windows. Other locals call it the German Water Tower. It's a piece of infrastructure installed by the Nazis that has been used pragmatically ever since their departure. Only later does another islander explain it was built as a lookout tower for the Luftwaffe. Alderney's accommodation with these concrete monuments is one of its most intriguing characteristics.

Today, we mostly escape to small islands, but once we fled from them. As often as islands are hailed as utopias, they have been dystopias, and there is a long history of turning islands into places of incarceration. In the early 1800s Van Diemen's Land, later Tasmania, was established as a penal colony. Alcatraz, Robben Island, Devil's Island, Pianosa Island and dozens more followed, all over the world – three on the Isle of Wight alone. Islands still make convenient prisons today. Gross abuse can be hidden away. The prison on Rikers Island in New York is plagued by violence. In 2001, Australia's government established a 'processing centre' for refugees on the Pacific Island of Nauru. I visited the island when the camp was first established and felt as disillusioned as D.H. Lawrence had, in the Pacific. For a few decades, Nauru was implausibly wealthy, thanks to the mining of guano for fertiliser, but by the turn of this century the birdshit supplies were running low and islanders saw economic salvation in 'offshore processing'. Since accepting its role as Australia's jailer for stateless people, Nauru has become a purgatory of sexual and physical abuse, hunger strikes and human anguish.

Will the larger, continent-sized island Australia have its day of reckoning for this cruelty? Amends can't always be made. They haven't been for what happened, on the cusp of living memory, on Alderney.

Geologically, the Channel Islands do not belong to the British archipelago. Alderney lost its connection with the Cotentin Peninsula, a little finger jutting out from continental Europe, at the end of the last ice age, barely three hundred generations ago. It is sixty-three miles from Weymouth, the closest piece of mainland Britain, but just eight miles from Normandy. After he took refuge on Jersey, Victor Hugo described the Channel Islands as chicks that had strayed from the supervision of the mother hen. (Expelled from Jersey for insulting Queen Victoria, he then resided happily on Guernsey until, with the restoration of the French Republic, he returned to his own mother hen in 1870.)

Given its geography, Alderney's status in the world as a self-governing Crown Dependency, not part of the UK but still a possession of the British Crown, shows the strength of political desire. The British monarchy has clasped the Channel Islands to its breast for nearly a thousand years. There was no conquest. Ebenezer Le Page, the fictional Channel Islander-hero of G.B. Edwards's cult novel, *The Book of Ebenezer Le Page*, says history 'began in 55 BC when Julius Caesar landed in Britain; and I remember AD 1066, because that was the year we conquered England'. Real Channel Islanders like to repeat this fact. William, Duke of Normandy, gathered reinforcements from his islands on his way to victory at Hastings. Although King John lost Normandy to the French in 1204, he kept Jersey, Guernsey, Alderney, Sark and Herm. This may resemble a quirk of history but to the Ridunians – from Riduna, the Latin name for the island – as Alderney islanders are known, it matters. Their charmed but also oddly deprived life depends upon it.

The island by day is as entrancing as by night. 'It is the boundedness of the smaller island, encompassable in a glance, walkable in one day, that relates it to the human body closer than any other geographical conformation of land,' wrote John Fowles. Alderney is rounder and more intimate than the northern British isles I had visited; easily explored on foot or bike, unexpected sea views all over, and yet still possessing Tardis-like hidden vales, pockets of pines, windy headlands and achingly beautiful coves of pale sand.

With its more forgiving French climate, it has a population of 2,000, far more than similarly sized Eigg or Rathlin, and these mostly elderly residents seem unusually cheerful, bustling along the small roads in tiny silver Suzukis, eschewing seatbelts and leaving their engines running when they pull up wonkily on the pavement outside the Post Office. They are surrounded by spectacular drifts of wild flowers on the clifftops in summer – thrift, squill, prostrate broom, Portland spurge, Alderney cranesbill, bastard toadflax. Alderney's latitude, geology and long history have bequeathed it an unusual concentration of plant species in such a small space: more than nine hundred. The island is famed for its seabirds – gannets were one beneficiary of war, establishing a colony on the island in the 1940s, possibly because they were displaced from Lundy in the Bristol Channel after it became a bombing range – and the greater white-toothed shrew, a sinister-sounding carnivorous rodent found on Alderney, Guernsey and Herm and in Ireland, but not on the British mainland. Occasionally it can be spied devouring dead rabbit carcasses after dark.

Even though I'm visiting in mid-December, the island's pastures are verdant-green, and the gorse sparkles with yellow flowers. The words of Alexei Ikonnikov, a Russian slave labourer during the war, encapsulate the charm of the Alderney I experience. 'I liked the air – it was very soft and salty and had a strong smell of grass,' he remembered. 'I liked the stone houses around the harbour and the little gardens they each had. I liked seeing the other islands in the distance. I always had this idea that Alderney was a place where people before the war were happy and free, and when the war was over, they would be so again.'

My introduction to Alderney's extraordinary history is a Vin d'Honneur, a commemorative drink in the Island Hall to mark the seventieth anniversary of islanders returning home after the war.

I mix with elderly guests around teas on a trestle table that flies a plastic Union Jack in its centre. We stand for the island president's toast. It gives me a shock.

'To the Duke of Normandy, our Queen.'

I'm also surprised by the ardour of 'the Duke of Normandy's' message, relayed by the Governor General of Guernsey, the larger, similarly semi-autonomous Crown Dependency to which the Ridunians are bound.

'To my most loyal people on the island of Alderney,' says Elizabeth R via the Governor General's mouth. 'I am most grateful for your assurances of continued allegiance and I welcome this opportunity of affirming the close ties that have existed for so long between the Crown and the people of Alderney.'

There are intakes of breath and 'Oh lovely' from the rapt audience; delight intensifies when it's announced that the Alderney flag is flying on the Ministry of Justice building in London as part of the commemorations.

If Elizabeth R sounds slightly paranoid, as though Alderney might re-attach itself to Normandy at any moment, perhaps she is simply keeping up the good work of her great-great-grandmother, who did much to establish the fortified character of the island. Garrisons were placed on Alderney by the Romans and Henry VIII too, but this home of humble French-speaking Norman farmers was changed most dramatically by the Victorians. A perceived threat from France, who built the port of nearby Cherbourg so large it would house their entire naval fleet, triggered Alderney's building boom in the 1850s: a long breakwater, a new northerly harbour and twenty-two Victorian forts and batteries to protect it. The island's population exploded to 8,000, including many Irish labourers and two royal visitors: Queen Victoria, accompanied by Prince Albert, approvingly inspected her realm's new defences during a holiday excursion from her favourite island, the Isle of Wight. Like so many expensive military deterrents, it was redundant before it was complete, the French were no threat, and Gladstone predicted these 'follies' could help an enemy in the future. He was right.

I attend the Vin d'Honneur in the hope of meeting residents who remember the German invasion of Alderney. In less than a week in 1940, the island's character was utterly transformed. Surprisingly, perhaps, few Channel Islanders had considered themselves a Nazi target that spring. They were so small, and seemingly irrelevant. When Ridunians heard gunfire and saw black smoke rising from the Cotentin Peninsula, however, they realised they were within touching distance of world war. It would be 'repugnant' to abandon territory held since the Norman Conquest, Churchill harrumphed, but his government quietly decided it could not defend the Channel Islands and would withdraw its troops. But it failed to tell the islands that it had withdrawn until four days after the event – and its failure to inform Germany of this demilitarisation almost certainly caused the unnecessary deaths of forty-four people, when the enemy bombed the capitals of Guernsey and Jersey before invading.

When British troops were evacuated from Alderney and boatloads of refugees from Cherbourg began arriving, the anxious islanders were faced with a decision: should they stay or go? There was no such agonising choice on much larger Jersey and Guernsey, where it was impractical to remove everyone. Such was the intimacy of Alderney, though, that there could be no civilian rule by its 1,450 islanders under a German occupation; they would be overwhelmed. And yet many older, Norman-French speakers were reluctant to leave their homes for a foreign country, England, that they had never visited.

On 22 June, the islanders assembled on their cricket field where they were addressed from the back of a lorry by Frederick French, the Judge, or chief minister. In a memorable scene in *An Island Story*, a musical dramatising Alderney's evacuation and homecoming, he appeals to them to stick together, and leave together: 'We are a small island. When the sun shines, it shines on all of us. When it rains, we all get soaked.'

There was a show of hands and, ten years after the evacuation of the Scottish island of St Kilda – though in rather different circumstances – another small island population voted to abandon their home. They had an hour to pack, one suitcase each.

'Going away was no problem, except we had to destroy our pets and animals,' remembers George Baron, who was sixteen and a half at the time and is still an extrovert, jokey man with a sharp memory. 'All the bulls and the stallions had to be destroyed. The cattle were let loose. There was no time to bury what you killed. I saw my father in tears. Killing your pets was the worst.' Churchill had ordered it: he didn't want to leave a larder for Hitler. Miriam Kidd, who has a wide-eyed, smiley face, exactly as she was in old photos when a girl, was just six. She remembers being told she must leave her ginger cat. Taken in a lorry to the harbour, she saw the corpse of a cat shot dead against a wall. It could have been hers. 'That was my last memory of Alderney,' she says.

Alderney was emptied. On 2 July, the Luftwaffe landed at the airport, and a very different island came into being.

Alderney's people became refugees in England. 'My mother said she sat in the stern of the boat with me in her arms and she sobbed her heart out all the way to Weymouth,' says Patsy Martel, a cheery woman who was nine months old when her family left. Many children had been evacuated before the adults at the start of the war. They boarded at schools or lived with foster families while their parents spent the war working in factories in Glasgow, Bury or Birmingham. They expected to be away for six weeks, says George Baron: 'It was six years.'

When peace was declared, the islanders could not simply go home. In their absence, Alderney had become a bleak and dusty ruin of barbed wire and derelict buildings, so devastated by war that civil servants proposed it should become a permanently uninhabited firing range. During the Allied invasion of France the island was bypassed and supply lines cut, and emaciated German soldiers struggled to survive until the war's end, burning bits of houses to keep warm. The Germans fitted the entire island with mains electricity and piped water, and planted potatoes, but they had also sown a more malevolent crop: 30,317 mines. The only British soldier to die on Alderney was killed after the war, when defusing a mine.

Judge French and other islanders agitated to be allowed home, and eventually the British government relented. On 15 December 1945, eighteen months after D-Day and six months after VE Day, 110 abled-bodied people, possessing practical skills in construction or farming, were shipped back to Alderney.

'Coming back was the worst,' remembers George. 'To be honest, everybody wanted to come back home until they got here. They couldn't believe it. Some of them stayed on the boat and went straight back to England. It was ruined.'

A modest arch bearing a banner saying 'Welcome Home' had been erected by British soldiers, who lined up by the harbour. Songs were played by Guernsey's Salvation Army band. 'I couldn't understand why all the old people were very tearful,' says Patsy Martel, then six. 'To me it was a huge adventure, having never seen the sea.' Those who remembered pre-war Alderney were indeed distraught. 'Hell couldn't look any worse,' remembered Joyce Buckland, who was seventeen at the time. The island was dominated by concrete fortifications constructed by slave labourers. Rats and fleas had taken up residence in former homes, which had been looted and abandoned without roofs or floors. And a number of residents reported the same strange phenomenon: there was no birdsong.

By the end of 1945, a quarter of Alderney's pre-war population had come home. For the adults, the place was a mess. For the children, it was a playground. 'We were running absolutely wild, especially

The sea around Barra could turn 'a richer ultramarine than any stretch of water on this side of the Mediterranean', declared Compton Mackenzie (below) who made his home among the 'aristocrats of the democracy' on this fabulous Hebridean island.

Cleadale, 'the rebel stronghold', on Eigg – a beautiful, inspirational beacon of independence (above). The 'Pensioners' Skateboard' facilitates entry to the Tomb of the Eagles on Orkney (below). Wellies by Eigg's Singing Sands beach.

The cosmopolitan Lower End of Rathlin, Northern Ireland's only permanently inhabited island.

Alderney islanders call it 'The Water Tower' (below) but it's actually a Nazi lookout for the Luftwaffe. Pitching my trusty tent alone on St Kilda (right).

'The islands seem to float suspended between earth and heaven in a crystal globe' wrote Compton Mackenzie of halcyon Hebridean days. Walking on Hirta towards the uninhabited island of Soay is intoxicating. But tourist brochures omit St Kilda's military installations (below).

The barns to the left of this Ynys Enlli farmhouse are where the modern-day hermit Sister Helen Mary set up home. St Martin's, Isles of Scilly, (below): an island of flowers where children roam free.

Island transport is always thrilling (clockwise from top right): Barra's beach airport; dogs ride on quads on Ynys Enlli; Alderney's supermini is the golf buggy; I hitched a lift on Viv Jackson's Massey Ferguson on St Martin's.

Clockwise from top right: Colin Evans, the eloquent boatman of Ynys Enlli; Liam McFaul, a modest Swiss Army knife of a man who is RSPB warden, organic farmer, fisherman, fire officer and coastguard rescue on Rathlin; Miriam Kidd with the cat that had to be killed on evacuating Alderney – Miriam looked just the same when I met her; Donna pipes off the Glaswegian boys (and me) as we leave Eigg.

Osea (above) – full of surprises – and its neighbour Ray Island (below): This Essex coast is wild and will always be so.

the boys,' says Patsy. They picked up German helmets, sat behind German guns and took aim at cargo ships in the bay. One boy lost a finger when he threw bullets into a fire and they exploded.

The British government devised a unique postwar experiment for Alderney: communism. Both the paper records and the real boundaries of the old Norman strip fields had been destroyed during the occupation. A commissioner was appointed to re-establish land-ownership, but this would take time – it actually took until 1964. Providing each individual farmer with equipment seemed wasteful, and so they were all forced to work together to produce food. 'Things were organised in London by civil servants,' says George Baron. 'They thought all the farmers would get together as a communal farm – no way, no way. Farmers are farmers. They all had their own way of growing, looking after cattle.' Or, as another islander, Royston Raymond, put it: 'The farming didn't work because the farmers were all Norman-French and the Norman-French are a particularly stub-born lot.'

Having to abandon Alderney to the Germans was a cruel experience. The islanders' determination to return home, and their resilience when they got there, is what the people of Alderney celebrate on 15 December, their Homecoming Day.

It is a warm and spirited celebration of community, by the com-munity. But as I drink tea and listen to the older folk, I wonder about the tales *not* being told. The seventieth anniversary's grand events – the unveiling of a memorial plaque containing Judge French's evacuation instructions, the premiere of the musical remembering their evacuation and return, and the showing of an excellent documentary containing memories of the homecoming – all concern the years 1940 and 1945. The bit in the middle is blank. At the Vin d'Honneur I ask Norma Paris, one of Alderney's ten elected politicians, why there isn't more recollecting of the Nazi occupation and the dead slaves.

'Older residents,' she says, 'keep quiet about it because it was a very traumatic thing to come back and find the island wrecked, but they've grown proud of what they've done [to rebuild] – and so they should be. They were very forward-thinking. They wanted to get on with things and put it behind them.' It sounds like part of an answer.

I spend the night in a B&B I booked because I'd spotted that it was the former farm where a Russian slave labourer called Georgi Kondakov ate pigswill to stay alive during the Second World War. Just as I found at the bunker inside the fake headland, there is no trace of malignancy, or of Georgi's suffering, within these white stone walls. Not every old building conjures up a sense of the past. The old farm is now a lovely place, run by a charismatic potter called Moira Sleeman, who plays a starring role in the musical and is also the island's part-time reporter for the BBC.

I read of Georgi Kondakov's plight in his letters to an islander called Brian Bonnard, who published them in an excellent book a quarter of a century ago. Discovering that Brian still lives on the island, the next morning I walk downhill from the B&B, past a tennis club and a sprawl of bungalows built in the 1960s and with names like The Anchorage and Sea Change; from gardens stocked with spiny New Zealand cabbage plants, I get fine views of a milky-turquoise sea.

Behind the two porches and three front doors of The Twins stands the stooped, meticulous figure of Brian Bonnard. His bungalow is named after its builder's twin aunts, from whom he had hoped to inherit a fortune. Brian's wife Jean was also a twin; they wanted two sets, but never did have any children. Les Jumelles, the Twins, are also the two peaked rocks we watch from Brian's window at half-tide, as his living room rustles to the tickings of his clock collection: cuckoo clocks, antique clocks, digital clocks, an atomic clock and a clock with an ornamental robin that chirps on the quarter-hour.

Brian is a botanist by training, and he and Jean retired here in their early fifties, some years after she beat cancer and her surgeon told her to go and live somewhere warm. Brian is proud of his wife. She was an inspector of schools, had a photographic memory, three doctorates and a PhD in homeopathy. She had learned to fly and had undertaken an RAF parachute jumping course, qualifying after a 10,000-foot leap. She also did 'mysterious work for the Foreign Office' and would disappear at a moment's notice; Brian didn't know what she was up to, and never asked.

Jean was the one who put him in touch with Georgi Kondakov. Seized during the German advance into Russia, Georgi was taken to a bleak island which the Germans called 'Adolf'. His fellow slaves told him it was English, and called it 'Aal-der-new'. Returned to Russia after the war, Georgi went to work in a factory, and never understood where he had been imprisoned until he met a British businessman at a trade fair who scoffed when Georgi told him he'd been held by the Nazis in Britain. They talked further and the businessman eventually guessed his place of incarceration, pronouncing it 'Ol-der-ni'.

In 1989 Georgi's story was published in a youth edition of *Pravda* under the title: 'Island of Death in the Channel'. Befriended by a journalist, Galina Chernakova, who offered to translate, Georgi sent a letter to Alderney's government asking if they knew of someone who would exchange letters with him, and they passed it on to Jean Bonnard, who was then honorary curator of the Alderney Society's excellent museum. Brian and Georgi started writing to each other, and in 1990 a visit was arranged. The Cold War was thawing, but Brian still had to go to the Russian Embassy in London to collect Galina and Georgi, a short man with an eager-to-please smile. When they reached The Twins, Brian remembers how Galina struggled to produce a polite translation of Georgi's reaction. 'The first thing he said was "Oh, this was the place where the Germans kept their tarts."' Brian's bungalow had been built within the walls of the slave labour camp where for fourteen months Georgi endured a nightmare.

*

Georgi Kondakov was sixteen in July 1942 when he was taken by the invading German forces from his Russian village. He believed that a childhood coping with the Soviet famine of 1932–3, when an esti-mated six million people died, prepared him well for Alderney. His first impression was of stony roads, and books, clothes and papers, torn and muddy and scattered everywhere. *Das Arschloch der Welt*, as the German soldiers called it, 'the arsehole of the world', was an un-popular posting. 'I always liked wind and storm. But there is so much of it, and constant lack of peace makes everything an effort,' noted Gerhard Nebel, a German author with suspiciously liberal views who was dispatched to Alderney in 1942 to assist with the construction effort. On Hitler's personal order, Alderney was covered with a greater concentration of fortifications per mile of coast than any other point along his Atlantic Wall, stretching from Norway to Spain. Operated by the Nazi's ruthless forced-labour group, the Organisation Todt, four camps – long wooden huts where workers slept in bunkbeds – were constructed. Each – Helgoland, Norderney, Borkum and Sylt – was named after a German island. By 1944, German officers were talking of the Führer's *Inselwahn* – island madness – a fixation on the Channel Islands. They were his 'laboratory' for Anglo-German rela-tions. Images of German soldiers on the very English-looking streets of Jersey and Guernsey were a valuable propaganda tool.

When Georgi was placed in Helgoland, alongside a thousand other mostly Russian and Ukrainian slave labourers, he was quite fortunate, although it didn't seem that way at first. Every day, he was woken at six. In winter it was pitch-black, but they were forbidden to strike a match. There was no time to wash. They were herded to work, usually for twelve hours, fortifying Alderney with cement. They turned grey with cement, and Georgi wore cement sacks for clothes. He and his fellow slaves constantly endured lice and parasites and epidemics of boils and diarrhoea. There was one lavatory in Georgi's camp. If they needed the toilet at work, a German guard called Otto made prisoners crap on his shovel. 'If he liked the heap, he said "*Gut!*" and allowed you to bury it. If not he would hit the man with the same shovel,' remembered Georgi. They lived under the constant threat of violence. Guards would beat them with rubber hoses or they'd have to dash through a narrow passage with guards on either side whacking them with sticks.

Georgi's most compelling memory of his island prison, he told Brian Bonnard, was one sensation: hunger. His daily ration was two thin slices of bread and a bitter ersatz coffee made from acorns and barley. On their two days off each month, the slave labourers received no food at all. His luck lay in the fact he was assigned to a mobile works group, which gave him opportunities to scavenge. The foremen would let them go to the sea's edge at low tide and they'd grab anything: crabs, limpets, seaweed, even the occasional vegetable washed ashore from a passing ship. Prisoners were rewarded if they caught rats and Georgi traded his rats for cigarettes, which he then swapped for bread. Those who went hungry in order to smoke usually died, but Georgi wasn't a smoker. At night, he escaped the camp and entered the pig farm that became my B&B seventy-three years later.' Here he devoured pigswill and found biscuits, flour and bread.

Brian admits he was 'a little bit sceptical' during the two years he corresponded with Georgi, until the Russian arrived on his doorstep. The two of them drove all over the island, and when Georgi remembered something 'just around the next corner' he was always correct. One particular stony beach used to be sandy, he said, and he was right. 'He couldn't have seen it on a map or in pictures, or been told such details,' says Brian. 'I had to revise my opinion. He had obviously been to all the places.'

The accuracy of Georgi Kondakov's memory is supported by ample evidence. Gerhard Nebel noted in his diary the arrival of Russian workers wearing evil-smelling rags and wooden shoes on 7 August, which matched the day Georgi said he arrived on the island. Another old German soldier, Gustav Dahmer, noted how Russian prisoners scavenged food waste and that four to six men died each day on this 'godforsaken island'. In many ways, Georgi's letters underplay the horror. His camp was designed for work, not for punishment or death, but such was the corruption of local officers taking workers' rations, their Nazi-ideology-based contempt for life and the frenzied war-work schedule, that death was an everyday occurrence. In the final two months of 1942, 116 prisoners' deaths were registered, mostly Ukrainians and Russians. The commonest causes of death were dysentery and malnutrition. These official records are unlikely to be comprehensive. A false-bottomed coffin was found on the island. Deaths were concealed.

Sylt was the most sinister camp on Alderney. Built for political prisoners, it was the only concentration camp on 'British' soil, overseen in 1943 by the SS *Totenkopfverbände*, the Death's-Head Brigade. According to Otto Spehr, a German police officer imprisoned on Alderney for helping enemies of the state, one fellow prisoner was hanged. Others, who fell ill, were pushed outside the camp fence and then shot for 'escaping'. Another German testified that he saw thirty-nine prisoners killed in one incident. He also identified two who were hanged. A Russian slave worker saw one man crucified for stealing. A Channel Islander who worked on Alderney told British military investigators that a German chauffeur amused himself by shooting Russians scavenging potatoes from the fields.

Towards the end of Georgi's fourteen-month imprisonment on Alderney, eight hundred French Jews were installed in a camp-within-a-camp in Norderney. Married to 'Aryan' Frenchwomen, they were considered 'half-Jews' and spared the gas chambers. They were forced to beat each other. They named Alderney *le rocher maudit*, the accursed rock.

Brian Bonnard casts doubt on Georgi and others' recollection of bodies being tipped off the end of the breakwater because subsequent dives never found any remains, although the Channel's strong currents could have washed any corpses away. Historians are also sceptical about stories that slaves were systematically buried alive in the foundations of Alderney's anti-tank walls. In her history of the Channel Islands during the war, however, Madeleine Bunting identifies three correlating accounts by survivors – who never met – of an Italian slave labourer who fell between the wooden planks being filled with concrete. The German foreman refused to stop work and the Italian was buried alive.

One of the British officers who after the war investigated the 'wicked and merciless' crimes on Alderney said the 389 burials of slave labourers on Longis Common were a 'minimum conclusion'; Georgi estimated that number died in his camp alone. Bunting estimates between 1,000 and 1,200 deaths on the island; Bonnard does not disagree, but notes that most would probably have died of starvation, dysentery or simply overwork and would not have been deliberately killed. Alderney witnessed the greatest mass manslaughter on British soil in modern times.

At odd moments, Georgi Kondakov's memories match those of islanders with whom he shared this space in close succession, as if they were hotel guests taking the same photo from their hotel room window. 'I remember Alderney to be grey and gloomy. There wasn't a single bird singing,' he wrote to Brian. Occasionally, for Georgi, the island offered some solace. During one nocturnal raid on the pig farm, he halted for a moment by the sea. 'It was tremendously beautiful. It was shining with myriads of small fires. The edge of the surf looked like foam on fire. Sometimes a lightning flash would run across the water, shining with peaceful light.' The surf sighed, and he resisted 'an unbearable desire in my inner depths to plunge into this sea of lights'.

This bioluminescence was a moment when the horror was transcended by the natural beauty of Alderney. As Hitler's fortifications neared completion, Georgi was redeployed to a camp in France, which he escaped to join the French Resistance. On his return to Russia after the war, he and his fellow slave labourers were accused of working for the enemy, and he endured four further years in a Stalinist labour camp inside the Arctic Circle.

When he arrived back on Alderney in 1990, he was overwhelmed to be presented with a bunch of flowers, for the first time in his life. People gave him a 'wonderful reception' says Brian. The island's president asked him to address the States, its mini-parliament; people talked to him in the street and lavished him with gifts; by the end of the visit, his one suitcase had become eighteen. Surprisingly perhaps, when he returned home he was permitted to take all his gifts with him.

Georgi likened the force that pulled him back towards his prison island to a childhood urge to 'peep behind the curtain' when you know that the danger is not real any more, but it was a traumatic visit nonetheless, and after he returned to Russia Brian did not hear from his friend for a few months. When Georgi wrote again, he said: 'I now understand why Alderney has always been, and remains, the place of strongest attraction to me. I think it was there, during the war, that I lost my former self, brought up in pre-war Russia. The man who was transported from Alderney to France in October 1943 only looked like the boy brought there in 1942. His inner world, his habits and outlook on life, everything, remained on the island for ever. Yes, I think my genuine, my original self, lies hidden somewhere in Alderney.'

Georgi Kondakov, who passed away at his home in Russia in 2008, found traces of his old life, if not his self, on Alderney. I wander the island looking for traces of its past, too. It takes a while to get my eye in, and then the concrete constructions are everywhere. On the horizon west of Brian Bonnard's bungalow stands Fort Tourgis, a derelict Victorian building occupied and modernised by the German invaders, just as Gladstone had predicted. Further east, the sand dunes around Longis Bay are supplanted by a vast concrete anti-tank wall, which might be mistaken for civilian sea defences and provides a handy windbreak on the beach. That the swooshing curved three-storey German naval range-finder tower is known as 'the Odeon' is not simply another example of the islanders' fondness for euphemism: it genuinely resembles a fine modernist cinema. Painted white, it could be a cool beach house. Most of this Nazi architecture was constructed by pouring concrete between wooden boards, which gives the yellow lichen-speckled walls a planked texture popular among concrete-loving modern architects. The buildings I find most sinister are those which have been subsumed into suburbia: a magnolia-painted chalet-bungalow built on the concrete foundations of a German bunker, a chalet originally constructed in the style of Adolf Hitler's mountain retreat at Berchtesgaden for the Nazi commander of the Sylt camp, which has now been relocated and turned into a luxury bungalow. Standing skew-whiff in one hedgerow is a rusty Nazi-era iron fence post with curved hooks for barbed wire. It is sharp to touch and just looks *nasty*. I find one comforting fact among these malevolent ruins: Alderney's dry Nazi bunkers have proved a perfect hibernation hole for the rare large tortoiseshell butterfly, another islander driven to extinction on the mainland.

The physical traces of the German occupation have lingered long after 1945, and so have emotional threads. One or two people experienced both Nazi Alderney and native Alderney.

When I listen to islanders' memories of returning to their ruined homes, one woman, Doris Curth, sounds slightly more positive. She was sixteen when she came back with her mother and father in 1946. Their house wasn't too bad, she says, it just needed a clean. She volunteered on the communal farm. 'It was nice. We all worked, all the locals. One of the German workers could play the accordion and we'd have singsongs at lunchtime.'

Later I join the islanders in their – German-built – cinema to watch a documentary showing memories of homecoming collected by a local filmmaker, Charlie Gauvain, and I suddenly realise that Doris Curth's sunnier view of Alderney might be linked to the fact that she fell in love with a German soldier. None of the history I'd read before had mentioned there were German PoWs on Alderney after the war. Curious to find out more, I walk down the hill towards the harbour to find the low-ceilinged fisherman's cottage where Doris lives, flowery hanging baskets alongside the ancient shell of a Hillman Imp in the front garden.

Like most Alderney residents, Doris looks younger than her eighty-five years and talks phlegmatically, rather than nostalgically, about the past. Working on the communal farm was ideal, she says, because she loved gardening. 'We never went home to lunch, we sat in the fields with the Germans. There was a crowd of girls and a few of the German boys.' Doris first saw Karl Curth on the day she arrived home. There were fourteen PoWs living in a camp close by and he was part of a group heading out to work that morning. She didn't really notice him, but another PoW later told her that Karl had said, 'Oh, I like the look of that one.'

While several thousand German soldiers were taken from Alderney to prisoner-of-war camps in England, around four hundred with practical skills – carpenters, plumbers, electricians – were made to stay on for a year to repair the island. When residents returned, Guernsey's postwar Lieutenant Governor advised them against fraternising with the enemy. He reminded them that these German soldiers had destroyed their properties, and noted the dead slave workers buried above Longis Bay. But the war was over and residents and Germans worked together to rebuild the island. Alfred Gaudion, a tall, softly spoken older islander, tells me he and his father cut hay with German PoWs. 'They seemed quite normal to us. They were just part of everyday life. All the hard cases had been moved out by then, I should imagine.' His older brother Peter remembers one PoW pointing at a group of three young German soldiers and whispering, 'Nazi, no good.' After some weeks, the British authorities took the three men away. Islanders liked the Germans because they told them more about what occurred on the island than the British government, which was reluctant to admit there had been a concentration camp on its soil.

Living near the PoW camp, Doris saw 'quite a bit' of them. 'It was a small island. There weren't a lot of people here.' She started saying hello to Karl, who was twenty and a plumber. 'He told me when we met, "I'm Charlie." Later it was "I'm named after Prince Charlie." He used to joke about it.' The Germans weren't allowed in the pubs so they went to the cinema together. 'They *had* built it, after all,' says Doris.

They took it slowly. Charlie went to England in 1947 to labour in a brickworks. Back on Alderney in 1948, he got a carpenter PoW friend to make a sewing box and gave it to Doris as a present. They required special permission from Guernsey's Lieutenant Governor to marry. Was it controversial? 'There were a few people who said things, but not to me. Nobody was nasty, but you heard the whispers, "Oh she's getting married to a German, I wonder what her parents must feel", but my parents were happy.' Doris and Charlie tied the knot in her mother's house that May. They couldn't marry in a church: Doris was pregnant. I mention how some men run away if they discover their lover is pregnant. 'It must've been true love,' beams Doris.

They were married for forty-three years, until Charlie died. 'My married life was good. He really was a lovely man,' she says firmly, taking two framed photographs from her living-room shelves. They show a cherubic-faced boy in a German soldier's uniform. Charlie was seventeen and a half when he went into the army. 'He had just finished his apprenticeship as a plumber and then he was called up.' He spent most of the war in France, says Doris, but never spoke about it, 'and I never pressed. I've always said, he was young and sent to war; the British were young and sent to war. It wasn't the everyday people who wanted war, it was government and officials.'

Doris and Charlie settled on Alderney. 'We had little ID cards and we had to report every year to say he wanted to stay in Alderney. He had the choice of going back or staying but he didn't go back home,' says Doris. 'I told him if we have to go home I'll come with you because we're married, so don't hang back. But he always told me he'd spent so much time here that here was home now.' They moved into Doris's current home in 1952, had four children, and one of their ten grandchildren carries on the family plumbing business. Charlie loved swimming in the sea, played football for two island clubs and founded Alderney's air rifle club. 'He got on with everybody. People always said to him, "What religion are you?" He said, "I belong to them all" because he worked in all the churches – English, Catholic, Salvation Army.'

Jersey and Guernsey were spared the destruction wrought on Alderney, but perhaps psychologically the Ridunians had an easier time of it. They did not live alongside the German invaders during the war, with all the awkward compromises that entailed. They have not faced allegations of collaboration, or insults concerning the women who had children with German soldiers, which have created a prickly defensiveness about the occupation on Jersey and Guernsey.

I was curious to understand why Alderney's years under the Nazis were not part of the island's official story. The emphasis on the trauma of leaving home and then returning to a devastated island looks myopic when placed alongside what occurred on Alderney in the years between. When I ask George Baron about the atrocities that took place during the war, he replies: 'To be honest, a lot of it is made up, a lot of it is rumours.' This sounds a bit like denial. Perhaps that's what it took for the returning islanders to turn the entrance pillars for Helgoland camp into the gateposts of a bungalow? Or paint a grim-looking German building with bobbing boats and fluffy clouds and use it as a recycling centre? Or buy the chalet built for SS commander Max List and turn it into a detached bungalow decorated with cedarwood shingles and seashells?

Such questions overlook the grinding austerity of the postwar era. The bungalows built on bunkers look like an accommodation with the occupier, but are simply an accommodation with poverty. The Ridunians couldn't smash up every Nazi building, not only because they were superbly constructed, but because they themselves were so poor. The islanders can hardly be condemned for making use of this wartime building boom.

Seventy years on, Alderney has a smattering of wealthy residents – the only ones I hear about are a multimillionaire self-published author and the zebra owner – but it lacks the wealth of its big-sister islands. Ridunians love telling how Jersey and Guernsey describe it as the 'Cinderella' Channel Island, pointing out that Cinderella had two ugly sisters. Its in-between status means it has no access to Lottery money or EU funds to turn each German fortification into a memorial or tourist attraction. Just as islanders have to rub along with neighbours they don't really like, Alderney has to rub along with its past. I realise it was thoughtless of me to expect their homecoming celebrations to recall the brutality of the Nazi era. Alderney's residents have as much responsibility for the actions of those temporary islanders of seven decades ago as a homeowner has for the actions of a burglar who tortures people in her home while she's on holiday.

When I ask about the reluctance to talk about the Nazi past, almost everyone supplies the same answer. 'People wanted to forget,' says Doris Curth. They were also discouraged from doing any digging by the British authorities. Any denial by the Ridunians is rather less significant than government denial. After the Germans evacuated Sylt in 1944, the prisoner Otto Spehr escaped his transportation through Belgium by stealing a plane and flying to Britain, where he worked for the BBC's German service during the last months of the war. He was reprimanded for mentioning the Alderney camps on the BBC and made to understand that 'the British did not want to know that there had been a concentration camp on British soil'.

Four men were prosecuted for war crimes on Alderney: a Soviet slave-labourer-turned-guard was sentenced to twenty-five years' hard labour in Russia; two German officers were given prison sentences in Paris in 1949 after being accused of subjecting Jews to 'systematic ill-treatment'; and a member of the SS was executed in East Germany in 1963. But the British tried no one. Fifteen suspected German war criminals were released without trial from British PoW camps. Several lived quietly in Germany into the 1980s. The mass killings on Alderney were an embarrassment to the British. The Cold War reduced the likelihood of British and Soviet authorities working together to investigate the abuse and murder of Russians and Ukrainians on the island. And so Alderney's time as a prison island has slipped from view.

Before I catch the plane back to the mainland, I take a walk. I want to see how Alderney's dead slaves are remembered. The bodies of Georgi Kondakov's fellow labourers were removed from the island and given a proper burial in the 1960s by various international war grave commissions, but a local family erected a stone memorial on an elevated spot above the former graveyard. 'In memory of all foreign labour who died in Alderney between the years 1940–1945,' a plaque reads. 'They also served.' Anniversary services have been held by Russian and French representatives of the deceased, and every year in May the people of Alderney hold a well-attended memorial ceremony in memory of the prisoners. Nevertheless, Alderney remains a corner of the Third Reich forgotten by all but a trickle of Nazi obsessives and bunkerologists who pore over the specifics of each fortification without much thought for the victims who built them.

On the high south-west of the island, mostly given over to the small airport, is another little-known memorial. Not far from the cliffs, and a long way from any tarmacked road, stand three concrete gateposts. These mark the entrance to SS Lager Sylt, the only concentration camp ever built on 'British' soil. A small grey marble plaque is fixed to one post: 'Some 400 prisoners died here between March 1943 and June 1944,' it reads. 'This plaque was placed by ex-prisoners and their families, 2008.'

Inside the gates are mounds of bramble, dull purple in midwinter and echoing with the metallic warning call of wrens. Apart from a jutting lump of concrete brightened with lichen the vivid yellow of Channel Island butter, the only visible structure is a concrete hut with a large flat circular concrete roof resembling the Art Deco Tube stations of the northern reaches of the Piccadilly Line. The doors to this elegant building, unusually for a small island, are locked. Through the windows I can see dusty black tyres and drums marked 'Flammable'.

One of the island's noisy Trislander planes drops in, engine spluttering twice, like a machine-gun. I turn back towards the airport shed, anticipating its fuggy conviviality, but my head is full of this camp. Suddenly I see in a different light the curved corrugated sheds surrounded by electric fencing that keeps Alderney's free-range pigs from ranging too freely. It is 2.30 p.m. and virtually dark. The slitty peepholes of the Water Tower gaze down at me again. It is time to go home.

7

The Family Archipelago

St Martin's, Isles of Scilly, 0.92 square miles, population 120

'Even islands like to keep each other company'
'The Man Who Loved Islands'

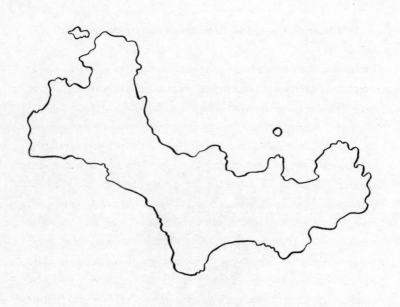

I return to the *Scillonian* after stowing our car on a Penzance side street and step into the ominous first frame of an unfolding horror movie. It is pouring with rain and the ship lurches at anchor. I find my little archipelago strung out on seating in the prow, staring at the TV, miles from any ventilation. Ted (previous seafaring experience: none) is rampaging through Babybel cheeses and a punnet of strawberries. Esme (previous seafaring experience: a boat trip across a Norfolk harbour to see some seals during which she clung to me and cried for Mummy) is scoffing muffins. So is her twin, Milly, who at least tolerated the seal-watching trip. The ship's lounge smells of coffee, cheese and warm dog. The children should be sat by a window, or outside. But all the other seats are now taken. And the kids have peeled off their wet-weather gear. It isn't going to be easy to get them on deck, if required. This won't end well.

I'd checked the forecast the previous night. Wind, near-gale force 7; sea, 'rough, very rough' at times. A few days earlier I'd phoned my dad's friends, Helen and Viv, in whose chalet we were staying for an Easter holiday. 'I'm so sorry, you're not going to have a very good crossing,' says Helen, as if psychic. I seek reassurance from the ferry booth attendant at Penzance harbour. 'It's been worse,' she says in the soothing manner of a doctor to a patient with a terminal illness. 'But I think it'll be a bit choppy. I'm sorry.'

'I'm sorry,' repeats the woman in the *Scillonian*'s café when I hurry there to better prepare my offspring for the coming ordeal: the café doesn't stock those little elasticated wristbands that my dad believes dispel all seasickness.

They're mumbo-jumbo anyway, I say, defiantly. I've vomited on Irish sea ferries, Baltic sea ferries, a Greenpeace boat off Greenland and, most humiliatingly, on a replica of Captain Cook's *Endeavour* as it navigated the monster swell of the Wash near Skegness. In recent years, though, I've found my sea legs, or at least a tactic for staggering across the ocean. Guinness is good for you, Compton Mackenzie was told on his rough crossing to the Isle of Man, but I don't require booze or tablets or ginger sweets or magic wristbands – I need to stand outside and fix my eye on the horizon. I tell the ship's café lady I'll just take my children outside. 'Outside works for four in ten but what about the other six? You take your children outside and it doesn't work and they'll never go on a ship again and you'll have to fly them to Scilly each summer and you'll be cursing those air fares.'

Canvassing views on seasickness is like a particularly futile online debate, everyone with a different, equally unsubstantiated, equally depressing, view.

We are not completely unprepared. We've taken conventional seasickness tablets. We also have Nanny and Grandad, Lisa's mum, Jan and her husband Rob, to lend a hand. It is as impossible to assess if someone will prove a capable seafarer as it is to guess if they can roll their tongue, but I like the look of Rob today. He's quietly confident and remembers a rough ferry during a holiday in Cyprus when he stayed up drinking all night while everyone else was sick. Lisa has no experience of the sea whatsoever, perhaps because her mum doesn't do ferries. I put Jan's wariness down to her characteristic modesty. Perhaps it will all be OK?

We rock away from the old stone jetty on our twenty-eight-mile cruise across one of Britain's roughest patches of water. I pop outside to taste the salty air and watch the white houses of Penzance slide away in the rain. Five minutes later, I return to the family. It is not OK. Jan is gulping for air. Lisa has nearly passed out. Ted's face matches the green waterproof suit he refused to put on.

I grab him and hurry up a flight of steps to the rear deck. We sit on a wet wooden bench. After a few ups and downs, Ted projectiles strawberry and Babybel chunks over me. I peel off his sicky trousers and wrestle on his green suit. He must be feeling ill because there's no resistance. The ship wallows in a serious swell. A wave breaks over us.

The second frame of the horror film is like a teen party where everyone falls, obliterated, at the same time. Conventional chit-chat is replaced by silence. Parents run past, grasping children, coaxing them to vomit somewhere sensible. Hoooooaaaarrr, shouts a man on the port side, addressing the waves with bile. A gloved steward scurries back and forth, tearing paper towels from a big blue roll, wiping up. Pensioners puke into paper sick bags, terribly discreetly. I'm in awe of their neatness. No one else is splattered with vomit like me. One lady rises with a bag fat with sick, as if blown up with air, and delicately deposits it in a bin. Milly, Esme, Jan and Lisa all vomit and then slump on their seats, comatose, unable to speak. 'Let me help you with those,' says another lady, taking Lisa's bags of sick as if they are yummy cookies. Islanders – British mainlanders – are so kind in a crisis.

Rob is fine, as are the numerous dogs on board. I sit outside, under cool seaspray with warm little Ted. Whenever he vomits, I fail to catch any in the mean-necked little sick bag. I prepare myself for a third, more violent, scene of horror, but instead find I'm experiencing something unexpectedly lovely. The ship turns and creaks as the waves question its fittings. At the top of a crest it drifts for a second, like an inattentive driver on a corner, then dives. The beast of an engine grinds, stinking of warm diesel and hot oil. Ted falls asleep and we ride the waves, his sicky top on my sicky top. I gaze at his deathly-pale jaundiced face and feel a surge of love. Up, down, up. We rock with the ship, clasped together. We can't do anything else. Our movement feels like an eternal moment on the pale-green ocean. I don't want him to feel sick, but I also don't want this to end.

After several hours, we slip into quiet water, and people straighten themselves like daisies turning towards the sun. The murmuring restarts. A series of low reefs rise above turquoise water. It is so exciting. I've never before visited England's greatest archipelago, the last stubby granite tips of a half-submerged chain of hills that form the south-west peninsula: between fifty-four and two hundred islands, depending on which rocks you count. They stretch, in the form of the sunken outcrop of Haig Fras, sixty miles beyond Land's End.

'Do you know what it felt like?' says Lisa, accusingly. 'Like I was in labour. I thought I was going to pass out and my clothes are all wet from having the sweats. We are never doing this again.'

'That,' says Jan, who is not given to making a fuss about anything, 'was one of my worst family experiences ever.'

In a floppy daze, we hover on the stone jetty of the Scilly capital of St Mary's until called to the little boat to St Martin's, which bustles across the turquoise shallows that perhaps only six centuries ago flowed onto low ground to separate the inhabited islands of St Mary's, Tresco, Bryher and St Martin's.

I tell the children this boat will be much better, without really knowing whether it will, but navigating the shallows between the islands is as smooth as a train ride.

'There's our taxi,' jokes Rob, as we approach a low rain-swept quay on rain-obscured St Martin's. He points to a tractor parked on the quay alongside a couple of scruffy Mitsubishis. It *is* our taxi. Viv Jackson, Scilly islander, is collecting us in his little red Massey

Ferguson 135 from 1965. It has lights like eyes, which give it an eager-to-please appearance, and behind its small white fibreglass cab it holds out a metal tray, like an anxious butler.

Viv, white-haired and possessed of strong hands etched like elephant hide, suggests we pile our bags on the tiny metal tray. He places a plank of salvaged timber on top of the luggage, then beckons me to sit on the plank. My four-year-old girls must balance on me, sitting on the plank, resting on the luggage, squashed in the metal tray. Jan and Lisa glance at me, alarmed, but, as captains throughout the ages know, seasickness muffles mutiny. Viv says we'll be all right and he looks dependable. I don't realise that he doesn't actually have a driving licence, not for a car anyway.

Speeding in the open air at 15 mph brings back other joyous small-island arrivals: the lift on Fredrik Sjöberg's *flakmoped* on Runmarö, and that time I'd travelled to Tuvalu to write a story about climate change drowning the coral island communities of the South Pacific. We face backwards and watch St Martin's unfold through the rain. We chug up a corrugated concrete track to Higher Town, where terraced stone cottages open onto the street, and expertly swing around tight corners between tall, slender hedges of evergreen pittosporum. These hedges are windbreaks, planted in recent decades, and are called 'fences'. They have been planted against the old stone walls, which are called 'hedges'. Between them are tiny bulb-filled fields.

An old man in yellow oilskins is bent over a row of daffodils, an image that could have come from any time in the last century. There are narcissi everywhere and, like on Eigg, everything is flowering simultaneously: dainty pink lilies, enormous tree lupins, bright-purple spikes of agapanthus, three-cornered leek in every hedgerow. Blackbirds sing through unusually orange beaks and sparrows dart with pieces of straw between theirs, like ruminating old farmers. Little geranium narcissi growing in hedgerows, white with orange centres, waft a vivid scent, as powerful as perfume squirted straight into your nostril.

Viv slows through puddles so we aren't splashed by the big rear wheels turning next to our heads. We pass a wooden shed that is the Post Office/shop and another shed that is the coastguard/fire station. The fire engine is a tractor. St Martin's is absurdly, dinkily, pretty but it is not twee. There are scruffy barns and haphazard piles of buoys and old lobster pots, and roadside crates of eggs and flowers with honesty boxes beside them.

We turn up a steep sandy lane, through a dark thicket of ancient Monterey pines, and bounce to a halt by a grey wooden cabin with a spectacular view west over the archipelago. The cloud clears, and the shallows turn a turquoise-green I've never before seen around Britain. Are we on a coral atoll? No wonder it's a place of legend. Scilly is not the Cassiterides, the islands where the Phoenicians obtained tin and kept a jealous secret for more than five hundred years – these lands were almost certainly Cornwall, and when Julius Caesar landed in Britain in 55 BC he was unaware he had reached the source of the raw material that made the helmets, shields and breastplates of his soldiers. It is probably not the Celts' Avalon or Glasinnis, lands of the dead inhabited by holy men, despite an unusual preponderance of Neolithic burial chambers. Nor is it Lyonesse, a fabled land west of Land's End lost to apocalyptic flooding and sometimes called Atlantis. It is a small archipelago mostly owned by the Duchy of Cornwall; struggling to make its way in the modern world, per-manently obscured by forecasters' bottoms on the weather map of Britain. And yet Greek and Latin mythology persistently points to a paradise somewhere beyond the Straits of Gibraltar: the Isles of the Blest, the Hesperides, the Elysian Fields, the Fortunate Isles. It could be Scilly. British mainlanders have long been tantalised by this archipelago when it periodically materialises at the western horizon of Land's End, just as the most alluring islands always do, 'an eternal stone armada of over a hundred ships, aloofly anchored off England', as John Fowles put it. 'Mute, enticing, forever just out of reach.'

*

The following morning, we are all full of the joys of terra firma as our island holiday opens with a bright day. Milly, Esme and I run down the sandy track underneath the old pine thicket, past the barns and glasshouses belonging to Viv and Helen, who live at the bottom of the hill in a stone cottage that was once the island slaughterhouse. Some children are bouncing on a trampoline, breathlessly singing 'Shake, Shake, Shake It Off' as I pause to admire the contents of Viv's wooden barn, where the tractor that brought us here and another 1945 Massey Ferguson 135 are parked. Beyond is a great stack of timber, fish crates, pink floats, buoys, flex, blue rope, green rope, yellow oilskins, string, nails, screws, bolts, widgets and gadgets. There are barrels, spare tyres, an old bike; biscuit boxes, plastic crates, a garden fork; ear protectors, tarpaulin, a tonne bag; pallets, ladders, rollers, strimmers, a workbench and a wire animal trap.

Viv is further down, in a glasshouse on the left-hand side. The one on the right belongs to Helen. The one at the road junction belongs to Henry, Viv's brother. Viv shows us the saplings he's growing: peach, pine, sycamore. He likes to slip the latter into hedges. 'What are you planting those weeds for?' other islanders ask. 'There are lots of aphids under sycamore leaves,' replies Viv. 'They are not weeds, they are for the birds.'

Then Viv casually reveals he planted the huge Monterey pines on the lane. Those ancient trees? That dense thicket? 'I planted them when I was about fourteen,' he says. He didn't ask anyone's permission, he just did it, visitors liked it and donated money for more trees, and so began his unofficial career as the Scillonian who planted trees.

The girls and I step into his Monterey grove and scuff about, chasing chickens and collecting cones. 'There. Full's eye!' calls Esme as she throws a cone at an imaginary target. It's almost the first time I've seen them free to potter about in the world beyond our garden.

Nothing grows beneath the pines but their shelter is a balm when the wind tears at you, which it does most days.

I find Viv later, in his barn, and during five minutes of chat he makes a bird box out of pieces of driftwood. 'It's for a spotted flycatcher,' he says. Conversation always returns to birds. A lot of greenfinches nest in the pines, he says, which he planted as a kind of giant bird house. Goldfinches too. Long-eared and short-eared owls overwinter here (no owls breed on Scilly) and nightjars rest here. 'I've always been into bird-watching. The knowledge they have in their heads to travel the world from here to Africa, and they do it until their lives end. Fantastic, absolutely fantastic,' he says. Does his love of birds come from his dad? 'I never saw him. He was a London man and he went back to London.' Not every island romance works out. When Viv was a boy, the St Martin's population was a hundred, a little less than today, and he was one of twenty-one pupils at the island school. He left when he was fifteen and went straight onto the farms.

St Martin's people traditionally farmed flowers, which provided the closest thing to prosperity the islands had known. Scilly was poor for much of its history. The islands were written off as 'excrescences' by that great nesomane Daniel Defoe on his nation-building tour of Britain in the 1720s. In the early nineteenth century, islanders petitioned parliament to relieve their 'extreme distress'. Like so many small islands, Scilly lost its young men to careers at sea, but returning Scillonian captains probably brought back the first bulbs to decorate their gardens. These flourished in Scilly's temperate climate and in 1867 a St Mary's man, William Trevellick, sent a hatbox of flowers to Covent Garden Market via the trains that had begun running from Penzance to London that decade. It is said that the handsome price fetched by his floral hatbox so stunned Trevellick that it kick-started the flower industry.

Scilly White, Sunrise, Golden Spur, Golden Mary, Golden Harvest, Emperor, Empress, Cheerfulness, Magnificence, Soleil d'Or –

the varieties of narcissi and daffodils speak of growers' competitive striving. The challenge was to grow strains that could beat rivals to market and flower in time for Christmas. Their competitors were the similarly temperate Channel Islands, Cornwall and the glasshouses of the Lincolnshire Fens. Scilly's seasons came early, especially on St Martin's light, dry, warm soils. Straw would be burned over dormant bulbs in the summer, to bring them on. Some islanders 'forced' their flowers in glasshouses heated by coal-fired boilers. Men and women would spend autumn evenings with hammer and nails in the packing shed, making up wooden boxes. From November to March, women worked in the glasshouses, tying the flowers as their babies played in a box below. The flowers were then sent to St Mary's to catch the *Scillonian*, scheduled to meet the train at Penzance, which sped them to Covent Garden or Birmingham. After the daffodils, the farms would grow irises and ixias in May and chrysanthemums in the autumn.

By the time Viv went to work, the golden era was over. Before the Second World War, St Martin's twenty farmers could earn two and sixpence for a box of twenty-four bunches, equivalent to a day's wages. During the war, flower sales were as good as halted because the land was given over to potatoes. In the 1950s, the ground became 'bulb sick' from intensive flower-growing, while small farmers were sickened by the belated introduction of income tax and VAT. Despite the arrival of the first labour-saving tractors on the island, some farmers quit in the 1960s and their families left the island; others scaled up, demolishing walls and increasing the size of their fields, which reduced shelter and increased storm damage – the perennial problem for every Scilly flower grower. The introduction of pittosporum trees from New Zealand helped reduce the destructive force of the winds. But they couldn't prevent the gale force of globalisation, and most fields are inactive now. Cheap foreign imports made Scilly's small-scale bulb business uneconomic. Viv's brother Henry is the last Ginnick, the nickname for St Martin's inhabitants – St Mary's men and women are

Bulldogs. St Agnes's are Turks, and Tresco islanders are Caterpillars, perhaps named after moonlit files of smugglers – to farm flowers and dispatch them to the mainland the old-fashioned way. Today, a box of fifty bunches fetches £20 at best.

'There's a lot of land on the island that used to be farmed that isn't any more,' says Viv. The little fields are overgrown but still bright with the old cash crop, mixed with pale-blue Spanish bluebells and yellow Bermuda buttercups. Even the rubbish dump on St Martin's sprouts a casual wealth of bluebells and daffodils, growing like weeds. Viv and Helen's house is filled with huge bouquets of narcissi and dainty dark-pink lilies. 'You can always depend on him for flowers,' says Helen. 'They are easier to get here than most places,' says Viv, looking pleased.

Helen and Viv farm 32 acres and twenty-nine ewes, the biggest sheep farm on the island, a scale dauntingly modest for any mainlander. Since the 1970s, each farmer has been allowed to build two chalets for holidaymakers; Helen and Viv have built one. Ladders rest against many high pittosporum hedges: whenever he needs to feed the sheep, Viv climbs up and cuts armfuls of green shoots. There is a pleasing economy to everything they do, but the world beyond forces them into uneconomical manoeuvres, just as Sarah Boden has experienced on Eigg. The couple live in the old slaughterhouse, but mainland regulations prevent the operation of a new one in such a tiny place. So they must send their lambs by boat to an abattoir in Falmouth, which is expensive for them and stressful for the lambs. The meat is brought back to the butcher on St Mary's, who can finally market it as 'St Martin's lamb': costly for everybody.

We settle into an easy regime. In the morning, I hold up a finger, estimate the wind direction and head for the sheltered side of the island. If we can't immediately see the beach, it always arrives surprisingly quickly. The edge of St Martin's is never far away. The western flats offer views of Tresco, St Mary's and the spectacular island pillar of the Bishop lighthouse far beyond; the eastern coves of Great and Little Bay curl below open moorland sprinkled with liberated daffodil blooms. In the afternoons, we walk up the island's main track to the Post Office. We smile and chat to strangers. For visitors, small islands are like steam trains: a retro treat where everyone waves, as I'd found on Eigg.

For the residents, children are a serious business. Viv tells me there are eleven pupils at the primary school; the crucial index for the health of this small island is on the rise. I knock on the door of the terraced cottage where Gladys Perkins lives. She is initially suspicious when I explain I've been enjoying her memoir, *Times Remembered*. 'You're not cribbing things from my book are you?' she asks, a tiny woman in a tiny cottage, ninety this year, sight fading but still firing an extremely penetrating look from her bright-blue eyes. We have a frank chat, author to author. 'Of course a book doesn't have a sell-by date,' she says: in this land of perishable flowers, she's impressed by their economic longevity. Compton Mackenzie's obscurity has caused me to ponder the lack of longevity in publishing, but perhaps I need to look upon literature with Gladys's positivity.

What is the most important ingredient for a successful small island?

'The school,' says Gladys emphatically. She talks about its pupils, and the toddlers and babies behind them, as if they are bulbs. 'There's lots of little ones coming on, which is very good.' Like Rathlin, St Martin's has recently enjoyed a baby boom, which has become an island joke. The winter of 2013/14 was 'a wet rough winter', says Viv. 'A lot of breeding had to go on.' Other islanders reckon it is because the island pub shut for a couple of years. But there are also settlers from the mainland, young families seeking free-range lives, and the new are welcomed by the old. 'Suddenly there aren't very many Scillonians left,' says Gladys, 'but you get people who've come in who settle and become good islanders.'

*

Small islands may be peripheral, but from Orkney in the Neolithic era to Alderney during the Second World War, they frequently pitch up in what Esme would call the 'full's eye' of history. Scilly traded with Mediterranean civilisations, sent flowers to London, and hid French spies on fishing boats during the war. The centre came to the periphery again in the 1960s, when the prime minister Harold Wilson holidayed here.

In 1967 another event struck Scilly which radically changed Britain's relationship with its marine environment. Gladys Perkins saw it happen. She spotted the big tanker from her kitchen window at breakfast time. The *Torrey Canyon* was gliding past St Martin's as close as the much smaller Scillonian ferry usually came. 'Then the coastguard rang my husband to say she'd gone aground on the Seven Stones in broad daylight,' she remembers. 'I couldn't believe it, I suppose these things happen. Seven Stones Reef is notorious, really. That was a bad day.' The *Torrey Canyon* was carrying crude oil. A disastrous spill began as St Mary's lifeboat worked for thirty-two hours to rescue the Italian crew. Every drop of its cargo, 119,328 tonnes of crude oil, was spilled. The air across Scilly reeked with oil but, fortunately for them, the prevailing wind and tides pushed the slick eastwards. The Royal Navy dispatched jets to bomb the wrecked ship. St Martin's islanders climbed the hill to watch the flames leaping into the sky. 'We could see all the number of times they missed it,' says another elderly inhabitant, Rodney Ashford, who was Gladys and Derek's best man. 'We thought, blimmin' 'eck – these are our defences and there's a blimmin' great supertanker stuck on a rock and they can't even hit that.' Scilly escaped its pollution but thousands, perhaps millions, of oil-slicked seabirds died as the huge spill devastated the wild coasts of Cornwall, the Channel Islands and France. The clean-up took years. Some of the oil was decanted into an old quarry on Guernsey, where it still reeked, darkly, more than forty years later.

*

Scilly was once famed for its flowers and is still remembered for its daffodils, but the flowers for sale on the mainland are now grown elsewhere. St Martin's in spring is an isle of abandoned fields still defiantly in bloom, like smoke still trailing from the chimneys of an abandoned factory.

Surprisingly, older folk don't mourn the wilting of the flower trade. 'It was a lot of hard work,' says Gladys. 'I wouldn't say it was profitable. It was what there was, it was what you did. After the war, it went downhill.'

In Gladys and Derek's black-and-white wedding photo, they are towered over by Rodney, who farmed in Middle Town for sixty-five years before moving across the road from his old friends. Here he lives, hardly stooped at all, in a low-ceilinged cottage. He isn't sentimental about the daffodils, either. They 'are all the same', he says. 'I never liked flower farming but there was no option. It was a hard life. I wouldn't say many people made a good living. When you had a good season you had put a bit aside but when you had a bad one . . .' He packed it up in 1991. It got harder and harder, he says, from the moment income tax was slapped on in 1952.

The flower industry has bequeathed Scilly a unique appearance, but I don't realise how much of St Martin's physical character is shaped by a much older force until Gladys and Rodney mention the D-word: the Duchy. Except for the island of Tresco and a few freehold properties here and there, the Isles of Scilly belong to the Duchy of Cornwall. They have done since the Duchy was created in 1337 by Edward III for his son and heir, the Black Prince. The stamp of the Duchy is not immediately obvious. It is more about absence: there are no cottages with bright-yellow window frames, none of the hippyish look of the houses on Eigg; there's no ugliness, but there's no flair either, nothing unexpected or out of place. The Duchy has a keen eye for conservation. Window frames, for instance, must be wooden, and white. 'Prince Charles will not have PVC windows,' says Rodney. The serenity of St Martin's could have been obliterated by mass tourism, golf courses and marinas; and some islanders, such as Gladys, are grateful for the Duchy's protective role. Rodney isn't so sure.

Most Scilly Islanders are tenants, just as Compton Mackenzie was a tenant of the Crown on Herm and Jethou. Viv and Helen don't own their farm or chalet; Gladys doesn't own her cottage; neither does Rodney. They pay rent to Prince Charles, or Charlie, as they call him. An ancient feudal relationship still shapes the character of Scilly and its islanders, and Gladys considers this changing bond in her memoir. All male tenants used to be invited to an annual Duchy dinner, held in the Sunset restaurant on St Mary's. If there was a rent review, the Duchy's land steward would stroll around the farm with the tenant. 'They were largely considered to be a benevolent landlord,' writes Gladys. 'Nowadays the Duchy has declared itself a business and employs professionals who are expected to maximise returns from the estate, leaving less room for the personal touch.' It doesn't sound too bad: tenants still receive a Christmas card and sometimes a present from their landlord; Gladys has been invited to two garden parties at Buckingham Palace as well as a bash at Highgrove to celebrate the 650th anniversary of the Duchy. Nevertheless, she feels they 'govern from a distance these days'. Rodney says the same. The tenants' Duchy dinner used to be a 'good outing' and at least you met the land steward twice a year on rent days. 'You'd pay your rent, get a cigar, and there was something personal about it. It also gave you a chance to have a good go at the land steward,' he says. 'Now the rent's just paid through the post.'

Rodney is very positive about St Martin's, particularly its young families, but when I ask if the Duchy is good for Scilly, he pauses. 'I don't suppose anybody loves their landlord.' Every islander has a different lease – some have three years, some twenty; some are responsible for the upkeep of their property and pay less rent; others aren't. Divide and rule, say the islanders. 'The Duchy are very clever because everybody's lease is different and they all have different conditions, so you never know where you stand. It's all a bit feudal.'

St Martin's is a long way from the property-owning mainland, and even further from the island-democracy of Eigg. If permitted by the fairly arduous planning controls, Scilly leaseholders can build a new house or chalet, but must then pay rent to the Duchy. If an islander improves her property, the Duchy can raise the rent. If an islander moves away, his asset returns to the Duchy. 'If we spend money on chalets to increase our income, the Duchy wants a cut of it,' says Rodney. 'We have to spend money on foundations and electricity and then pay the Duchy. No, I'm not spending another penny on Duchy land.' Instead, some years back, he saved up and bought a holiday home on the mainland, just outside Penzance. His face lights up. 'I loved that little bungalow. That was freehold. That was my little bit of England! To have that little freehold, that was – ooh! We made a lovely profit when we sold that one on the mainland.'

I wonder what Compton Mackenzie would have made of it. He was drawn to islands partly because of their potential to circumvent the bureaucratic authority of the mainland. A formative memory for Monty was a boyhood trip to France. He'd become an eager butterfly collector; he'd caught swallowtails and Camberwell Beauties and pinned them in fourteen cork-lined cigar boxes, nailed up tight. On his return, suspicious customs officials at Southampton chiselled open each box, trashing his collection; he was left with a lifelong distrust of officialdom. He never fitted easily into schools, armies, organisations or institutions, and his rampant individualism was fired further when the authorities prosecuted him under the Official Secrets Act for publishing his memoirs of First World War spying. That crisis precipitated his flight to the island of Barra in the 1930s, where he nurtured a violent hatred of what he called 'the little man' – everyone from an anodyne civil servant to Hitler – and fought to preserve island individualism against the controlling reach of the mainland. Many small-island escapees are doing something similar. Many small-island owners seek control over their own little domain. D.H. Lawrence was alive to this irony; Monty, less so. I've not yet found one of his rants against bureaucracy to contain the reflection that during the First World War he helped invent a humongously bureaucratic visa system.

Scilly islanders have one alternative to the Duchy, and what it stands for: their island of Tresco. I peruse it from our chalet on St Martin's: dark trees across the light water. Everyone has an opinion about Tresco. 'Oh, that's different,' says Gladys Perkins when I ask her about it. 'It always has been different,' says Rodney Ashford. 'They don't belong, do they?' says Viv Jackson. Helen Smith tells me about a day she visited and heard a mother of two children who were misbehaving in Tresco's Post Office say, 'I wish nanny were here. She'd know how to deal with you.' When Compton Mackenzie bought Herm, he aspired to create a garden 'which might compete one day with Tresco, and Tresco has the finest garden in Europe'. (When he switched to Jethou, he planted another lavish temperate garden, inspired by Tresco, acquiring seedling acacias and various echiums from Basil Leng, a renowned plantsman, who brought them from the Isles of Scilly.) Forty years before me, John Fowles canvassed Scilly opinion about Tresco. 'It's not island,' said a native of Bryher contemptuously, spitting over the gunwale of his boat.

One bright morning, we walk to the pier and take the daily boat to Tresco. St Martin's residents bemoan their boatman retiring because the boat, which now links them to all the other islands, is run by Tresco's boat service. 'It hasn't half gone downhill,' grumbles one islander. 'You feel bottom of the pile.'

Baby Ted is grumbling too. 'Boats isn't very good for me,' he says sombrely. But this miniature voyage is fine. It looks like we can skip over the sandbanks from St Martin's to Tresco, and our boat slows to a glide in places because the water is so shallow. Dropped off at the south end of the island, we follow a straggling line of tourists heading for Tresco Abbey, a large stone house with a tall castellated tower, hidden in the pines.

The story of Tresco's independence goes back years. For many centuries Scilly appeared more burden than asset for the Duchy, who leased it to various lesser aristocrats. By the 1820s Scilly was poverty-stricken, wrecked by crop failures, taxes and absentee proprietors. Curiously, its struggles were also blamed on the fact that the law of primogeniture didn't operate on the islands. When a tenant died, his farm was divided equally among his sons, leading to ever smaller farms that could not support a family. In 1834, the Duchy awarded a ninety-nine-year lease on the islands to Augustus Smith, an energetic, paternalistic member of a family of bankers who was keen to 'improve' Scilly. Smith got to work: he reallocated farmland to create viable farms, insisted that only eldest sons should succeed to each tenancy, and offered building work to the unemployed, who knocked up roads, schools, a new church, an extension to the quay, and a new home befitting the new Lord Proprietor of Scilly, who became known as 'My Lord', 'the Governor' and even 'the Emperor of Scilly'.

This home was Tresco Abbey, sheltered behind the walls of a ruined priory. Within those walls, and blossoming in Scilly's temperate climate, Augustus Smith started a garden of plants collected from all over the world, many of them by the islanders Smith educated to become ship's officers. His successor, his nephew Thomas Algernon Smith-Dorrien-Smith, had a love of hyphenation and Monterey pines, which he planted to provide a gale-resistant shelter belt for Tresco Abbey's blooming gardens. Shortly after Algernon's son, Major Arthur Dorrien-Smith, succeeded his father in 1918, the lease for most of Scilly reverted back to the Duchy, but the Major clung on to Tresco and was granted a new ninety-nine-year lease. Augustus Smith had made education compulsory on Scilly long before the mainland, and his successors inherited his sense of duty. Gladys Perkins remembers that when she was a child the Dorrien-Smiths came over every year to St Martin's with a large Christmas tree, which they would put up in the schoolroom. The children would dance around it and then choose a present, 'the Tresco treat'.

The Major's grandson, Robert, has run Tresco since 1973, despite being allergic to the Soleil d'Or narcissus, which sustained the island's economy for so long. He is friends with Prince Charles, who stays with him when visiting his dominion. Both operate the same sort of stable, benign rule, but there is an important difference between the Duchy and the Dorrien-Smiths: while the Duchy ultimately administers Scilly from the mainland, Tresco's landlord is an islander. It's probably accidental that his predecessors created a garden that became a tourist attraction, but this at least solved the financial conundrum facing every small-island owner in the twentieth century. While other small-island owners went bankrupt, the Dorrien-Smiths survived by turning every tree and blade of grass to the service of holidaymakers. 'Eccentricity permeates the place,' noted the *Financial Times* in 2013 when granted a tour of Robert Dorrien-Smith's private residence. Maybe so, but dedicating Tresco to tourism turns it into one of many thousand island resorts. These are single-minded places: rather like a ship or an oil-rig, all residents are unified in one purpose, which rapidly diminishes an island's idiosyncrasy and imaginative power.

We pay to enter Tresco Abbey gardens, and are catapulted into another world. Red squirrels chatter and swing like monkeys through skyscraper conifers. Vast evergreen pohutukawas, New Zealand Christmas trees, cast cool shade over thick trunks of shaggy bark. There's a bamboo thicket, lurid pink camellias, spiky-leaved exotics from Mexico, and shrubs from South Africa, Colombia, Australia. It could be almost anywhere in the world and any time of year with its May, July and August blossoming. High above, the wind sends white clouds over, fast, but among the shelter of Algernon's pines there is not a whiff of a breeze. Ted toddles ahead on the gravel path, loose-limbed, as if directed by a puppeteer. Sparrows flit out of nest holes in the fibrous grey trunks of palm trees, and what sound like parrots screech everywhere. Esme and Milly discover the screeching is made by golden pheasants, stupid-looking birds with an astute interest in picnics. We sit on the grass and suddenly the past collides with the present and I'm celebrating my seventh birthday again in the Royal Botanic Gardens of Melbourne, eucalyptus leaves rattling in the wind 'like a bunch of rusty keys in the hand of a caretaker', as Compton Mackenzie put it (he was not a fan of eucalyptus).

I adore the mad ambition of Tresco's gardens. It is a typically visionary Victorian achievement that turns its back on the locale and the local flora, but is true to the spirit of Scilly: both island and garden are outward-looking places, animated by global trade. It is obsessively well tended, the throw-it-all-together profusion of shapes and textures meticulously trimmed, with uncompromising little notices revealing the long Latin names for each species and variety, which mean nothing to me and other visitors lacking botanical training.

The rest of Tresco resembles any grand estate in England that opens its gates to tourism. Workmen in Tresco polo shirts busy about in golf buggies through the perfectly groomed landscape, and streams of perfectly groomed families in polo shirts flit about on bikes. Cut-glass accents debate little fingerposts painted in the green of the Tresco estate, which point to the shop selling olives and fine wines or the splendid café overlooking a beach of white sand. Unlike St Martin's, there are no messy little farms or chaotic barns. Every cottage is immaculately renovated and the prettiest are available for hire at eye-watering prices. Rodney Ashford admires this bustling, well-tended island: when a gale blew down trees all over Scilly, he says, Tresco tidied up the mess far quicker than St Mary's. There are one or two locals here, but Tresco is mostly inhabited by staff and does indeed seem a place apart. While the rule of the Duchy ensures that almost nothing is for sale on the other islands, every piece of Tresco is on offer. Holiday islands must sell themselves to survive; and islands and islanders are slowly, inexorably diminished.

Looking back at St Martin's from Tresco's jetty, I can see a band of green-black trees following a cleft up the middle of the island – Viv's Monterey pines. We catch the boat back on a full tide this time and it's a relief to return to the simplicity and tranquillity of St Martin's, with its rutted concrete track speckled with tiny shells and its wild edges of bluebells and gorse. The weather rolls in from the west, grandly, and rain comes drumming on the tin roof of the chalet as chickens peck-peck around the door. 'You see those rocks?' says Esme. 'I always think they're shaped like a boat.' She's right. In the shallows between St Martin's, St Mary's and Tresco is a low rock with high crags at each end that could be a container ship but is called Guthers Island. Every islander I meet knows the tide times, and the tides are getting bigger during our spring break. Later in the week there's a six-metre tide: a low enough ebb to walk to Guthers.

The first Scillonians probably walked to their homes on the outer islands. Islands are created by what we today call disasters: earthquakes, and great floods. Four of the Isles of Scilly may have come into being relatively recently. In 1755, a great earthquake in Lisbon produced a tidal wave in Scilly. But the archipelago was probably formed some centuries earlier with the gradual rising of the seas, which flooded the low central plain that once linked St Martin's, St Mary's, Tresco and Bryher. The Romans referred to the 'Scilly Isle'. Another clue is that old Cornish names are found on the islands' outer edges, while the names along the inner shores are Tudor English. Old field boundaries can still be seen on St Martin's eastern beaches at low tide.

In September 1970, John Pickwell of St Mary's walked from uninhabited White Island to St Martin's and then on to Tresco, Samson and Bryher. On the next tide, accompanied by a local policeman and the very tall chaplain of the isles, he waded the most difficult stretch from Tresco to St Mary's. 'The only person to walk to St Mary's was the vicar,' remembers Viv. 'They say he walked on the water.'

Today, it's more difficult because of rising seas, but there's still an annual expedition between St Martin's, Tresco, Samson and Bryher. 'With the tide running on your legs it's very, very tiring. The water can be up to here,' Viv gestures to his waist. That doesn't sound too scary, but if you take your feet off the bottom and swim, you'll be swept away by the current. Viv has saved two people from drowning in the tidal rips off St Martin's. Does he swim for pleasure? 'No,' he says. 'I don't like getting my feet wet.'

Thursday dawns like in the children's picture book, *The Day the Tide Went Out . . . and out . . . and out . . . and out . . . and out*. The turquoise sea between St Martin's and St Mary's and Tresco empties like bath water, exposing silver sand and islands of black seaweed. It appears an easy walk to Guthers on a bright spring day. I'm not dressed for treacherous tidal sands when I set out across the flats, and I remove my shoes and socks to walk barefoot. Soon my feet are burning. The sand is so coarse, mixed with crumbs of jagged shell, that it stings my soles. I zigzag between groupings of exposed rock: Pigs Ledge, Moths Ledge, Broad Ledge. Between them are pools and ribs of sand, a plaster-cast of ripples in the water. Pieces of kelp lie on the sand like sleeping crocodiles. There's a half-eaten crab, meaty middle gone, and enigmatic crumbs of beach rubbish rolled into abstractions. I expect to wade across fast-moving tidal channels but the sea really has disappeared; I reach Guthers via just one patch of ankle-deep water.

Shadows dance on the sand from twenty herring gulls, rising from their island, voicing their displeasure at my arrival. The granite pillars at each end are speckled with canary-yellow lichen, and look exactly like the tors of Dartmoor or Bodmin Moor of which they are a continuation. In between the tors is a low field of wild sea beet, the finest I've ever seen, and I stuff my pockets with the rich green leaves, which taste better than spinach. A wren surprises me, darting among the rocks. Does it really live out here? Compton Mackenzie regarded wrens as 'the tutelary creatures' of Jethou. These tiny birds are becoming my island totem; they seem to be more ubiquitous than the showy seabirds. I'd love to stay here with them and camp, as the solitary human islander, but have to hurry back before the tide cuts me off.

That afternoon, I call on Daph Perkins, a lovely woman who wears gold studs in each ear and says everything with the delight of a young girl. She moved to a coastguard cottage on St Martin's when she was thirteen and her father quit his ice-cream business on the mainland for coastguard duties. Seventy-six years later, she still lives in this elegant Victorian bungalow with glorious views over St Martin's Flats. 'It doesn't seem possible does it?' she says. 'Crumbs!'

I've never met her before, but she has been watching over me. 'I put the glasses on you this morning out on the flats,' she says. 'I thought, whoever is that? I stayed and watched you walking back because I thought, oh heck, I hope they know the tides.'

She has an equally clear view of her arrival on the island. 'Hardly any mainland people visited in those days. Two or three of the children must have heard we were coming and stood up on the rock, and looked at us as we came up the track, thinking Who is this?' In addition to coastguard work, her family took over the Post Office and, between tying flowers, milking cows and helping out with dozens of other island tasks, Daph worked 'up there' – it was fifty yards from her front door – in the shed cum shop, for fifty-five years. 'We started off with postcards and of course the awful cigarettes. Then orange squash and Heinz baked beans and we gradually built it up.' The post arrived three times a week and was collected three times a week. Daph stamped each letter – 'I reckon I've date-stamped enough letters to stretch from here to America' – and sewed up the mailbags. She had to empty the island's two telephone kiosks of pennies and bag them up, which took ages. And she'd deliver telegrams too. She would have known everything. 'You must never report any Post Office business,' she says gravely. 'You couldn't go telling other people what someone's got in their savings accounts or what was on a telegram. You have to be very careful, especially in a small place. It doesn't do to say what you shouldn't be saying. It's horrible if you fall out with somebody.' It's an echo of the old secrecy on Rathlin. I once asked an islander on Lundy how everyone got on. 'Carefully,' was her reply.

The holidaymakers from the mainland hear more island gossip than the natives, thinks Daph, 'because they talk to people'. Many of the same families return each year; she remembers tiny children coming into the Post Office for ice-creams who now bring their children, or grandchildren, for the same. 'They all say, "Ah there's nowhere like it." I was sitting on the beach and a visitor said, "Where would you get anywhere better than this?" She thought it was the most beautiful place in the world. We all do. We all think we're jolly lucky.'

We sit in her living room, sun streaming through the windows, old paintings of St Martin's on the walls, and I'm struck by her self-contained joy and peace. It reminds me of the Waterboys' classic song about the person who stays at home, deeply rooted, and doesn't just see the crescent, but the whole of the moon.

Daph seemed to possess a gift that most of us lack, or at least an appreciation of what she had, and I wondered how much of it came from staying so loyally rooted to this elevated spot, high on a rock, surrounded by the light of the ocean. She never married, but she was not alone. Her brother, Derek Perkins, married Gladys round the corner, and another brother, Terry, lives nearby. Like most islanders, she seemed more keenly aware than many mainlanders of the interrelatedness of things, and the world beyond her own.

On England's greatest archipelago, I can't escape the sense that each island is a sibling, with all the rivalry, empathy and intimacy that incurs. Before I say goodbye, and before we take the *Scillonian* again on what turns out to be a mercifully smooth passage back to Penzance, Daph tells me how every household on St Martin's used to own a boat. Sundays were special because she and her family would take their boat and go picnicking. They'd head out to the Eastern Islands or Samson or Teän or St Helens. 'You see the world from a different angle,' she tells me. Hopping between islands as part of life, like that, must bequeath a robust sense of self and a strong sense of the other. Does it enhance an awareness or a sense of detachment? Perhaps even a kind of second sight? I glance at my girls, who came into the world five minutes apart and, as usual, are sitting together on the ferry home. Perhaps being an archipelago islander is like being a twin. You have a keen sense of the other from birth. And you are never alone.

8

Lost Land

Hirta, St Kilda, 2.4 square miles, summer population 15

'The elements! The elements! His mind repeated the word
dumbly. You can't win against the elements'
'The Man Who Loved Islands'

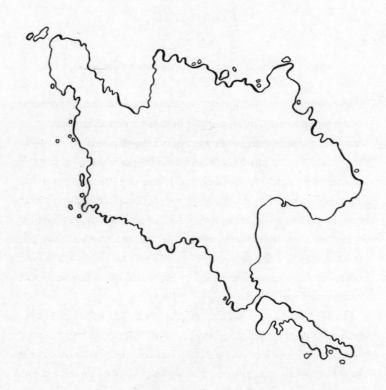

Tourists jostled into the iron shack that served as a Post Office, desperate to send cards that bore the St Kilda postmark. They complained loudly when the postmaster, Neil Ferguson, ran out of penny stamps and then ha'penny stamps and then three-ha'penny stamps. It was their last chance to post a card! The mailbags taken down to the steamship anchored in the sheltered bay were the heaviest they'd ever been. Ferguson could be forgiven if he had rather weightier matters on his mind, though. The following day, he and his thirty-five fellow inhabitants of the archipelago of St Kilda must leave their island home for ever. Human life would be extinguished on Britain's most isolated inhabited island.

The St Kildans, or the Hiortaich, as they were called in Gaelic, worked long into the night rowing their belongings out to their evacuation ship. Sailors from the Navy stood by: they'd offered to help but the islanders wanted to do it their way. Most of the Hiortaich's meagre possessions were left behind: beds, chairs, chests, old pots, fishing gear, pets. Despite the National Canine Defence League offering to rehome the island's large population of dogs, a stone was tied around the neck of each one before it was thrown off the stone jetty. When a boat visited the island a few weeks later, the harbour was bobbing with dead dogs.

The last residents rose early on the morning of 29 August 1930, put on their best clothes, said prayers and deposited a small heap of oats and a Bible in the eleven inhabited houses. At least one Bible was left open at the Book of Exodus. The islanders stacked their fires with coal and turf before they left. When these died down, it was probably the first time for a millennium that no fire burned on St Kilda.

The crossing was calm. The children played hide-and-seek on deck; the adults stood in the stern and watched these mighty hunks of granite, basalt and gabbro, the ancient core of an old volcano, diminish over the horizon. A few waved. Tears finally came when they reached the small port of Lochaline 140 miles away on the Sound of Mull. For many, this was not only their first glimpse of the mainland, but the first time they had encountered a tree, a car, even a pig. A large crowd gathered to meet them. This island at the edge of the continent was at the centre of events. The evacuation of St Kilda was big news. EXODUS FROM ST KILDA! ISLANDERS LEAVE THEIR HOMES WITHOUT TEARS went one headline. Most of the arrivals were resettled close to Lochaline where, bizarrely, given their treeless previous life, the men were given jobs working for the Forestry Commission. Some moved further afield, to Glasgow and beyond. One senior islander, Finlay MacQueen, told another: 'May God forgive those that have taken us away from St Kilda.'

St Kilda is the most famous island – or islands – in Britain. It may be the best-studied few square miles in the world. Hiort, as it is known in Gaelic, is an archipelago containing Hirta (in Gaelic, Hirte), Boreray (Boraraigh), Soay (Sòthaigh) and Dun (Dùn). It is the most peripheral of British isles, fifty miles west of the Outer Hebrides, a hundred miles from the Scottish mainland. Plenty of islands lost their people in the early 1900s, particularly the smaller isles of the Outer Hebrides – Berneray, Mingulay, Sandray, Taransay, Scarp and

Boreray – but St Kilda has become the generic example of small-island extinction. A pinprick on any map, alone in the Atlantic, it is much more prominent in many mental cartographies, an object of obsession and longing – 'as much a place of the imagination as a physical reality', as Madeleine Bunting says in her tour of the Hebrides. St Kilda is Britain's only dual World Heritage Site, protected for both its nature and its culture; and archaeologists, geologists, ecologists and historical anthropologists have pored over it, subjecting it to more than seven hundred books and scholarly articles. Its story is told and retold, polished and revised, mostly by outsiders like me, who wonder: Were the Hiortaich unique, or rather like us? And why, after so many generations of habitation, did they abandon the home they loved?

Many visitors revere St Kilda for its superlatives: for having Britain's highest sea stacks and sea cliffs, 430 metres high, twice the height of England's biggest at Beachy Head; and for being home to the most important seabird colony in north-west Europe. Others seek it out because it's hard to reach. Some idealise it, believing it was a superior society, crushed by the careless stampede of the twentieth century.

Most of St Kilda's five thousand annual visitors are day-trippers, but I arrange to camp. Anyone can do it, but you must be self-sufficient: carry your gear, bring your food, remove your rubbish. I'm seeking an inkling of what it was to be a St Kildan, a fuller sense of what it is to be an islander. But no one is permitted to boil puffin for a traditional Hiortaich breakfast these days, so I take pasta and tuna and a pot of Aldi's instant noodles as a treat. I leave behind my laptop because there's no phone signal and no means of contact with the wider world, unless I attach a message to a small vessel fashioned from driftwood and the inflated stomach of a sheep and cast it into the Gulf Stream, as the Hiortaich did when needing to send a note to the mainland. It's surprising how often these mailboats worked, although they did occasionally pitch up in Norway. Because it is bigger than

Alderney and St Martin's, St Kilda disrupts my trajectory of moving to ever smaller islands, but I decide I must visit in May to maximise my chances of actually landing on this notoriously inaccessible place. I also assume that it will feel much smaller than it actually is, alone on the ocean. Here, I'm mistaken: islands are enlarged by the scale of the sea that surrounds them, and the heaving Atlantic around St Kilda makes it even more monumental.

The character of its population also marks a turning point on my island journey. Everywhere I have visited so far has permanent inhabitants, ranging from tens of thousands to a hundred. Although humans have resettled St Kilda, they only live there in shifts. It's a place of work, not a home; a community more like a ship or an oil-rig than an organic island society.

I take the easiest, cheapest route, driving 647 miles from my home in Norfolk, crossing the bridge that renders Skye an almost-island, to catch a fast boat from Uig pier. Inevitably, Skye is also one of Compton Mackenzie's almost-islands: when his burgeoning Scottish nationalism inspired him to move from Jethou to Scotland, he tried to buy Flodigarry, the former home of Flora MacDonald, the young Jacobite heroine who helped Bonnie Prince Charlie escape Scotland after his defeat at Culloden. Monty was defeated by money, however: the house was too expensive.

Dizzy from my day-long drive, I reach Uig and call an automated phone line to check the sailing to St Kilda. My trip the next morning is cancelled. The sea is calm here, but it's too windy on St Kilda to land on the main island, Hirta. Several years ago I met Kate Tristram, a historian on Lindisfarne, who told me how some prospective visitors to that tidal island became angry when told they could arrive or depart only at a certain time, because the tide covers its causeway. The sea is a useful check on human pride. I must wait. I fall asleep in a caravan by the pier as cuckoos call and rain drums on the roof.

The boat is cancelled the next day too, and I have to unpack my beautifully assembled rucksack. I cheer up when I meet Lena and Göran Nordendahl, a Swedish couple who hail from the same Stockholm archipelago as Runmarö, where I was first told about the man who loved islands. They live on two of the islands there. They like the simplicity of a life without electricity, running water, Internet. On their islands, they wear a single set of clothes. 'You don't have all these choices every day,' says Lena. They had, of course, just visited St Kilda.

For the third consecutive day, the boat is cancelled; I wonder if I've driven all this way for nothing. And then, miraculously, on the fourth day, the boat departs. I'm fortunate: for another couple on the trip, this is their eighth attempt to reach St Kilda.

Crossing what the Scottish poet Douglas Dunn calls 'the moody jailer of the wild Atlantic' is four hours by boat, banging through the swell at 25 knots, enveloped in greyness. First, we speed over the Minch, which Compton Mackenzie once claimed 'has probably had more triumphs over the weakness of the human body than any other stretch of sea of similar size in the world'. I start to hallucinate islands almost immediately – but there, hulking to the north, are the Shiants, the trio of uninhabited islands that inspired Lawrence to write 'The Man Who Loved Islands'.

'To most people the Shiant Islands mean nothing,' wrote Monty after he bought them at auction after the death of Lord Leverhulme, the soap magnate from Lancashire who purchased the whole of Lewis in 1917. 'To some they mean the most acute bout of sea-sickness between Kyle and Stornoway as the MacBrayne steamer wallows in the fierce overfalls that guard them. To a very few they mean a wild corner of fairyland, the memory of which remains for ever in the minds of those who have visited their spellbound cliffs and caves . . .'

Monty spirited the Shiants into his orbit with his characteristic combination of luck and charm. He learned of their impending auction by chance while dining with a couple of newspapermen in

Glasgow in 1926, and 'spent a restless night' on the sleeper back to London 'thinking about them'. The Shiants did not appear terribly inviting – 475 acres, no buildings, numerous seabirds, leased to a sheep farmer for an annual £60 – but Monty, who had never visited them, immediately grasped their majesty: soaring columns of basalt to rival the Giant's Causeway and three million puffins, guarded by the treacherous waters of the Minch and its Blue Men, reputed to wreck every boat if the captain cannot answer in rhyme the verses they shout to him. So only a poet – such as Monty – can sail to and live on the islands, reported Faith in her memoirs; she was, as ever, loyally supportive of her husband's extravagance.

The expected price was £1,000, which Monty couldn't afford. Nevertheless, he dispatched Charles Boyte, the brother of his secretary Nelly, to bid up to £500. Bidding opened at £300 and rapidly rose. But as soon as Charles gave his last nod, £500, the hammer went straight down. It was a miracle, said Faith. Actually, Monty's good fortune was due to an incompetent auctioneer who believed Charles was a representative of Lord Leverhulme's son who had secretly instructed him to ensure he obtained the islands as a sentimental memorial to his father. Monty was delighted. His 'mere possession' of the Shiants changed him, considered Faith, giving him 'what he had wanted from a boy when his dreams had been all of Scotland'.

Although Monty rarely visited the Shiants, they were his 'talisman of Scotland,' according to Andro Linklater. Monty's vision of the islands and their inhabitants – basking sharks, Atlantic seals, 'mattresses' of sea pinks and a thousand thousand oblivious seabirds – was purely Romantic. His descriptions of the Shiants may have been so ecstatic, of course, because they also gave him his second wife Chrissie and his third, Lily, via his friendship with their father, Malcolm MacSween, who grazed sheep on the islands.

Monty's purchase of the Shiants also gave D.H. Lawrence what he required. I can picture his glee when he heard the news. First Herm, then Jethou, and now an uninhabited Outer Hebridean rock; Monty appeared hell-bent on a trajectory towards island madness. His relationship with Faith was troubled: debts, and affairs, were mounting. Would this garrulous dandy really retreat to solitude in north-west Scotland? Lawrence now possessed a truth stranger than fiction. Here was the perfect finale for his morality tale about the rise and fall of a man who loved islands. Monty invited Lawrence to both Jethou and the Shiants on several occasions but Lawrence, perhaps feeling a pang of guilt, did not go.

Lawrence had gathered most of his material the previous spring, 1925, when he returned to Capri and found Faith living there alone. He dined with her and probed her about how Monty was faring on Jethou. They talked 'more frankly than I would have allowed anyone else to do' because, said Faith rather guilelessly, she knew that Lawrence ultimately loved Monty. 'To me that night,' she wrote, 'he seemed an angel and I gave him some of the secrets of my heart.' She wasn't the first, or last, to have her confidence betrayed by Lawrence. 'I like to write when I feel spiteful. It is like having a good sneeze,' quipped Lawrence, and he repeatedly 'skimpoled' his family and friends in his fiction, observed the biographer Harry T. Moore. Dorothy Brett, Katherine Mansfield and particularly his friend John Middleton Murry all felt 'the cut of his satire'.

Lawrence actually wrote two short stories about Monty, and the first to be published was 'Two Blue Birds'. Reading it, I feel sorry for the Compton Mackenzies. It begins: 'There was a woman who loved her husband, but she could not live with him. The husband, on his side, was sincerely attached to his wife, yet he could not live with her.' A devastatingly sharp sketch unfolds: of Faith's 'gallant' affairs in the sun and 'clever and enigmatic' Monty, a washed-up novelist with an adoring secretary to whom he dictates for ten hours a day. Just as in real life, the impractical wife helps her husband into debt but is also an astute critic who worries that adoration is not good for him and that his work is 'getting diffuse and poor in quality'. They watch two blue tits fighting and the wife has a row with the secretary before withdrawing with the words: 'I'm afraid no man can expect two blue birds of happiness to flutter round his feet, tearing out their little feathers.'

When Lawrence's new story appeared in 1926, Faith immediately realised she was its source. It is a vicious satire at the expense of the Compton Mackenzies, which she described as 'a malicious caricature of Monty, and a monstrous perversion of facts'. Monty, however, took a different line. With a characteristic reluctance to reflect on his inner world, he insisted there wasn't 'the faintest resemblance to her or me'. He was roused to offence, though, by the short story that was about him alone: 'The Man Who Loved Islands'. When he read it in a newspaper in 1928, he threatened Lawrence's publishers with an injunction if they included it in a forthcoming volume of short stories. 'But it's not meant to be Monty,' Lawrence complained. 'I was well aware of that,' Monty wrote in his memoirs, 'but if Lawrence used my background of a Channel Island and an island in the Hebrides for one of his preposterous Lawrentian figures the public would suppose that it was a portrait.' So Monty prevailed, and what he dismissed as a 'lunatic story' was not published in book form in Britain until after Lawrence's premature death in 1930. By then, Monty could meet it with a jokey critique, scorning Lawrence for suggesting that cowslips could grow on a granite island when they prefer lime.

During an interview in 1950, Monty was generous enough to admit that Lawrence's short stories possessed an artistic validity, but for the victims they were falsifications. Lawrence deployed 'a trick of describing a person's setting or background vividly, and then putting into the setting an ectoplasm entirely of his own creation', Monty argued. These caricatures 'against photographic backgrounds' distorted the truth about his former friends. I'm not so sure that Monty's public denial of his place in 'The Man Who Loved Islands' reflected his true feelings. In some recess of his mind, Lawrence's intelligent, un-forgiving critique must have struck a chord. Monty's very conscious engagement with island society on Barra was a repudiation of the misanthropic egotism of his fictional counterpart Mr Cathcart. And, just as he did on Barra, Monty also briefly became a champion of the rights of Gaelic-speaking small-islanders on St Kilda.

Our little boat lurches through the Sound of Harris and past Berner-ay and Pabbay, which had been deserted like St Kilda. An hour and a half beyond, a tiny grey triangle of rock appears on the horizon. It isn't a hallucination this time, because the seabirds have grown in number. Gannets in groups of five, six, eight, move like synchronised swim-mers in immaculate white, following the contours of the swell with a perfectly coordinated float, soar and beat-beat-beat. Experienced mariners reached St Kilda by following the birds. The Hiortaich fore-cast the weather by their movement. In the seventeenth century, one of the stewards who regularly sailed from Harris to St Kilda to col-lect rents from the islanders watched a gannet miscalculate its dive for fish, plunging into the open boat. It descended with such force that it died with its beak and head impaling the wooden hull, wings almost stretching from one gunwale to the other. Fortunately for the steward, the gannet's head securely plugged the hole it had made in the hull, and the feathered bung remained in place until he reach-ed Hirta.

The triangle of rock draws closer – an islet, Levenish, beside which emerges a much larger land mass: Hirta. In its shelter, the swell drops and we ease into Village Bay, a natural amphitheatre between two mountains, filled with buzzing insects that turn out to be puffins. The grassy slopes are covered in daisies, which are actually the heads of fulmars. The rocks all around are stained with guano as pale yellow as a gannet's head. Not many species have colonised this remote mountainous island – just two human-assisted mammals and 180 flowering plants compared with 600 on the Isle of Skye – but St Kilda's wealth comes from the sea. West of the British archipelago, the continental shelf drops away to deep ocean and up this edge rise nutrient-rich waters that support vast reserves of kelp, plankton, fish and seabirds. Humans once completed that food pyramid, and we are fascinated today by the Hiortaich's unusual diet: not fish (the sea was usually too hazardous for fishing), but seabirds. A 1764 census recorded ninety islanders each devouring '36 wild fouls eggs and 18 fouls' daily, which I can't quite believe, but other documents record that 89,600 puffins were slaughtered for meat and feathers in 1876 alone, and the typical adult ate about 115 fulmars each year. Puffin was boiled with porridge oats to liven up breakfast.

Today, the seabirds are unharvested and St Kilda is home to the largest British colony of puffins and fulmars, the largest Leach's storm petrel colony in the eastern Atlantic, and the second-largest gannetry in the world.

Wobbly with the swell and with gratitude, we are decanted into a little Zodiac – to minimise the risk of accidentally introducing rats to the island – and putter over to the small stone pier. We walk up the ramp at Village Bay, and our first vista is not of the ruined cottages that are St Kilda's public image, but of a low mass of olive-green prefabs like the mobile classrooms of my childhood. It's ironic that after the 1930 evacuation, the island was uninhabited for just twenty-six summers. This mountain in the Atlantic was too useful to ignore indefinitely. It was reoccupied in 1957 when the island was given to the National Trust for Scotland and the RAF built a concrete road zigzagging up the mountainside of Mullach Mòr to service a radar station. The station is now operated by a private contractor, QinetiQ, which tracks missiles test-fired from Benbecula. An air-and-sea danger area that extends 260 by 95 kilometres into the North Atlantic is cleared of boats whenever a missile needs firing. 'Please don't go in these buildings, you might never come out,' says Kirsten

Dallas, the National Trust for Scotland ranger whose job is to meet all arrivals. 'We don't know what happens in there.' Between the low prefabs, ships' containers and oil tanks is a taller chimneyed unit containing diesel generators that emit an incessant grinding hum. These are omitted from the tourist vision of St Kilda, but they sustain modern life here.

On the slopes above are the buildings that sustained the older life: dotted all over the hills are hundreds of cleits, windowless huts of tapered stone with green turf roofs: storehouses for fish, turf and everything else that got the Hiortaich through the long winters. Their curved walls remind me of the beautiful beehive structures I've seen in western Ireland, built by Celtic monks. In Ireland, some of these clocháns have been used into modern times, and the St Kildan cleits were deployed until the islanders' hour of departure. Beside and inside them tread Soay sheep, a dainty brown breed probably introduced by the Vikings. Gaggles of lambs gather on the cleit roofs, dancing around like teenagers at a party. Since the evacuation, these beasts have roamed wild, munching Hirta's heather and orchids into permanent miniature. Unlike most domesticated breeds, they shed their fleece naturally; during their late-spring moult, the Hiortaich simply pulled at their ginger-brown dreadlocks to obtain soft, waxy wool, a process known by the lovely word, 'rooing'. In southern England a few years back, commercial farmers hailed a 'new' self-shearing breed of sheep, which they believed could save them a fortune in shearing costs. Not for the first time, 'relics' from the periphery may be an important part of the future for the centre.

Day-trippers fan out in a frenzy along the elegant crescent of single-storey stone cottages built in a style familiar across Scotland and Ireland's west coast. The trippers are limited to four hours on the island, but as a camper I have the luxury of time. The cloud lifts and I erect my little tent in the empty camping field and hang my food in the cool interior of a cleit, surprised to feel a breeze wafting through cracks – a deliberate design to dry whatever is stored inside. I hope my hung food will evade the attentions of the island's third mammal (after sheep and humans): the St Kilda field mouse. When the people left, the house mouse quickly died out, but the more independent field mouse thrived in its niche.

The first I see of another islander is the vermilion insides of its mouth. Singing loudly, bouncing between the cracks of a cleit, the St Kilda wren is sparrow-sized and brightly speckled, having evolved into its own subspecies during its time here. Assured, noisy and distinctively large, the wrens hold Village Bay in a series of territories. Islands are places of giants and pygmies and the wren is evolving to be larger, while the sheep get smaller. Would this wren's descendant, like a mighty eagle, one day clasp sheep in its claws? Scientists studying the Soay sheep have linked their shrinking to warmer winters: they no longer need to be so bulky to survive.

The wren is accompanied by the retching-into-a-tin-can chat of the fulmars. The epitome of elegance in flight, wings spread so flat they look like gliders, they are less graceful on land, squatting on rocks around Village Bay, chuntering and complaining. Compton Mackenzie reckoned they possessed 'a cold disdainful eye'; he preferred kittiwakes, 'the prettiest and daintiest of all the gulls'.

The trippers depart and I join the fulmars, sitting on a rock, surveying the scene. I'm rendered motionless by an evening that unravels like tissue paper, becoming softer and softer. The land darkens, but the sea shows all patterns of light. Silver traces of current wiggle like snail trails over the calm Atlantic. The sun spins cumuli into gold and the clouds cast golden shadows on the blue water. The gold turns pink, purple and then the palest of grey. I feel a great weight pressing upon me and submit to it, long before the dusk has darkened.

Soft rain wakes me soon after 5 a.m., and I wander the ruins of Village Bay. Our disputed portrayal of Hirta's human history reflects both poles of small-island life: as prison and as utopia. For some tourists who arrived on the first steamships in 1834 – 'Come and See Britain's Modern Primitives,' said adverts – the Hiortaich were wretches whose small society was a reproach to our great civilisation. Others believed they were noble savages. 'If this island is not the Eutopia so long sought, where will it be found?' wrote the geologist John MacCulloch after visiting St Kilda in 1819. 'Where is the land which has neither arms, money, law, physic, politics, nor taxes? That land is St Kilda.' And so Hirta's abandonment is either the march of progress or an indigenous morality tale, a miniature version of the conquest and evisceration of Native Americans and Aboriginal Australians. Were these cultured, innately communal people enslaved or liberated by global capitalism?

Pausing to roll between my fingers a tendril of greasy Soay wool, I stand within the ruined walls of a 'blackhouse', one of the older traditional homes superseded by the mid-Victorian cottages – which, at the time, were cutting-edge for the Atlantic coast – and try to picture life in the early 1800s. Here, in a single oblong room, protected by two-metre-thick walls and turned side on to the relentless south-westerlies, lived a typical Hiortaich family. Were I visiting them, I would crawl through the low doorway, most likely retching because the floor would be piled high with cow dung and the claws and beaks of rotting gannets, puffins and fulmars. Manure emits heat, and by pressing it into the floor throughout the winter they created something not unlike underfloor heating. In the gloom illuminated by a fulmar-oil lamp, I might have bumped into the family cow, stabled at the bottom end of the room, its slurry draining away from the coffin-like sleeping-hollow at the top end. In the middle was an open turf fire, but no chimney. The fire burned continuously. Its smoke turned the insides of the house black, acted as an insecticide, smoked the puffin carcasses hanging in the eaves, and applied a layer of tar to the inside of the thatch, thereby repelling the annual rainfall of fifty inches – double that endured by people in southern Britain. There was no oven and little furniture, and despite the billions of feathers available, mattresses were fashioned from straw. In summer, the islanders removed their flooring and spread it on the fields to invigorate their oats and, later, wheat, barley and potatoes. Martin Martin, in 1697 one of the first visitors to document life on St Kilda, claimed that such was the fertility of the fields that barley yields were the largest in the Western Isles.

Victorian tourists were wowed not by the Hiortaich's farming, but by their crag-climbing. The women undertook much of the hard labour – milking cows, tending sheep, grinding corn, weaving, cooking – but only the men performed astonishing barefoot climbs to capture seabirds and collect their eggs from the vertiginous cliffs.

I leave Village Bay and make a day-long circumnavigation of Hirta, feeling my way along its edges. Periodically, I drop to my knees and peer over the cliff, grey-green lichens as prickly as a doormat under my hands. A kaleidoscope of fulmars turn against the dark water, crying over the white-noise menace of surf meeting rock a stomach-lurching distance below. The cliffs aren't always sheer, but I can no more scale them than fly like a fulmar. We mainlanders live on the flat. Land is horizontal. Here, half the island is manifest in the vertical. If your terrain is half-cliff and you don't climb, you are only half alive. And the Hiortaich climbed to stay alive. 'The inhabitants look as if they had been all tarred and feathered, for their hair is full of feathers and their clothes are covered with feathers,' wrote John MacCulloch in 1819. 'Everything smells of feathers.'

A sustainable harvest of seabirds supported life on St Kilda. Gannets, or *guga*, were a staple of earlier times, but after the 1750s the islanders ate more fulmars, which provided fatty meat said to taste like beef. Fulmars – 'foul gull' for their habit of vomiting a stinky fluid over intruders – also provided an oil sold on the mainland as medicine, reputed to possess similar properties to cod liver oil. Another cash crop was fulmar feathers, which the British army used as lice- and bedbug-resistant bedding in the nineteenth century. Tough seabird flesh was observed to be good for the islanders' teeth. They also ate plenty of eggs, particularly gannet and guillemot, often keeping them for six to eight weeks to improve their flavour. Other species – oystercatcher, tree sparrow and especially the egg of the St Kilda wren – were blown and sold to collectors.

I admire the guillemots huddled on ledges, their backs turned to the water, and am reminded again of Compton Mackenzie, who wrote: 'There on one narrow ledge you will see seven little Eton boys turned to the wall in disgrace.' Of course, Monty visited St Kilda. With his knack for finding his way to the centre of events, he pitched up in June 1930, two months before the evacuation. He'd gone to meet Faith's brother, Christopher, off the *Dunara Castle* steamer when it docked at South Uist. They bumped into the MP for the Western Isles who was on his way to St Kilda, and decided to accompany him. Disembarking on Hirta, they were strolling along 'the straggling little street' when they saw a fishing cruiser drop anchor and a prostrate figure being carried ashore. It was Tom Johnston, Under-Secretary of State for Scotland, and the man responsible for St Kilda's evacuation. He was violently seasick. Once Johnston had staggered to his feet, he talked with the islanders about their leaving, 'to which they were strongly opposed' claims Monty in his memoirs. This was not what Johnston told the House of Commons five days later: he confirmed that the government would grant the wishes of a petition signed by all householders to be removed from the island. Monty was furious. 'Mr Tom Johnston landed on St Kilda with a mind obscured by sea-sickness and he was in no condition to appreciate the real state of affairs on the island,' he wrote to the *Oban Times*. The government-funded evacuation was a 'pusillanimous admission' that it was 'incompetent to deal with the problems of modern Scotland'. Monty campaigned against the evacuation of St Kilda. But a decade later, he declared that the government had been right; why he changed his mind, he never explained.

There is a giddy experience to be had in wild places, which Alasdair Gray in *Lanark* describes as being 'drunk with spaciousness'. It is intoxicating to walk along An Cambir, the north-western arm of Hirta, where it stretches towards the uninhabited island of Soay, and it is also invigorating. I share a drunk's exaggerated sense of his own reach, but I imagine I can see and feel with new precision, which is not a characteristic of the inebriated. I have the light, the air and the landscape to thank. Monty wrote of the 'clarity' of Hebridean days when 'the islands seem to float suspended between earth and heaven in a crystal globe'.

I climb to the highest point of Hirta, above the three white eggs in concrete cups belonging to the radar station. They could be an art installation, an aesthetic response to the eggs all around us. The last cloud vanishes as a stage curtain lifts, and suddenly is revealed the full grandeur of this world. I can only gasp at its splendour. A vast expanse of empty sea glitters for miles around. Then, along the eastern horizon emerges a chain of islands. In the foreground, the low islets of Haskeir. Beyond are the mountains of Harris, and the hummock-backed hills of North Uist, Benbecula, South Uist. Further away to the south, a paler grey, is Barra. Beyond it, perhaps Vatersay or even Mingulay. I can't see another soul, but through binoculars I can identify human traces: buildings, surf on a long strand, a lighthouse and more eggcup radar stations to match St Kilda's.

An arena so vast makes us feel tiny, which is a profoundly comforting sensation. But I don't feel as alone, far out in the Atlantic Ocean, as I imagined I would. The clarity of the land in view makes St Kilda appear comprehensively bound to the isles of Britain. It belongs to the British archipelago in a way that Alderney and the Channel Islands do not. This may be the ultimate island, and yet I'm struck by its relatedness.

The many chroniclers of St Kilda still debate its historic closeness to the mainland. The Victorians saw the Hiortaich as Britain's version of an undiscovered Amazonian tribe, marvelling at their isolation and uniqueness. This perception is enduring. 'The St Kildans can only be described as St Kildans and their island home little else than a republic,' argued Tom Steel in *The Life and Death of St Kilda*, one of the twentieth century's more reliable popular histories. Recently, though, a revisionist view has taken hold among Scottish historians that emphasises St Kilda's close connection to the Western Isles. For instance, when smallpox decimated Hirta's population in 1727, reducing it to four adults and twenty-six orphans, the island was repopulated by crofters from Skye and the Outer Hebrides. For centuries, St Kilda was enmeshed in the clan economy; its chief clan, the Macleods, lived on Skye and treated St Kilda as a farm, together with the Hebridean island of Pabbay. Islanders paid annual rent: barley, eggs, tweed and particularly feathers, which proved a useful cash crop. Historically, tourists tended to travel straight to St Kilda and so overlooked the fact that its language, culture, religion and politics, from its devout Free Church to the daily meetings outsiders called its 'parliament', were shared by the islands of the Outer Hebrides.

Seeing these isles so visible on the horizon emphasises the impossibility of insularity. St Kilda is equally visible to the islanders of North Uist, Harris and Benbecula. The Hiortaich would have been more outward-looking than most lowlanders: they were certainly granted a clearer view of life sixty miles away than anyone living in, say, Cambridge. Those islanders who never travelled to their Hebridean neighbours would have interrogated peers who did for news and stories. And for centuries, there was a steady stream of adventurers, entrepreneurs, academics, officials, do-gooders and dreamers sailing here.

Nevertheless, the Hiortaich were not servants of the British realm in the way that mainlanders were. When James IV of Scotland passed an Act declaring that its islands were under his rule he excluded St Kilda because it was so remote, he claimed, that he couldn't guarantee its safety. After Bonnie Prince Charlie and his Jacobite rebels were rumoured to have fled defeat at Culloden to hide on Hirta in 1746 – a nice example of how mainlanders see small islands as fugitive places – soldiers set out in pursuit. They found the Hiortaich had no idea who the Young Pretender was, and were similarly oblivious of King George. In 1815, visitors noted the islanders knew nothing of the Battle of Waterloo. In the spring of 1838, St Kilda's minister belatedly caught up with Victoria's coronation the year before and hurriedly changed references in the prayers from 'His' to 'Her' Majesty. Unlike the men of the Western Isles, the Hiortaich were never pressed into military service and never lost anyone in battle.

Today, there's a St Kilda Club. It even has its own tie. The comments in the visitors' book at Hirta's cottage museum reveal the intense bonds people form with the island long before they reach it. 'Waited 40 years for the weather to come out here! Not disappointed!' write a couple who sailed over in their own boat. 'Finally made it after decades of longing,' say another. 'I have waited for 50 years,' reveals Björn Tobrustrom from Uppsala, Sweden.

During my three days on Hirta, the dozen or so QinetiQ staff keep a low profile. They are not permitted to talk to visitors about their work, which mostly seems to consist of playing chess in the sunshine and driving a Land Rover up the zigzag track to check on their giant eggcups. Another group of temporary islanders are more forthcoming. Volunteers for the National Trust for Scotland must apply and pay for the privilege of spending two weeks painting window frames and repairing other bits of the World Heritage Site.

'It's my eleventh time, I've got it bad. My wife thinks there's more than feathered birds out here,' says Stephen MacDonald, a burly Scot with a shaven head who is a building contractor on the mainland. Whenever I see him up a ladder applying pitch to roofs or fixing the chapel's tiles, he cheerfully reminds me he's forked out £860 for this busman's holiday.

He's a lovely bloke, and I warm to him even more when he points to the mountains I've just descended and says that An Cambir is his 'favourite place in the world'. His desire to reach the archipelago was sparked by his dad, a sailor, who told him many tales of St Kilda. When his first application to join a Trust working party in 2002 was successful, Stephen realised his dream. 'It sounds corny but the moment I set foot on that pier, I felt I'd been here before,' he says. He visited the little graveyard in Village Bay and discovered that MacDonald was one of the most commonly found surnames on the island.

Stephen remains deeply attached to St Kilda even when living his ordinary life on the mainland. 'This place should have a public health warning because it can affect you in so many ways,' he says. He reckons he has ten thousand photos of it. When he glimpsed it from the air by chance during a flight to America, he got really emotional. Best of all, one day driving through his home town he passed a Range Rover and was startled to read its registration: SK11 LDA. He turned round and followed it. When the driver stopped, Stephen apologised for pursuing him and asked if he could buy the numberplate. The man said it was a courtesy car belonging to a dealer. So Stephen went to see the dealer who shrugged and said it meant nothing to him, and Stephen could have the plate for the £80 it costs to switch it. Retelling this tale, Stephen sounds almost offended. 'I can't let you do that,' he told the dealer, 'people would pay a fortune for that plate.' So he gave the man an envelope containing £500. Stephen could have sold it to another member of the St Kilda Club for £2,500, but of course he hasn't.

He adores the island's wilderness, but also deeply respects the old islanders. 'I've got nothing but admiration for the St Kildans. They were a simple people, but extremely resourceful,' he says. 'Everybody had everything. It was almost like a little utopia.'

Stephen repeatedly stresses my good fortune with the weather. The daughter of a nineteenth-century missionary recalled a storm so severe it left every islander deaf for a week, and Stephen has endured twenty-four hours at sea in storms involving 'endless bags of vomit', to reach St Kilda. One September he was undertaking building repairs on Hirta, and the evening before he was due to depart the ranger asked when he was leaving. 'I said, "Friday". He said, "You're not. There's a storm coming in." That night the storm was like a steam train going over the roof. I could feel the pressure in my ears. I opened the door and it was just a maelstrom. I looked down the street and the roofs were undulating.' He felt 'like Robinson Crusoe': high winds and poor visibility stopped even a helicopter from landing for twelve days, although at least he had QinetiQ staff for company. They are used to the storms: during the winter of 2015, assailed by 144 mph winds, all fifteen employees had to be airlifted to safety by the coastguard as the waves smashed through their prefabs.

It's impossible to conjure up such conditions on the bright days I roam St Kilda. I'm mostly alone, but I don't feel I'm bestriding this world with the benign, godlike gaze of the man who loved islands. I'm in thrall to a higher island ruler. My lairds first announce themselves by tearing a hole in the air – two great skuas, or bonxies, a name derived from the Norwegian, *bunksi* or *bunke*, meaning 'dumpy body'. There's no sign of plumpness as they pursue each other down the mountainside at peregrine speed. Half-gull, half-buzzard, all-bully, these magnificent chocolate-brown creatures waddle proprietorially on the mountainside like murderous ducks. When I approach, they emit a low, duck-like 'quooork!', and take off. A winged shadow passes overhead and suddenly there's a vwroooosh of air through feathers and a bonxie dive-bombs my head from behind, pulling up a few centimetres before it can whack me.

On my way through the empty valley of Gleann Mòr, I'm attacked by eleven more bonxies. At first I'm conciliatory. 'Easy,' I murmur. 'You're the boss. This is definitely your home, not mine.' But I'm rattled by the rapid assaults. I throw my left hand (to save my right, writing hand) in the air when another approaches and shout: 'Yah!'

'Quooork!' the bonxie replies with sinister nonchalance.

I decide they are territorial bullies. The bonxie has a shocking reputation. It's a pirate and a robber, and it harasses gannets until they vomit up the fish they've caught. It will kill most things, and scientists studying it on Hirta believe its booming population is diminishing the number of storm petrels and Manx shearwaters.

I learn that I've misunderstood this ruler of St Kilda when I meet the island's ornithologist, Gina Prior. A young-looking woman with dark hair and glasses, she is actually the most experienced National Trust for Scotland employee on the archipelago. She first came here when she volunteered in 2003 to assist ecologists who study the Soay sheep. 'You know it's quite special in terms of the ecology, but it's really hard to explain the feeling when you first set foot on the island,' she says. 'Some people come and go and that's it. For others, it really gets into your soul. You almost become addicted to the place.'

On the morning I intercept her, she's due to take a boat to Dun to mark puffin burrows. For the last thirty summers, Gina and her predecessors have weighed and measured the chicks inside a hundred puffin burrows. It is not a sunny picture. Puffins require a reproductive success rate of around 70 per cent each year to sustain their colony, but on St Kilda it currently hovers around 40 per cent. Other seabirds – gannets, Leach's storm petrels, Manx shearwaters – are suffering similar declines. When the monitoring of kittiwakes began in 1994, there were 513 nests on St Kilda; in 2015 there were just four, each containing a single chick. Fulmar nests declined by 37 per cent between 2002 and 2015. The archipelago is a pristine, protected environment, but no island is an island.

As we talk, Gina glances at the sky. Innocuous wisps of cloud are gathering over Hirta's hills. 'It just doesn't look quite right,' she murmurs, and postpones her trip to Dun in the eternally flexible manner of Hiortaich past, wise enough to know we can't defy the St Kildan weather. Instead, she begins her annual count of the one bird that is thriving on St Kilda: the bonxie.

She kindly allows me along as her assistant. 'You better take this,' she says, pulling one of two bamboo canes topped with a little red flag from her rucksack. I guess it's to mark nests, but Gina shows me how to fix it to my backpack so the flag flutters above my head: a dive-bomb deterrent.

She's had bonxie talons tear at her face. One time, a bonxie smashed her glasses. On another occasion, a bird made her lose her balance on a steep slope, fall and badly bruise her arm. This year they've evolved a new tactic: they shit on her head.

We climb Oiseval, the hill behind Village Bay, and a raven croaks overhead. Raven v bonxie, who would win? 'Always the skua,' says Gina, recalling the time a snowy owl took up temporary residence on Hirta. 'That got a hammering from the bonxies.'

I consider the bonxie to be the quintessential creature of St Kilda, the master of its uplands, so I'm astounded when Gina tells me they are not much more St Kildan than I am: they arrived here only in the 1970s. By 2012, there were 151 pairs on the archipelago. 'They've just got dinner around every corner,' she says.

Gina climbs the hill with a deceptive ease, me puffing behind. This is the least hazardous of her bird counts: more treacherous is scrambling to the artificial nestboxes on the cliff edge to monitor Leach's storm petrels. Gina is a self-taught St Kildan climber. Each season, it takes her a couple of days 'to settle into the whole cliffs thing – to be not afraid to fall', she says. She climbs alone and is casual about previous accidents – tumbling down a hillside and breaking her ribs, being squashed by large stones falling on her – but wears a tracking device she can use to alert the coastguard if she requires rescuing. She's never needed to yet, and is very conscious of the expense of a rescue. I realise that the issue of inconveniencing the authorities has never occurred to me as I've shambled around St Kilda: I'm still a long way from thinking like an islander.

Two bonxies loiter by a cleit on the slopes above us. 'What are you guys doing?' whispers Gina. She suspects they are guarding a nest. I had assumed the bonxie's dive-bombing was aggressive territoriality, but Gina explains that I was attacked so badly because I was obliviously tramping right past their nests, which are on open ground. The dive-bombing bonxies are simply good parents.

One of the birds above us gives that low 'quooork' call again, which Gina tells me is an alert. The bird's mate descends for a gentle dive-bomb. The little red flags keep her a few metres above our heads. When the pair retreat to higher ground, we scour their vacated territory and eventually spot a bowl-shaped scrape in the slope. It contains two huge eggs, about twice the size of a hen's. They are warm and very beautiful, dark olive and adorned with Jackson Pollock splatterings of chocolate-brown and grey. Gina kneels, pulls callipers and scales from her rucksack, and deftly weighs and measures each egg. She moves quickly because she doesn't want to keep the female from incubating her eggs for long.

Scientists identify the main cause of seabird decline on St Kilda and other isles as climate change. Warming temperatures are making our northerly seas less suitable for the plankton at the base of the food chain. So there are fewer sand eels, fewer larger fish and fewer seabird predators. Changing fishing practices, particularly stopping fishermen from throwing their 'discards' overboard, are probably contributing to the decline of certain species such as kittiwakes, which are surface-feeders. The impact of the bonxies is tricky to assess, says Gina. A study has found they do predate large numbers of petrels on St Kilda, but most of these seem to be non-breeding adults: given the bonxies' kill rate, the petrel population should be plummeting to zero, but it isn't. Even though the bonxies are decimating the petrels, the predator is still rarer than the prey.

We spy another couple of bonxies on the hillside. Splat. One has fired a large poo at my right shoulder. Individual birds have notice-ably different personalities, says Gina; some are more aggressive than others. The dive-bombing continues so we know we're close. Sure enough, we find another nest of two perfect eggs, like painted orna-ments. Within minutes, we are enveloped in thick cloud. Gina was wise not to head out to Dun, but now she doesn't want to disturb any more incubating bonxies because the rain will rapidly cool their eggs. We gingerly descend the slopes to Village Bay.

'Some people think they are coming to escape from life and people and learn about themselves,' says Gina, of St Kilda's summer residents, 'but it's surprising how many people you encounter, and you have to be personable and communicative.' I mention the complexity of the archipelago, not only its human history, but its geography. To know every rock or crevice would take a lifetime. That's why Gina returns each summer. She hasn't got to the bottom of it yet. 'There are still many parts of the island that I don't know,' she says. 'There are still so many places where I want to go.'

The weather is worsening, but the Atlantic is still calm enough for the trippers and so I have to leave on the day boat while I can.

I pack my tent. The Soay-grazed grass is pressed shorter where I lay. In a couple of days, there will be no trace of me on Hirta. But St Kilda leaves an indentation on me. Remembering the sense of elevation walking on An Cambir is like recalling another life.

I notice after Alderney and St Martin's that my island sojourns turn my home on the fringe of a suburban village into something claustrophobic and noisy. All I hear on my return is traffic. Anyone raised on the grand arena of a small island must feel a mighty tug to return. I try to imagine what the Hiortaich felt in 1930 as they prepared to leave their homeland for ever. Their departure is still fiercely debated by historians, in large part because – extraordinarily, given all the studies of St Kilda – there is not one book written by a St Kildan in their native Gaelic. The abandonment of the Irish island of Great Blasket in the 1950s is similarly famous, but given clarity by a small library of memoirs written in Irish Gaelic by the islanders themselves.

The argument over St Kilda, crudely put, is this: did the Hiortaich jump or were they pushed? Most outsiders who examine their decision emphasise the push aspect. Through the nineteenth and early twentieth centuries, the money-driven mainland corrupted the purity of the periphery. Stephen MacDonald's view of St Kilda is typical of those who see the islanders inexorably drawn into an all-conquering market economy. 'The death knell for St Kilda was when modern man found them,' he says. 'When they learned the power of the penny they were doomed.'

Apart from capitalism, the external force most frequently blamed for pushing St Kilda's human society to extinction is religion. In 1697, Martin Martin – who is more reliable than many visitors because he spoke Gaelic – depicted a cheerful people who loved song and poetry and were religious even though they had no resident minister. In the nineteenth century, when the dour evangelism of the Free Church of Scotland was making a dramatic impact on the Highlands and Islands, ministers arrived on St Kilda. 'Many a fiddle was dramatically broken across the knee, and gay voices and feet were stilled to conform to the gravity now thought to be desirable for salvation,' wrote Frank Fraser Darling, looking back from the standpoint of the twentieth century. Not only did this new puritanism make island life less joyful, writers such as Tom Steel argue that by reducing their time at work, 'a highly organised, strictly managed, puritan and often harsh religion' actually hindered the Hiortaich's ability to support themselves. By the mid-1800s, islanders were attending church virtually every day. 'The Sabbath is indeed a day of intolerable gloom. At the clink of the bell the whole flock hurry to the Church with sorrowful looks, and eyes bent upon the ground,' wrote John Sands, a Victorian visitor-author who has since been shown to have borne a grudge against the island minister of the time.

Revisionist historians argue that outsiders such as Sands and Steel have misunderstood the religion of the Islands. In a recent essay, Donald Meek accuses them of portraying St Kildans as South Sea islanders falling victim to missionaries. In fact, Meek argues, the evangelical Protestantism that spread through much of the Hebrides did not seek to destroy Gaelic language and culture. He emphasises that the most important voices are the St Kildans themselves, and they can be heard in the memoirs of the Reverend Donald John Gillies, who was born on St Kilda in 1901 and emigrated to Canada in 1924. Gillies shows that the Church provided a Gaelic education and gave practical help to islanders. The islanders' faith also strengthened the cohesion of their community.

Meek believes, essentially, that the Hiortaich jumped. By the early twentieth century the disastrous rates of infant mortality had been arrested by modern medicine, but the arrival of troops on St Kilda during the First World War made the mainland more alluring. Once connected to the outside world, the Hiortaich could better imagine new ways of life. When the war ended and the Navy departed, alongside the regular post and food supplies they provided, many islanders also emigrated. The population shrank by a quarter and continued to fall until there were too few men of working age to support the community.

Some observers maintain that the government of the day should have supported St Kilda better. If the island were imperilled today, one might hope the mainland would offer grants for the improved connections the Hiortaich required, such as a regular mailboat and a new jetty. But in 1930, officials still saw 'backward' St Kilda as an embarrassment and an inconvenience: the authorities even charged the islanders for a meal on the boat that evacuated them.

The concerns of the last Hiortaich were a more extreme version of islanders' worries today. On St Martin's, I meet elderly residents who say how difficult it is to obtain healthcare or visit hospitals on the mainland since Scilly's helicopter service was scrapped. On St Kilda in 1930, an attempt to get a pregnant islander, Mary Gillies, to hospital was delayed for two weeks because of bad weather. Gillies, who was also suffering from appendicitis, was eventually taken by ship, but died in a Glasgow hospital on the same day as her thirteen-day-old baby daughter. That month, May, the islanders decided to leave. A message was sent to the authorities to 'petition' for their evacuation. And what about Compton Mackenzie's evidence that the Hiortaich didn't want to leave? He probably only spoke to one or two of the older men, such as Finlay MacQueen, who had second thoughts. One islander, Lachlan MacDonald, later explained that 'the older people agreed to leave, but when the case came to push and they knew they were going, well, they would rather stay, but they had signed the petition'. Faced with the islanders' plea, the government in Westminster could hardly insist that they stay.

When St Kilda was vacated, the Scottish Office rebuffed more than four hundred inquiries from nesomanes pleading to resettle the archipelago. And the mainland has been unable to stay away. An empty island, possessed of culture, complexity, character – what a marvellous gift for the rest of the world. Tourist steamers continued to visit throughout the 1930s and several of the Hiortaich actually returned and camped in their derelict homes during the summer, catching birds or guiding visitors. Rachel Johnson, the last of the living Hiortaich, who was eight when she was evacuated, died in a Scottish nursing home in 2016, so no individual truly belongs on St Kilda any more. No one can lay claim to it and everyone can lay claim to it. The island becomes a destination for all kinds of hopes, fears and theories. The fate of the Hiortaich is viewed as an indictment of the past and also a warning for the future in an era where extinction plays on the mind.

The tour boats that visit St Kilda soften the blow of departure by cruising to its mighty sea stacks before heading back to the mainland. I had already admired Stac Lee and Stac an Armin, the highest sea stack in Britain, from the heights of Hirta, but being slooshed around them in a small boat is a surreal experience. The swarming birds, the slap of ocean on rock, and the slender silhouette of Stac Lee towering above us is as improbable as the computer-generated imagery of a fantasy film.

I'm struck by the impossibility of living in this world without possessing an unquenchable sense of a force much more powerful than yourself, of being the recipient of a whopping dose of majesty and vulnerability. No wonder the Hiortaich cleaved to community and religion. Leaving all this behind must have been an acute loss that could not be salved.

I stand alone on the deck of the little boat and watch the archipelago recede into a grey murk. On the horizon beyond the dark rock triangle of Levenish is a spectacular city of clouds, cumulus piled upon cumulus. Of course, these islanders believed in a heavenly power, such as God. From a distance, the profile of Hirta, Soay and Dun eventually resembles a woman lying on her back in the Atlantic, before the archipelago morphs into a single blur. It takes one hour and fifteen minutes' sailing until this solid ground is finally lost to cloud and spray. I turn and enter the cabin, which is resounding with pop music played by the captain as we thud across the Minch. It suddenly feels as neat and tidy as a cruise across a lake.

9

The Saintly Tadpole

Ynys Enlli, or Bardsey, Wales, 0.69 square miles or 440 acres,
permanent population: 6

'The souls of all the dead are alive again, and pulsating
actively around you. You are out in the other infinity'
'The Man Who Loved Islands'

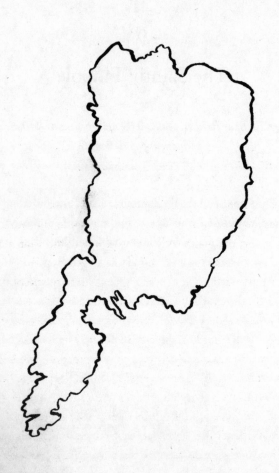

'Do you like singing?' says Sister Rosalind Mary.

Yes, I reply, because I do.

She asks if I know a particular hymn. I look blank.

A multitude of flying ants are trapped inside the small sunlit window of the oratory, a feast for two spiders who wrap them up like corn on the cob. Outside, a sheep tears gently at the grass with its teeth. I attended a Church of England primary school, but my religious education is patchy and poorly remembered.

Sister Rosalind Mary invites me to choose a song, and I leaf through the hymnal. 'All Things Bright and Beautiful', I know that, but hope to find something more appropriate to our situation, two strangers, alone, and about to fill a pregnant silence by singing together. Um. The small nun with straight grey hair and glasses waits. A swallow chirps above the low hum of bumblebees at the fuchsia.

Eventually, Sister Rosalind Mary puts me out of my misery, rising from her wooden bench, crossing the broken flagstone floor of our tiny whitewashed cell, and taking a high-backed kitchen chair next to mine. She suggests something I've never heard of, holds up the hymnal for us to share, and opens her mouth. I don't recognise the tune. Time passes, slowly. Even by the fourth verse I haven't mastered the unpredictable ups and downs. I follow her warbles, softly, devoutly, and terribly out of tune.

The remainder of five o'clock evening prayers passes as if in a dream. Sister Rosalind Mary is both tentative and confident, happy to pause for a contemplative moment when I worry I'm not doing what I should be doing. The prayers are easy, though. She says the main bits and I, reading from the service sheet, reply: WE GIVE YOU THANKS.

> For your love for us, compassionate and patient,
> which has carried us through our pain,
> wept beside us in our sin,
> and waited with us in our confusion.

WE GIVE YOU THANKS. I really like the idea of love waiting for someone in their confusion. The words are beautiful.

Sister Rosalind Mary prays for Sudan and invites me to participate in a 'sharing of the day', ushering me onto solid ground at last. I tell her that an hour or so before I'd waded through horsetails as high as my waist to this oratory in the old cowshed, I swam in a tiny bay where grey seals conversed on the rocks. I felt disappointed they didn't swim closer and welcome me into their world but I enjoyed meeting them. She tells me of her satisfying day of meetings with humans and how she believes people have been very 'open' with her.

Then, with a dizzying whoosh, our intense service for two is over and we walk out into the sunshine, leaving behind the peaceful little room, its table decorated with bleached-white limpet shells and a crown of thorns fashioned from brambles.

I realise how rarely I'm in a one-on-one experience with a stranger that I do not lead. In my professional life, interviewing people, I tend to set the agenda. In my private life, I may at times be a passive consumer or a helpless subject – in a doctor's treatment room, say –

but that process is nonetheless centred on me. This one wasn't. As we slowly retreat from the intimacy of the service via some gentle chat outside the old hayloft where Sister Rosalind Mary is staying, I realise I'm inadvertently interviewing her, withdrawing to safer territory. She pins a service notice on Enlli's church gate during the one week she resides on the island in summer, but says she doesn't usually get anyone at morning and evening prayer. What qualities does she find on the island? 'There is the beauty, but it is the spiritual atmosphere,' she says. 'The first time I took a Eucharist last year I didn't actually have a congregation, but I had a sense that the chapel was full. It felt OK to be sharing that.'

Islands have been occupied for religious reasons almost as often as they have for penal ones, and Ynys Enlli has long served as a place of spiritual pilgrimage. Small-islanders were among the first and last to embrace Christianity in Britain. Iona, in Scotland, can claim to be an early capital of Christianity; the stubborn people of the Isle of Wight were among the last to submit to its strictures. Lindisfarne began as a franchise of Iona, its monks bringing both Christian teaching and a literary culture to Godless north-east England. I've visited all these fine islands but, like most of my fellow spiritual trippers, had never set foot on the holy island of Wales. Ynys Enlli, or Bardsey as Norse raiders named it, is famed as the resting place of twenty thousand saints. Far fewer mortals visit it each year because of the cobalt switchback of the Sound, a lethal stretch of water that has bestowed its Welsh name, the 'isle of currents', to the place.

Colin Evans is Enlli's boatman, and he and his tiny, extremely bright-yellow boat make quite an entrance as I wait on the slipway at Porth Meudwy, 'the Bay of the Hermit', a crack in the sheltered south-eastern rocks of Llŷn Peninsula. The harbour smells of bladder-wrack drying on lobster pots. Scattered among the boats and trailers are a mother with her tiny baby in a car seat, an older woman, two elderly men and an attractive young couple speaking Welsh. We are bathed in the unhurried calm of a perfect September day. Suddenly, very fast around the corner comes Colin, the drill-like thud of his motor bouncing off the rocks around us. As the boat approaches the surf, a man materialises at the wheel of a weather-beaten tractor and reverses a trailer into the water. The boat cuts its engine and slides onto the submerged trailer, Colin lashes vessel and trailer together, and the tractor carries them up the slipway, high and dry. I assume the small crowd is a queue for Enlli, but it is mostly an audience. People chat and exchange parcels and crates of shellfish under damp hessian sacking and then disappear; only me and the nice young couple climb aboard.

From the mainland, Ynys Enlli appears to be a bleak, unpeopled mountain of dark rock, and it is only when Colin's boat reaches its southern tip that its secret is revealed: a long tadpole-like tail of fertile pasture reaching westwards to a red-and-white striped lighthouse. Our landing in one of its low rocky coves follows a similar pattern to our departure: another old boy appears from nowhere on a tractor and hauls us out of the water. Colin explains he devised this system to provide a more reliable service on a crossing that is frequently cancelled because of the violence of the Sound. The island's farmers, Steve and Jo, can be stranded for two weeks at a time during winter because of the weather.

Enlli actually has a smaller resident population than St Kilda but it can claim to be a little more permanent because its warden, its farmers and the couple who run the Bardsey Bird and Field Observatory don't move on and off in shifts like the employees of QinetiQ. Its winter population of six is augmented in summer by Christine Evans, a poet, and her husband Ernest, the last of the old islanders, who can trace his family back to the eighteenth century. Enlli is owned and managed by the Bardsey Island Trust, a group of local people, academics and other interested experts, and the island is sustained by tourism, the

Trust's dozen or so former farmhouses and barns providing basic self-catering for the small number of devotees who worship this beautiful small place.

Rhodri Evans, the warden, shows me around my living quarters, Llofft Nant, a simply furnished two-roomed old barn. He is an artist, a watercolourist, and another of those professional islanders working as a warden – on Rum, in the Seychelles, on St Kilda. Enlli, he thinks, is more remote than St Kilda because the Scottish island's military base makes it accessible by helicopter. 'Islands are the same the world over. The challenges are: water – there's always a shortage – and little things get built up into big things. And the other thing about islands is that things take about five times as long here as anywhere else.' Islanders, he says, must be careful with each other. 'We treat each other very gently here.' Rhodri takes his leave, murmuring, 'He didn't do it deliberately' as I gaze from my kitchen window at the enormous black bags of silage dumped by the farmer in front of what would be a gorgeous view of meadows sloping towards the low cliffs and the sea beyond. It doesn't matter: beauty is more than what's visible. Swallows are feeding their young, chattering and whizzing low around the eaves, the sea sighs in the distance and a stable door creaks. A great calm settles upon me like the three heavy old blankets I pull onto my single bed during the chilly night.

The Bardsey Island Trust are island-lovers after the fashion of Adam Nicolson: there are no signs or bossy notices on Enlli. There are almost no trees either, but compared to St Kilda it is a supremely gentle place, during this week in September at least. Mynydd Enlli, the island's mountain at its eastern end, shields the mainland from almost every view; islanders must perpetually contemplate the great expanse of the western horizon. This is pin-sharp, much sharper than it is ever drawn on the east coast, and beyond is the palest of blue smudges: Ireland. Dotted along the mountain's lower slopes are a couple of ruins, a small schoolhouse and eleven grey stone farms, handsome Victorian buildings each with the same steeply peaked roof of purple-grey slate. Their barns, yards and old pigsties are enclosed by enormous battlemented stone walls. These farms were built in the 1870s by an enlightened member of the Newborough dynasty, who owned the island for four centuries. The landlord wanted to provide decent homes for the islanders, but the men who arrived to build the houses married the island's young women and the young Enlli men were drawn into labouring. So these 'improvements' accelerated an exodus to the mainland that left the eldest islander, Love Pritchard, declaring in 1925: 'We have not enough young men to row boats off for us and look after the cattle.' St Kilda's experience has been fairly universal for islands of this size.

Two choughs dance in the air as I explore Enlli's northern edge, pasture curving gently to an inaccessible shore of craggy rocks. A pair of seals, the male with a big Roman nose, bob in the water and gaze at me with moist black eyes. Most of the low earth hedges around the small fields are redundant now that the sheep and cattle are tended by one farmer, and the monumental stone gateposts look lonely, no longer linked to fences. By the sea, an old ship's rope has been twisted into the shape of a heart, held in place by the grass that coils around it. I sit on a beach of coarse grey sand and read about how I'm following sixteen centuries of pilgrims.

As succinct as any modern guide, Gerald of Wales described in 1188 'a small island occupied by some extremely devout monks'.

Either because of its pure air, which comes across the sea from Ireland, or through some miracle occasioned by the merits of the holy men who live there, the island has this peculiarity, that no-one dies there except of extreme old age, for disease is almost unheard-of. In fact, no-one dies there at all, unless he is very old indeed. In Welsh the place is called Ynys Enlli, and in

the Saxon tongue, Bardsey Island. The bodies of a vast number
of holy men are buried there, or so they say . . .

The ideals of 'the desert fathers', monks from Egypt and Syria, had
been brought by sea to the western British Isles by the fifth century.
Men and women took up an ascetic form of Christianity, removing
themselves from everyday life to become *peregrini*, pilgrims, who followed the 'way the saints went', as the poet R.S. Thomas put it. They
devoted themselves to a life of prayer, poverty and solitude, often in
contemplation of the sea, where forces of devilment were considered
the strongest. On the wind-blasted North Sea island of Inner Farne,
St Cuthbert built his cell walls so high he 'could see nothing except
the heavens above'. Enlli, set apart from the mainland but accessible by sea traffic and possessed of this contemplative, westerly geography, would have been a particularly perfect location. As Adam
Nicolson points out, the early Christian pilgrims sought out the very
best remote places in Scotland – fertile or seabird-rich islands such as
Canna, Barra, Taransay, the Flannans and the Shiants: 'Richness in
extremis: the definition of the Celtic church.'

Among the first, or possibly the second, generation of Welsh missionary saints to arrive on Enlli at the start of the sixth century was
Cadfan, who travelled from Brittany with twenty-five 'brothers' to
become the island's first abbot. His successor, Lleuddad, was said on
his deathbed to have decreed that islanders would die in order of
seniority, and that the soul of anyone buried on the island would
be saved. The sixth-century Welsh saints Deiniol and Dyfrig were
thought to be buried there, and Dyfrig's remains were exhumed as
holy relics for a new cathedral established at Llandaff near Cardiff
in 1120. Bishop Urban of Llandaff was an ambitious propagandist.
His *Book of Llandaff,* which sought to demonstrate the antiquity of
his new religious enterprise, was a 'clever forgery', writes the Bardsey
historian Mary Chitty.

I'm disturbed from my beach reading by a seal clearing its throat and unleashing the kind of vibrating brrrr that we make with our lips when we're cold. There's a lot of heavy breathing from my fellow beachgoers as they shift between rock and sea like bored sunbathers. Sitting here on my rock, I think of Elgar the Hermit, one of the most remarkable islanders to appear in Bishop Urban's *Book of Llandaff.* Unlike the saints in standard hagiographies, Elgar performs no miracles and the status of his parents is not mentioned, which makes his story all the more convincing. Born in Devon in the eleventh century, he was kidnapped as a child and taken to Ireland, where he became a slave to the King. He was forced to act as the King's executioner, and lived in fear of his own life until one day he fled Ireland on a boat. He vowed to do penance for those he had killed and, shipwrecked on Enlli, became a hermit. 'His was a life holy, glorious, chaste, with very little bread, threadbare clothing and a lean face,' said the *Book of Llandaff.* Elgar lived with a religious community and then alone for seven years, dependent on food bequeathed by the sea or brought by 'eagles' – it's for us to decide whether these were angels or real sea eagles dropping their prey. Elgar became famous when Caradog, a hermit and harpist from South Wales, visited him and 'found the servant of God living although lean'. Elgar told Caradog how the spirits of those buried on the island appeared to him in bodily form, especially Dyfrig and Deiniol: 'They always tell one what is true, and always promise what is right.' Helpfully, they also told Elgar where to find food: raw fish, herbs, water and, once, the body of a deer (which could have been washed across the Sound from Llŷn). Caradog urged Elgar to return with him to the mainland, but Elgar resisted; he later prepared his own grave in his oratory, then lay beside it to die. In 1120, alongside the exhumed body of Dyfrig, six or seven of Elgar's teeth were dug up and taken away for the glory of Bishop Urban.

The Book of Llandaff hailed Enlli for its fertile pasture, 'sweet flowing springs' and 'sea shore full of dolphins but free from any snake or frog', which was all true. But a rather outrageous claim is the one we have remembered: that twenty thousand saints, martyrs and confessors are buried on the island. A belief that anyone who died here would not suffer in hell encouraged 'coffin ships' to ply a brisk trade from Pwllheli and Barmouth. This saintly reputation lured even the conqueror of Wales, Edward I, who visited in twenty boats laden with wine to dispense as alms to the island. Enlli's moment as the nation's capital lasted for two days in 1284, when the government of England and Wales was administered from the island by Edward's entourage: his Queen, his chancellor and perhaps a hundred clerks, secretaries, grooms and other flunkeys, who lived there in tents. Two boys were paid fourpence for two days' work clearing nettles and gorse in preparation for their arrival.

The image of twenty thousand saints stuck because, like any good propaganda, it bore some relation to reality. Enlli was not known for its healing powers, but it was a place of spiritual cleansing, and nicely aligned with the older pagan view that we pass beyond this world over the western horizon. The word *sant* in Welsh means 'holy man' and not necessarily a saint, and over five centuries countless pilgrims and monks must have been buried on the island. In 1964, an eighty-six-year-old islander Tomos Jones remembered exposing 'many skulls and bones' when they ploughed the fields. Victorian builders, too, reported an 'incredible' quantity of human bones dug up during the construction of a new barn. I jump when I read its name: Llofft Nant, where I'm staying. My humble sleeping quarters are built over a cemetery of saints.

That night, Llofft Nant is extremely dark, but I enjoy the most peaceful, untroubled night's sleep I've had for months. The swallow family are chattering under the eaves as I wake, shortly before the sun appears over the mountain, at 9 a.m. This island does not rise early. A sheep coughs, and two ravens croak their way over. Water sluices against the rocks and from beyond comes the white noise of a great tide race. It runs from the north at 9 knots on the flow, still water meeting choppy water with a wiggly scribble on the surface of the sea. I wouldn't want to be tossed into this battle.

I climb Mynydd Enlli through a patchwork of heather, western gorse and European gorse, which is larger and has spread virulently since its introduction in Victorian times. I'm amazed to reach the top in fifteen minutes – once again, objects on small islands are always closer than they appear – and yet it still feels a significant peak, rising directly from a flat sea: a double impact of space and grandeur. I have three sheep and hundreds of flying ants for company. Silver Y moths and faded summer butterflies enjoy the sunshine; graylings, peacocks, a red admiral and a small tortoiseshell, circling the top of the mountain in a proprietary fashion.

R.S. Thomas wrote of waiting for a God who never came. Enlli is the reason the great Welsh poet of doubting faith ended up living at the end of Llŷn Peninsula. He first visited the island in 1953 on a secular pilgrimage to see its newly opened bird observatory. In the Middle Ages, three pilgrimages to Bardsey equalled one to Rome. Thomas said it should be the other way round, after two hazardous crossings nearly ended with his boat sinking.

Enlli's permanent religious community had been crushed centuries before by Henry VIII's dissolution of the monasteries. Legal documents from the time paint a picture of dereliction: it had 'no pasture, arable or meadow ground' after the monks' neat farms were destroyed by 'the great plenty' of rabbits – some four thousand. The island experienced centuries of piracy, private ownership and population slumps, all too characteristic of peripheral places. The island's rabbit population eventually declined too, dying out in 1996, but an unexpected human figure emerged once again: the noble hermit.

In November 1957, a meeting between two strangers in London set in train the re-establishment of hermetic life on Ynys Enlli. Mother Mary Clare was travelling to a convent at Burwash when she stopped off at Waterloo Station to meet, at the suggestion of friends, Father Gilbert Shaw, an elderly priest who worked in the slums of the East End. The pair found themselves talking intensely, for four hours, about the contemplative life. Father Gilbert had read of the desert fathers; Mother Mary Clare had felt during the Blitz in Cardiff that the only answer to evil was prayer. Both recognised that some people require solitude to attain a spiritual life, and could better serve humankind that way. Father Gilbert began providing retreats for the nuns of Mother Mary Clare's community, the Sisters of the Love of God, who were based at Fairacres, a rambling house in Oxford. He eventually became the warden there and was convinced, even as the communities of nuns and monks dwindled, that the contemplative life would grow. A visiting speaker, Father Derwas Chitty, who retired to the Llŷn Peninsula in 1968, believed that Ynys Enlli was the perfect place to pursue it. 'The island of hermits,' he called it. 'The island of solitude where one is least alone.'

The first solitude-seeking nun, Sister Helen Mary, thigh-length green waders under her voluminous habit, moved from Fairacres to Enlli in 1969. Born in Hastings, she had studied music in Vienna in the late 1930s, where before escaping back to Britain she witnessed the ill-treatment of Jewish women. She later taught at a school in South Africa, but felt called to an increasingly contemplative religious life.

At first, she spent summers in my barn, Llofft Nant, and returned to the mainland in winter. Then she found there were too many tourists wandering by Llofft Nant, which overlooks the ruined tower of the abbey, and so relocated to the old barns where I met Sister Rosalind Mary. Here, Sister Helen Mary established the tiny oratory. She called it Carreg Pig Kitchen, because that's what it had been. For eighteen months she had the support of Father Chitty, who urged her to read more about the lives of John the Prophet and other desert fathers. 'Get to know them as your friends,' he told her. When he read their sayings 'his face shone', she remembered: 'He knew them intimately, as individuals whose states of soul were open to him.' When her mainland mentor died suddenly in 1971, Sister Helen Mary travelled deeper into the solitary life, living without electricity, central heating or money, prising up the cobbles in her yard to grow potatoes, greens and soft fruit.

She would rise at dawn to think and meditate, wearing a blue long-sleeved 'morning dress' for domestic chores and a brown habit later in the day. She used an old pram to gather wood in and collected a dogfish from local fishermen every Friday, when she was permitted to eat fish. A saying of the desert fathers was 'Go and sit in your cell – your cell will teach you all things', and she would sometimes sleep in her little oratory, burning gorse on a stove to keep warm. Island-ers would see her out most days, in all weathers, creeping as close to the sea as she dared, to say her prayers. They believed she sometimes slept in a cave by the shore. Father Gilbert Shaw said, rather beauti-fully, that the work of a solitary was to stand 'holding things without being deflected by your own desires or those of other people'. Sister Helen Mary read widely in French, German and English, including the writings of Abhishiktananda – a French monk, Henri le Saux, who had established a place of prayer and meditation in India – and *Revelations of Divine Love* by the medieval mystic Julian of Norwich.

During her first years on the island, Sister Helen Mary sought strict silence and avoided conversation with islanders. But she would take the boat off the island to see colleagues, nuns from her convent who had settled on the peninsula. Sister Winifred lived there in a caravan, protected her habit with a veil and a green raincoat, and made tapes-try mats. Oblate Sister Anita, a refugee from Nazi Germany, saw the revival of the hermitic life as one answer to the horrors of Auschwitz. Sister Teresa knitted clothes for a local shop; she was given permis-sion to wear trousers and to keep a cat, named Sundar ('beautiful' in Hindi). Colleagues considered her 'a rebel and an individualist who

did not fit into community life'. The Enlli poet Christine Evans remembers Sister Teresa as 'a bonny country woman who loved to chat
and loved birds and the natural world'. Each year, Mother Mary Clare
would travel from Oxford to meet her sisters, and they would all
enjoy a picnic together. 'We sat for hours on the headland, contem-
plating Bardsey Island in comfortable silence,' recorded Oblate Sister
Evelyn Christina. Later, they enjoyed 'a very gay dinner and evening'.

The ascetic life led by Sister Helen Mary was driven by the belief that
disciplining body and mind, removing all things that distract the soul
from God, leads to clearer thought and a greater sensitivity to the
world and its people. But the islanders of Enlli offer a different view
of their resident hermit.

I'm picking curly kale from the splendid vegetable garden created
by Jo Porter, one-half of the island's farming team, when I first
spy Christine Evans over the wall. I recognise Christine from the
photograph in her excellent guidebook to Ynys Enlli. I tell her about
my island mission, and within minutes I'm sipping tea in her kitchen,
walking boots still on (there is no boots-off policy on small islands).

Christine was holidaying on Enlli as a young Yorkshire woman
when she met the islander Ernest Evans. They married and settled on
Llŷn Peninsula and the island, where they live in the summer months.
It takes me a moment to realise that Colin, the boatman, is their
son. R.S. Thomas was an admirer of Christine's poems, which express
with great subtlety the beauty of Ynys Enlli. Christine is an unusual
blend of poetic sensibility and complete lack of pretension. One of
the gadfly wives of the aristocratic Newborough family established a
tradition of anointing a local islander as 'King'; for me, Christine is
the modern-day heir, a modest island matriarch who seems to know
everything about everyone who has ever lived here.

We talk about the lighthouse which, like many now, stands dark,
unrequired in the era of GPS. It used to be Christine's torch at

night. 'You went for a walk and you'd just wait until the beam came sweeping around again.' Ernest enters the room and I ask them both about Sister Helen Mary. The Revd Donald Allchin, a theologian and warden of the Sisters of the Love of God in the late 1960s and early 70s, 'had this idea that Llŷn was extremely welcoming for solitaries', says Christine. 'We were just polite really. We'd had enough of them in the end. They are like twitchers – they are extremely focused on what they want. If they decide God wants them to get a lift into Pwllheli, they'll be standing in the middle of the road. They were very demanding. They only ever came to your door with a basket' – when they wanted something.

Taking a vow of solitude may seem easier on a small island, but it actually jars more with island life than with city life. 'How did Sister Helen Mary fit in?' asks Ernest, rhetorically. 'She didn't fit in. She was an outsider.' Islanders did not exactly feel the beneficence of her prayers; they saw an upper-middle-class woman blanking them each day. 'She used to ignore you when you went past on the track and yet when she wanted something she'd be down here knocking on your door,' says Ernest. 'If you want to be like that, go and live in the city. You can't be like that on an island.'

The nun's life of solitary prayer was not simply dependent on the support of her religious community. She had foisted herself upon an island that was now compelled to bear this burden, whether they welcomed it or not. Residents worried about her, too. 'She hated the idea of being looked after, but they felt responsible for her,' says Christine. 'If they went to check on her she'd be quite cross.' Helplessness together with forcefulness is not a popular combination, but the islanders continued to look out for her. As Sister Helen Mary grew older, locals persuaded her to hang a tea-towel on her gate each morning so they knew she was alive and well.

On one occasion, the nun was required to attend 'a conference of hermits' in Europe. Recalling this makes Christine laugh. 'She was first on the boat, even scrambling over sacks of lobsters to make sure she got aboard because God had told her to go.' Later, Sister Helen Mary requested a radio so she could pray about current affairs. 'I am here praying, I am keeping the lamp burning,' she once said. Christine has a different version. 'There was a great earthquake in Peru and I remember her coming down and saying "Can you tell me what the news is?"' When Christine told her, 'she was full of glee. She clasped her hands together and said, "I must go and pray for them."' After that, the nun got a radio so she could keep abreast of the latest disasters.

For the last century at least, every small British isle has been drawn into the cash economy. How did a hermit buy a radio? Sister Helen Mary had been a wealthy woman; she had handed over her family money to Fairacres when she joined, as is typical in such communities. The Sisters of the Love of God provided her with a small allowance, but she routinely returned hers because the Bardsey Island Trust allowed her to stay rent-free. Sympathetic visitors also left boxes of food with Christine and Ernest for her. They would write 'By kindness' on the label. 'It did get a bit much,' says Christine. The other nuns living alone on Llŷn became 'very spiteful' about Sister Helen Mary, according to Christine, because when she returned her allowance, Fairacres would ask the other solitaries why they required more money for their bus tickets and electricity and gas bills.

I can't help but smile at the idea of bitching solitaries; but such earthly foibles do not seem typical of the contemplative life. In later years, Christine feels, Sister Helen Mary 'mellowed a bit' and participated – a little – in island life. Once, when Christine heard that she used to teach the piano, she asked her if she missed music. 'She said, "Oh no, I'm surrounded by the sounds of nature."' The now elderly nun would ask if she could help Enlli's farmers, and she'd be told to pull the docks out of the hay, a thankless task which she would do in the heat of the day. Donald Allchin sensed that Sister Helen Mary 'grew into a great sense of discernment and liberty of spirit – it was beautiful to see it growing'. She became more willing to speak to visitors, and share her experiences of a life of prayer.

One day in the late 1980s, the nun fell ill and had to be airlifted off the island. Her community was increasingly worried about her but she was determined to return. 'I am quite well again and have been very glad to get back,' she wrote in a letter. 'I realise the need to enter more, even, than before into the silence and solitude here.'

Sceptics of solitary island dwellers such as D.H. Lawrence might question how much of this 'need' is really serving others and how much is the personal preference and individual egotism of the 'I-lander'. I guess the two are intimately entwined. Clearly, there are different kinds of I-lander, for Compton Mackenzie never really came close to fulfilling the prophecy of 'The Man Who Loved Islands'. He converted to Catholicism as a young man, when he also dallied with becoming a priest, but thereafter his faith was an unobtrusive part of his existence. There was no way he could have lived a solitary life, turned in on himself; he needed a nurturing secretary and a small community around him, an audience with whom he could face outwards. This was a man who had once opined gratefully that, on an island, 'the individual is not overwhelmed by his own unimportance'. Small islands enabled Monty to feel large.

By contrast, Father Gilbert Shaw described religious life as 'the process of self-stripping, that battle with oneself which St Anthony had known in the desert'. Sister Helen Mary certainly felt that the actual island itself supported her own struggle, however solipsistic or altruistic that might be. Enlli's spiritual fecundity was 'available to every contemplative soul', she wrote, 'a living reality, original, creative . . . hidden within the silence that clothes and speaks to the listening spirit'.

After she fell ill and was airlifted from the island to hospital for a second time, her community insisted that she return to the mainland. She died in 1992. Much later, Christine found her will in a box of letters. 'She hoped to die on Bardsey, but if she didn't she hoped to be buried here or have her ashes scattered here,' she says. Sister Helen Mary is buried in Oxford. I feel sad for her. No matter how dissident in life, an individual is at the mercy of the wishes of wider society in death.

No hermit has overwintered on Enlli since Sister Helen Mary died, but several hundred people have undertaken retreats. Various vicars and nuns stay in her loft for shorter periods, such as Sister Rosalind Mary who, typically, stays for a week in the summer as a visiting chaplain, providing services for the island as well as undertaking a more personal retreat. Several temporary chaplains have left short prayers in the oratory, where a booklet produced by the island's 'Spirituality Committee' explains how people have found Enlli a 'thin place', where the curtain between heaven and earth seems almost transparent. This is an echo of George MacLeod's description of Iona after he refounded a holy community there in 1938.

The busiest person on the island, Jo Porter, is also the driving force behind the Spirituality Committee, as well as the one who made the attractive woollen wall-hangings and cushions in the oratory. I hope to talk to her about it, but this proves harder than it sounds. Jo, a neat, slim, slightly hippyish-looking woman, is like the tiny wind turbine that whirrs in her garden. I bump into her at different times serving tea to a dozen day trippers ('daysies' – I'm a 'staysie') minding the shop filled with baskets and sheep's-wool hangings and slippers that she makes in the winter; mowing grass; checking on the sheep; tending her allotment, which provides family and visitors with vegetables all year round; or out roaming, monitoring the island's precious maritime heath and the chough habitat for the RSPB.

'There's a seasonal rhythm, which I like,' she says when I finally persuade her to pause for a cup of tea. 'It's really busy in the summer and quiet in the winter. In the quietness of the winter I do the more creative stuff – weave baskets and rugs and do the felting.' During rough winters, Jo and her husband Steve go a fortnight without a parcel drop or a chance to get onto the mainland. In the summer, their house is open more or less all hours to curious visitors, such as me. A small island compels its residents to be both gregarious and solitary. 'I couldn't live here all the time. By the end of the summer, I'm ready for the winter. By the end of the winter, I'm really ready to see people.'

And what of Enlli's spiritual qualities? It feels as though Jo takes a deep breath; like most people, I guess she's more comfortable talking about kale or choughs than Christianity. Eight years ago, she and Steve (paragliding in Spain when I visit) and their teenage children Rachel and Ben (about to head off to university) applied for the job of looking after the island farm, and moved from their home in Conwy. 'It's part of a call,' says Jo. 'Coming here is more than vocational, it felt like the right thing to do as Christians. It's what God wants us to do. We try to get away from dividing the spiritual from the vocational – work and prayer go hand in hand. It's not so much being in the chapel, it's just part of how we live.'

She found that the oratory had been neglected, and turned it into a well-loved little room. 'I felt it was right to have a space that was set aside for prayer, from Sister Helen Mary's days. A lot of people don't like the chapel but feel at home in the oratory. It's more of an unoffi-cial space,' she says. She holds 'informal and contemplative' 'Pilgrim Prayers' twice a week. Sometimes nobody comes; once, twenty people spilled out from the oratory into the courtyard. Jo finds that a growing number of spiritual seekers are finding their way to Ynys Enlli. She keeps a special rubber stamp in the shop, so pilgrims undertaking the North Wales Pilgrims' Way can record their visit. 'Many people who come here on holiday are still retreating from mainland life, and many have deeper questions and find this is a place to unravel things or find new directions or voice questions. Many people, even if they are not looking for it, have had encounters with something beyond them. Many people would say that's Jesus or God. It's a spiritual experience.'

Our modern, rather romantic interpretation of Celtic Christianity has its critics, but many of Jo's contemplative practices come from that period. 'It's a well that we're still drinking from,' she says. She believes the established Church often takes good care of the container, but loses sight of the contents. For spirituality to be alive, she says, it has to be more than going to meetings; on Enlli, this means incorporating prayer into daily life and following her calling, as an ecologist, to care for creation.

I struggle to ask if the island has a particular power, a kind of benevolent haunting from all the devout people who have made pilgrimage here, and Jo instantly understands. 'It's definitely a prayed-in place and you sense that. There's a similar feel on Iona, there's a sense of wholeness and ease in prayer and a peace that's beyond quiet. People put names to it like "the thin place" and I would definitely say it's a thin place.'

Shortly before I leave, I bump into the boatman Colin Evans, down by the harbour with a trailer-load of what appear to be bizarrely enormous batteries. They are exactly what they appear: huge backup batteries for the lighthouse, which Colin has maintained for years. He's moving them so that the Bardsey Island Trust can better store its solar-panel power. Although Colin works on the island tirelessly, he lives on the mainland with his wife and young children, and he's in the mood to talk. 'It's a great sadness to me that the island has lost its work ethic. It's all conservation. That's absolutely unsustainable,' he says, his words flowing forth like a sermon. 'These young men walk around the island and count the birds and they think they are doing a great thing. That's a hobby. Conservation as a philosophy is not just about wildlife, it's about culture and language and respect.' He feels that the disappearance of traditional farming, which has provided produce, incomes and jobs for the island, has been a sad loss. How could the island be managed better? 'It doesn't need to be managed, it evolves because of the changing nature of society. If you don't have development, what have you got – a museum? I'm very keen on sustainable development and I'm very keen on work. What the island produces in terms of fish and meat, it's the only thing we've got left, and both of these things have been very devalued. So we're stuck with tourism and this industry of conservation, which depends on rules and subsidies from elsewhere, which immediately makes the island dependent. The real conservationists are us. We've got our hands in the soil or the ocean to make a living, and we're vilified because we're "exploiting" the environment. Everybody else does as well, but they buy their halloumi from a supermarket where you can't *see* it is actually produced by people who exploit the land. How can we kick-start the island into how it once was, economically independent and proud?'

I feel humbled because I haven't hitherto recognised how wildlife conservation can undermine the independence of a small island as much as our global economic system does, of which it is part. I feel sad that Colin sees tourism as degrading – 'I suppose it can be a modern expression of a pilgrimage in a way,' he says reluctantly – but his words very precisely skewer holiday islands such as Tresco, where mass tourism causes a kind of annihilation and the island becomes a parody of itself. As Colin says: 'It's very hard to sell what we're selling and not have pieces of it taken away.'

'You're very aware of the other lives, the natural lives, and things seem to be in balance very well,' says Colin's mum Christine, of life on Enlli. She believes its power derives from the way it orientates each islander in perpetual contemplation of the westerly horizon. 'You only have to imagine the island facing the other direction and it wouldn't be anything,' she says, impressively brusquely.

Dancing around the fuchsia, the bees fill their bags with pollen and the air with their humming, a pair of stonechats bounce along the bramble-topped hedge, and Jo's son Ben tells me he's just seen a little owl, a 'furious gargoyle' as R.S. Thomas wrote, 'that is like a god gone small and resentful'.

Shafts of sunlight break through the cloud, turning patches of sea into pools of white gold. Rays like lighthouse beams point down to Earth. They resemble those adverts – 'It could be you.' This may be a clichéd image of spiritual transcendence, but the sun breaking through the clouds in the western sky over Ynys Enlli is a never-to-be-repeated transposition of light and colour, a completely original moment. Later, I watch a spectacular sunset. The red sun illuminates the horizon like a light above the threshold of a doorway. No great trail of pinky-orange leading over the dark water – just this, an illuminated doorway, beckoning us to a world beyond our own.

10

After the Party

Osea Island, Essex, 380 acres, permanent population 0

'The island was no longer a 'world'. It was a sort of refuge'
'The Man Who Loved Islands'

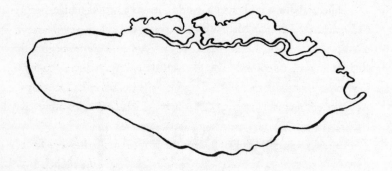

I swish through fields of waist-high cock's-foot and white campion, and squeeze between gaps in fat hedges of dying elm, blackberry and blackthorn. In the long grass of one field lies a discarded battery charger for a mobile phone. In another, a scrunched water bottle and Red Bull cans. There are bikes thrown down everywhere, Raleigh Chloes with chubby tyres for riding on gravel and sand. A tit chips its disapproval among the hawthorn berries as I climb a brambly sea bank and scramble onto an expanse of salt marsh.

The sea is a grey line on the horizon, and all is silent except for a gentle but strangely penetrating popping noise. Softer than rainfall, it seems to begin in the middle of my head. I glance around but can see no obvious source. Slippery green seaweed feels like a wet plastic bag and there's a fine unpicked harvest of samphire, more than I have ever seen, thick juicy limbs with joints like the creases on a baby's arm. Eventually, I trace a pop to a bubble that emerges from the purple mud and expires, followed by another, and another. The salt marsh is slowly exhaling, popping, the tide on the ebb.

I left my family and friends unpacking in the Captain's House to slowly circumnavigate this autumnal isle of abandonment. Under a canopy of adolescent oaks, I find a ruined, mildewed boat and an old campfire. I jump: there's a skin-headed man on his knees. He's motionless. I look again. He's actually a rubbery head and pink torso, designed to be punched hard in a gym. He's wearing a T-shirt that says 'Staff'.

Unsettled, I force my way through an overgrown blackthorn thicket and descend a concrete ramp, slippery with moss. It looks like an old wartime installation, but there are three relatively new ship containers, painted a discrete olive green. Their doors hang open. Inside is a mountain of old sports bags, keyboards, records, drums, amps, cables and defunct recording equipment. There are music books, boxes of old master tapes and paper-filled filing-cabinet drawers dumped on their backs. There must be a fortune squandered here in the damp. Resting on the floor is a frame containing a discoloured gold disc: 'Presented to Matrix Studios to recognise sales in the UK of more than 400,000 copies of the Go! Discs single, Dub Be Good to Me, 1990'. What a classic song. Plenty of people would want it on their wall. And here it is, being enjoyed by the mildew.

The Blackwater, a great salty estuary carved into the soft, low coast of Essex, is a generous creator of small islands. Mersea is the biggest, with a population of 8,000 who bustle fairly freely between home and mainland via a causeway that is covered only by the highest tides. Northey is much smaller, a few eroding fields and salt marsh, two houses and thousands of wild geese. Like so many islands, it was once owned by a notable idealist. As a young journalist based in Paris in the 1890s, Norman Angell reported on the case of Alfred Dreyfus, a French-Jewish military officer wrongly accused of treason. Dreyfus's incarceration on Devil's Island in French Guiana didn't deter Angell from imagining he might find peace on an island, and he bought Northey in 1923 and made his home there. Ten years later his work for the League of Nations earned him the Nobel Peace Prize.

Smaller still is Ray Island, a barely discernible whisper of hawthorn and blackthorn between Mersea and the mainland. And then there is Osea, a satisfying 380-acre oval five metres above sea level, with fertile fields, a small village and a private causeway of a mile and a quarter over which the tide draws back like a deferential butler to permit visitors for four hours in every twelve. Ninety minutes from London, or less via a small plane, Osea is a perfectly positioned object of desire for a wealthy individual who loves islands.

Before we encountered the unexpected drama of the causeway, a twisty single track exposed at low tide across the muddy channel between mainland and island, I had only viewed Osea from afar. I'd watched this moated fortress of dark trees from Northey. I'd also seen it glint in glossy magazines. Its scandalous past and intriguing present made it the most glamorous forbidden place I could aspire to exploring. 'The secret island where the A-list go to drink, strip off and party all night,' gasped the *Daily Mail* in 2013, painting a picture – aided by a couple of Instagram snaps – of a London crowd of 'fast-living' actors, musicians, socialites and supermodels retreating to the privacy of the island for hedonistic weekends. The names belong to the 2010s – Poppy Delevingne, Jaime Winstone, Tyrone Wood, Sienna Miller – but their story was that of every coterie of bright young things from every decade since the 1920s, with a dowdy audience – us – agape and envious, forever excluded from this sea-girt sanctuary by birth, breeding, money or temperament.

Paparazzi lenses cannot penetrate Osea. It is unequivocally private. The causeway is down a narrow private road through a modest holiday park of empty caravans and thick Leylandii hedges. Beyond a locked gate with coded entry is a long track leading over the sea bank and onto the causeway, once known as 'the hard'. This does not appear very hard, a twisting route over the mud, marked by small rocks with toupees of dark seaweed and tall sticks bent like fishing rods. These identify the causeway for boats at high water. During our crossing, a curlew stalks across the mud, unconcerned by our car; an oystercatcher calls and then, with a little spin of wheels, we're across a gravelly nicotine-coloured beach and onto solid ground. 'Osea – strictly private,' says one sign. 'Private,' says another. And another.

Five years before our arrival, a writer, Peter Caton, was unceremoniously ejected after he ignored these private signs. He was researching his book, *No Boat Required*, which is a tour of Britain's tidal islands, and was ordered off Osea by an officious islander who wouldn't answer his innocent questions or reveal anything about the business of Osea's Manor House, a fine Edwardian pile overlooking a small beach. Caton subsequently discovered it was the Causeway Retreat, an expensive private clinic for the treatment of drug and alcohol addictions and psychiatric disorders. It advertised helicopter transfers to the island (twenty minutes from London) and facilities including a gym, a recording studio, a cinema, a library and a two-hundred-year-old billiard table. 'Guests' included Amy Winehouse and Count Gottfried von Bismarck, the great-great-grandson of Germany's Iron Chancellor. Both have since died. Caton's wanderings clearly compromised the Causeway's security, but there was something oddly unprofessional about the paranoid reaction he encountered. Not long afterwards, the Causeway was prosecuted by the Care Quality Commission for breaching the Care Standards Act. A judge described the company running it as an 'atrocious organisation' and 'scandalously negligent, if not downright misleading and fraudulent', with standards that would 'shame a Third World country'. The Causeway Retreat was shut down.

This scandal must have felt like a recurring dream to Osea. Islands may inspire idealists but they also attract 'men of pleasure', as Daniel Defoe described the Londoners drawn to Osey, Osyth or Oosy Island in the 1720s, to shoot its 'infinite number of wild fowl'. Osea's idealistic moment came in 1903 when Frederick Charrington, heir to the London brewery company and a fortune of more than £1 million, bought the island. Thirty-three years earlier in Whitechapel, the nineteen-year-old Frederick had observed an ill-dressed woman clutching her children and beseeching her husband to come away from a pub. She needed money for food. The husband, enraged, knocked her into the gutter. Frederick went to help and was also punched to the ground. Dazed, he looked up and saw his surname on the sign above the pub. 'When I saw that sign, I was stricken just as surely as Paul on the Damascus Road,' he wrote. 'Here was the source of my family wealth, and it was producing untold misery before my own eyes.'

He vowed not to receive another penny from his family business and joined the Temperance Movement, opening a school and campaigning to 'clean up' boozy music halls in the East End. In a hagiography by a popular writer called Guy Thorne, Frederick was hailed as 'the most self-sacrificing and practical philanthropist of his day'. After three decades helping the poor, this 'kindliest, quietest, most gentle-spoken of men' decided to create a unique sanctuary, a holiday resort, a better world, a Temperance Island: Osea.

His vision was not an island hospital for alcoholics, but a peaceful resort where yachtsmen and nature-lovers could build their own holiday cottages, providing they signed a 'non-intoxicant' clause and vowed not to bring drink to the island. Frederick outlined Osea's charms to *Household Words*, the weekly magazine once edited by Dickens. It would be a 'perfect' retreat for those who required the removal of all temptations, not a prison but 'picturesque' mock-Tudor cottages – room for ten thousand homes, if required – arranged along double avenues of high elms, 'like Chicago'. Frederick purchased a steamer to run twice daily from Maldon railway station to Osea. The more sceptical-sounding *Spectator* reported that Frederick's project sought to determine whether abstinence reduced energy and whether teetotallers took to opium instead, but *Household Words* was won over: 'To be able to enjoy life on an island within forty miles of the metropolis, including sea-bathing, fishing and shooting, has the wonderful charm of novelty, to say nothing of its freedom from the pandemonium created by drinking trippers.'

By 1913, it appeared that Frederick's dream was realised. Osea was described in idyllic terms by his biographer Guy Thorne. Seats had been built around the trunks of ancient elms beside 'an old, flower-covered cottage', and a village shop 'where every necessary' – except booze – could be obtained. A convalescent home was nearly finished and there were billiards, badminton and roller-skating. A menagerie contained seals, kangaroos and black swans. At the Manor House, also built by Frederick, Thorne dined with 'members of the upper classes who have fallen into the drink habit', including eight from famous public schools and four from 'the great Universities'. Rather coyly, Thorne, also known by his pen-name Ranger Gull, didn't mention that it was a much-needed retreat for him too: when he lodged at another favoured bolt-hole near Land's End, he drank a bottle of whisky each day and was 'very bad' until he started on his next.

The fact that Frederick hadn't completed his convalescent home on Osea ten years after buying the island might betray that all was not as perfect as Thorne described. In reality, Frederick Charrington simply could not police the boundaries of his alcohol-free ideal world. Booze poured into Osea. Beer and spirits were routinely smuggled in to island 'patients' in a small boat from the Chequers Inn at the village of Goldhanger on the mainland. For easy retrieval, bottles were tied to a navigation buoy close to shore so frequently that it became slyly known as 'the doctor's buoy'. Osea was requisitioned by the Navy in 1917. The island's hotel manager, a former curate, died of alcoholism in 1924. Charrington eventually sold up.

One day in the mid-1960s Michael Cole, a young man the papers called a 'genius inventor', threw a newspaper article about the auction of Osea Island onto the desk of his brother David. The Cole siblings were pioneers in Cambridge's science industry, bright graduates who used their mastery of solid-state physics to devise laboratory instruments for high-tech companies.

On a warm summer's day not long afterwards, David motored over to Osea. 'I was driving across the causeway and there was an easterly wind,' he remembers. 'The smell of the causeway was wonderful – ozone, rotting seaweed, fish, oysters. A marvellous salty tang. I thought, God, I would like to live here for the rest of my life.'

I meet David in his graceful home, the oldest house on Mersea Island, seven miles as the gull glides from his great passion, Osea. David is eighty-three but looks just as sturdy and vital as he does in sepia shots of his schoolboy rowing team from the 1940s, which hang in his toilet. He is also a marvellous raconteur.

Osea has had more than its fair share of slightly unhinged men who loved islands, and David tells me about his predecessor, Major Alfred Allnatt. In the early 1920s, Old Bill, as his family and close colleagues called him, won a contract to feed and house labourers building the British Empire Exhibition, to be staged in 1924 (it also gave us the first Wembley Stadium). Major Allnatt leased fields in North Acton, London, for the contract, and by chance befriended a bank manager who ran a junior football team, which also played on the fields. The bank manager arranged a massive loan for Allnatt to buy the fields and turn them into an industrial estate. Old Bill became a billionaire in today's money.

He was shy of the spotlight, but he was not shy of spending his fortune. He too was an idealist and philanthropist: he dispatched 26,000 boxes of fruit jellies to almshouses each Christmas, and donated Rubens's *Adoration of the Magi* to King's College, Cambridge, in 1961. In a story reminiscent of Compton Mackenzie's loyal staff bidding for the Shiants, Allnatt obtained the painting when his PA Sylvia Saunders instructed the dealer at the Rubens auction to bid a much higher – world-record, in the event – figure than her boss had authorised. Saunders's typical duties included buying a shop to which

Allnatt had taken a fancy and playing bridge with him all night. He must have rewarded her handsomely because she was a wealthy woman by the time she retired.

Major Allnatt enjoyed his money too, buying racehorses and a colossal 101-carat yellow diamond now known as 'the Allnatt diamond', which fetched more than $3 million when it was sold by Christie's in Geneva in 1996. He also bought Osea. A short history of the charitable foundation he established tactfully describes Old Bill as an 'eccentric in a wonderfully English kind of way' who 'enjoyed a certain devilment'. He founded the Society for the Promotion of Old English Pastimes, and each year held a week-long 'Conventical' on his island. Employees were 'expected' to attend. According to the charitable foundation's official history, 'guests' had to take part in events ranging from tractor slaloms to mud-walloping, which entailed business associates digging in the mud at low tide in a frantic search for ping-pong balls.

David Cole has the unofficial version of events. After he bought Osea from Allnatt's executors, he found 'examination papers' that Allnatt had set for his guests, who had to dress as schoolchildren, sit in tiny chairs and take a general-knowledge test. Allnatt was the invigilator. He wanted to humiliate them by showing his cultural superiority, thinks Cole. 'He was a serious sadist. Mostly it was mental torture.' After a heavy dinner well-fuelled by Edwardian-vintage burgundies, Allnatt would force his guest-employees to strip off and swim round the pier. They did it, believes Cole, because they were getting such big bonuses. It reminds him of Graham Greene's novel about one fabulously wealthy Dr Fischer, who holds lavish dinner parties and elaborate games that tempt and humiliate the greedy. The cruellest of Allnatt's invented sports was revealed by the wife of Osea's farm manager, who David took on after the Allnatt era: staff had to run a relay race through the island's gorse and nettles in their underwear, while the Major pursued them brandishing an electric pig prodder.

'They were appalling stories,' says David, 'and I'm certain they were true because you couldn't make them up.'

After Allnatt died, David and Michael Cole bought Osea for a bargain £74,000. They took on the farm manager and his wife and a tractor driver and his wife, sought advice from the Ministry of Agriculture about modern high-yielding wheat crops, and began renovating its twenty-five houses. Some cottages hadn't been used since 1919; old jackets with letters in their pockets still hung inside. 'We restored the village completely,' says David. 'We didn't want it to look twee. We wanted it to look like a living, working place. There were always two or three families working on the island.'

David's wife, Hilary, and their two children stayed on Osea all summer, and David commuted to Cambridge in an Aztec, a fast American aeroplane. He built two grass airstrips on the island, 'quite short so you had to have a plane that would stop quickly'. It took seventeen minutes to get to work. Their thriving company opened an office in Paris; Osea was handy, says David, 'because I could go straight to Paris from there, just dropping in to Customs at Lydd'. One day he took off from Osea with Hilary and his younger son Adrian, then twelve, destined for the elegant French resort of Le Touquet. When the plane's passenger door swung open during takeoff, Adrian undid his seatbelt, climbed onto the wing of the small plane and pulled the door back in. Hilary, understandably, was 'hysterical', but they landed safely, fixed the door, and made it to Le Touquet in time for lunch.

David and Michael decided it would be fun to have a seaplane and were visited by a pilot–salesman, the Earl of Bective, whom David knew from school. 'The Earl Defective', as he calls him, landed in front of the Captain's House, David's villa overlooking the south shores of the island – where my friends and family were presently staying. The Earl's nickname came from an incident a few years earlier, in 1965, when he visited the Isles of Scilly while Harold Wilson was on holiday there. According to a waiter at the Atlantic Hotel on St Mary's, he was approached by Bective, who asked to be rowed out to the uninhabited island of Samson. The Earl grilled the waiter about his political views, told him he possessed a .38 revolver, and asked him to assassinate the prime minister. A fee of £5 was agreed, but the waiter became worried in the night and called the police. According to David's version of this story, the island's police officer thought it best not to disturb Lord Bective, but in the morning escorted him from Osea, telling him never to return. After a brief stay in hospital, the Earl was released; he denied the incident, and continued to serve in the House of Lords. Like so many whose lives briefly touched Osea, he later received treatment for alcoholism and manic depression, then retreated, sober, to a Philippine island where he married a friend of Imelda Marcos. His last speech to the Lords was in praise of Alcoholics Anonymous.

In the end, the Cole brothers resisted the Earl's sales pitch. They were rather preoccupied with their high-tech business after Michael learned how to grow single crystals of metal, a key advance in the electronics industry, and invented the Quantimet image-analysing computer, one of the most important laboratory instruments of the 1960s and 70s. They took over a rival business founded by Charles Darwin's son Horace, and their new venture, Cambridge Instruments, employed 1,800 people at an innovative campus-style HQ. Rather like today's dot-com entrepreneurs, they took on young graduates on big salaries and were feted for their progressive informality; there were no 'sirs' – from top to bottom of the company, all the employees used first names.

Unlike dot-coms their business was no bubble, but the Coles ran into trouble after the 1973 oil crisis caused a collapse in sales. Eventually, in 1977, David quit Cambridge Instruments and sold Osea to Cambridge University. In the mid-1980s, the university got in touch and asked if he was interested in buying back Osea. Hilary, 'a deadly negotiator', got it for a good price, and for nearly two decades the couple lived in the Captain's House. They sailed, watched birds and tended their island home. They planted several miles of hedgerows and six thousand trees, which were hard to establish because Osea is so dry and its ground-water slightly brackish, which means that many trees don't respond well to watering. They turned Osea's fields to grass for overwintering wild geese to feed on, and took on tenants, mostly bohemian middle-class families who sought a second home by the sea, including two concert pianists, a painter, a novelist, the former Labour MP Paul Boateng, and David Shayler, the former MI5 spy. 'A lot of kids were brought up there,' says David. 'It was a really happy place.'

One of his tenants was Nigel Frieda, the younger brother of the celebrity hairdresser, John Frieda. John and Nigel 'were very good-looking and both have a lot of charm', says David. Nigel ran the Matrix recording studios in Soho, where everyone from Adam Ant to the Smiths recorded, and later a business park in west London. 'I liked him. He was a pleasant guy. He always wanted to buy Osea but didn't have much money.' They eventually did a deal, and for a while David stayed on in the Captain's House. After Hilary died, however, his heart wasn't in it. 'I love it there. The birds are fantastic. I was very sad to leave, but I found living on Osea without her wasn't wonderful.'

After the Causeway Retreat shut, Nigel Frieda relaunched Osea as an upmarket holiday island and wedding venue for fashionable London-ers. I gain entry after persuading the *Guardian* that the island would make an interesting travel article, and Nigel's team agree to let my family and some friends stay in the Captain's House in early October. Passing those 'Private' signs encourages all my selfish private-island thoughts – This is mine, stay away! – as I glance back at the mainland's envious gaze. I have finally found the kind of perfectly propor-tioned small island that I can fantasise about possessing. Osea has a miniature civilisation, the village, at its core; a periphery of big hedges, grassy fields and young woodlands of oak, ash, maple and white poplars, planted by David and Hilary Cole; and a rougher exterior of blackthorn and bramble thickets. Wildest of all, the salt marsh with its mud, samphire and bushes of scratchy sea-blite. We can take this walk from civilised to wild on almost any small island, but the smaller the island, the quicker and more intense the walk.

We're met in the village by a friendly, skinny, exceedingly young-looking man with lots of tattoos, called Jonny, the site manager. Amazing place, I say. 'It's mad, isn't it?' replies Jonny. The village is a mix of single- and two-storey weatherboard cottages with low ceilings, sash windows and sweet names: Puffin Burrows, Honey Pot; and nicely furnished but cobwebby and closed up for the season. Jonny climbs into a Land Rover, spins down a narrow avenue of golden-leaved horse chestnuts, conkers spilling like chocolate jewels all over the gravel. We follow, he signals with his hand where we should park, and disappears around the corner. We never see him again. We're left alone to wander, the only guests on the whole island.

David Cole chose well. The Captain's House is a beautifully proportioned 1920s villa in the best position on Osea, high – well, three metres – on a little cliff facing south over the Blackwater. Nigel Frieda's designers have fashioned the interior in Old Colonial style, with black-and-white pictures of sailing boats on the walls and – now decorative – battered old suitcases with brass fittings. There are shelves of interesting books and old *National Geographic*s. I find a feature from July 1962 on Tahiti, the 'finest island in the world'. Paul Gauguin, a stockbroker better known as a painter, who abandoned Paris for Tahiti in 1891, is quoted: 'All the joys – animal and human – of a free life are mine. I have escaped everything that is artificial, conventional, customary. I am entering into the truth, into nature.' The manifesto for idealistic island hedonists ever since.

It is the season's end, after the party. Three days earlier, Osea must have hosted a big wedding. A trace of fun hangs in the air, like the name-tag of the previous guest, Carrie, still slung on our bedroom doorknob. Outside, a gazebo is surrounded by old confetti, and wedding chairs with padded seats are still stacked behind the house, getting wet in the autumn drizzle. Casually abandoned on the ground by a large shed-turned-nightclub are metal catering trays filled with leftover food from the wedding banquet. I remember David Cole mentioning there was once 'a massive infestation of rats' on the island.

We saunter along the southern edge of Osea to Frederick Charrington's three-storey Manor House, with its red-tiled roof and two little turrets at each end. The lights are on but no one is at home. According to rumour, Osea's annual electricity bill is £100,000.

Two hundred rooks call from the tall dark trees behind. On a grassy slope leading to a dinky shingle beach are white-painted wooden beach chairs, New England style, their paint beginning to peel. We lie back on them as if convalescing, wrapped in jackets, while the weakening autumn sun breaks through. Beyond the beach is the timber skeleton of a long-disappeared jetty.

Osea may appear dishevelled and yet, in the same breath, it is incredibly pure. A gulp of its air truly feels as if it contains twice as much sea-weedy, salty oxygen as standard. Frederick Charrington's biographer Guy Thorne breathed the same air. It is better on Osea than anywhere else, he pronounced, 'because of the "saltings". Just as the sea itself around the island is more salty than the sea of the free ocean owing to the deposits left upon the mud at low tide, so the air is more heavily charged with ozone.' Thorne recalled showing a yachting friend around Osea, who told him: 'I do not know Charrington, and he must be an odd sort of crank not to allow any drinks here. Still, I suppose he justifies himself upon the principle that his own private air is like champagne – it certainly is marvellous!'

We follow a track around to the village. There's a gym, lots of unlocked Raleigh Chloe bikes on racks – free for guests to use, and lose – and a locked office whose porch smells of weed. We go for an end-of-season dip in the outdoor pool and I find myself swimming alongside the drowned bodies of two mice and a pygmy shrew, the tiniest mammal in Britain. Then we mooch along to the games and cinema room, where we can sit in eleven seats (one has been ripped out) and play DVDs – *Napoleon Dynamite*, *About a Boy*, Hitchcock. Outside, an old red letterbox is sealed up but it still lists Osea's collection times: 'Mon–Fri: ACCORDING TO THE TIDE. Sat: ACCORDING TO THE TIDE. Bank holidays: ACCORDING TO THE TIDE'.

Not far from the real letterbox stands a fake one. It's inside a white-painted gazebo that stands by white-painted recliners overlooking a dark pond. 'This is a bit Gatsby, down here,' calls our friend Jen, cheerily. 'Where's my bullet to the head?'

I find that the door to the letterbox opens, and inside are unfranked envelopes with 'par avion' on them. I know I shouldn't, but I can't resist. I open a letter. It reads: 'Zero emotional baggage'. I picture the scene: group therapy by the foreboding pond, people writing down their problems and posting them, to shed them for ever. I open another. It contains a heartbreaking tally of personal failures and shortcomings. I feel bad for opening the letters, and sad. This island may have absorbed a lot of highs, but there have been lows too.

Circling back towards our house again, we find a walled garden with paths cut through long grass and trees bearing sharp, tasty little apples, rock-hard pears and rotten plums. I think of a poem by Robert Frost, in which he admired the orchards of New England and wished that some apples would always go 'unharvested'.

Lying in bed that night at the Captain's House is like being in a ship: all I can see through the windows to the south and west is water. At 11 p.m., a curlew calls on the muddy beach below. The next morning, the Blackwater is an elegant silver-green and the water looks lustrous, like good hair.

If Osea was a person she would be a great beauty, with a bad hangover. Take me or leave me, she would say with a shrug, not bothering what admirers made of her. I like this insouciance: this may be a holiday island, but it doesn't feel it is selling itself like the Scilly Isle of Tresco.

Wandering around Osea, so private and yet so nonchalantly open, makes us wonder about the people who have been here. Jen discovers that a friend of hers organised a ticketed party on Osea earlier in the summer. Buses brought people from east London. She gets out her phone and hunts down some photos on Facebook: dressed up, Osea shimmers, amazingly. A mirrorball hangs from a tree, there are clouds of smoke, raised hands, smiling people. 'It's just like a battered old party town,' says Jen, 'a place where you can be yourself.' Another friend, Jade, is reminded of her twenty-something days when she organised all-night parties. 'It feels like there's been a lot of intense madness here,' she says. 'It's like a playground for grownups. What do you want to do? Make your own fun. There's definitely been some fun had on this island.'

Eigg is also an island that appears to invite fun, but its hedonism is checked by the permanent residents, the parents and older inhabitants who must live through the mornings after. These islanders are also acutely aware of their pristine environment. On Osea there are no long-staying residents, and no such restraint. Just as deliberately as on Enlli, there are no notices on Osea, apart from a few hand-painted signs hammered into tree trunks pointing to outbuildings that have been turned into party venues: the Shack, and the Bomb Factory. There's an attractive absence of bossiness, no instructions, no rules. There may be fewer limits on what a person can do here than in any other place in Britain, which is part of its allure. Every guest can be a rock star and trash their island hotel with impunity.

Its owner, of course, must clear up the detritus, and the longer I stay on Osea, the more intrigued I become about Nigel Frieda. When I ask if I can chat to him, his people repeatedly tell me, vaguely, that he will be 'on the island' in a few hours or a few days. After a while, I suspect that Nigel doesn't want to talk, but shortly before the tides demand that he take the causeway back to his business in London, he drives up to the Captain's House in a Range Rover expensively customised by Overfinch. He's an extremely dashing man in his fifties, with silver hair and kind brown eyes. He rented a cottage here more than twenty years ago, he explains, and when the Coles came to sell he was 'in the right place at the right time'.

'The couple who owned it were big conservationists, planted thousands of trees, made all the gardens beautiful. They knew I wouldn't ruin it and would carry it on, be the custodian.' He first spent about three years 'doing it up', building a recording studio, then rented it to the rehabilitation clinic for six years. 'When they left I thought, What am I going to do with it? I didn't have a particular plan, but I had a couple of parties down here that went really well and it seemed to find its own direction from there.' Since then, he's played host to family holidays, weddings, corporate away-days and 'parties and little festivals, really boutiquey things'.

Nigel has worked in the music industry for decades. In the late 1990s he enjoyed pop success with the Sugababes, a band he masterminded, and he's still working with young singer-songwriters. The days when artists removed themselves from temptation to the countryside to record an album are over, now that albums are, basically, over. Is there still a demand for an old-fashioned residential recording studio like Osea's? 'You'd need to be a fairly significant band to do it, but for albums and people with a bit of a profile and budget, the record companies will definitely invest in it,' says Nigel; Tiny Tempah and Jessie J, Noah and the Whale, Jamie Woon and McFly have stayed on Osea in the past decade. More recently, fashionable electronic artists such as SBTRKT and The Weeknd have recorded or played secret gigs there.

I'm too cowardly to mention the dereliction and the abandoned gold disc when Nigel talks of his ongoing renovations, and so we stick to more comfortable conversational territory: how visitors appreciate the lack of 'Do this, do that' notices. 'You feel what is here. You wander around. It's like someone's house. When you drive onto the causeway you feel all the stress is over there,' he gestures towards the mainland. 'There's something about the island, it just relaxes you.'

And then he's gone, thundering over the conkers at speed on the big tyres of his Overfinch, back to the stress of London.

When I talk again to David Cole, he emphasises the burden of maintaining a small island. Osea has four miles of cliff and sea wall and one and a quarter miles of causeway track, scoured twice daily by the tides. 'That requires continual, weekly maintenance. You've got a lot of property. It's got the same level of aggro as you'd have on an estate of several thousand acres on the mainland, but with much less income.'

I now mention some of the dilapidation and the flaky paint. It happens quickly in the salt air, and, David says, if you're not a permanent resident it can be hard to find good people to maintain a small island. Tradespeople don't want to pop over to Osea because of the hassle of the tides and the salty water and air, which corrode their vans and equipment.

David is a wonderfully positive islander and sounds delighted to imagine 'lots of sex and drugs' on Osea. A few summers ago, he cruised over from Mersea Island to Osea in his launch with his son and grandson. 'We anchored off the Captain's House and found twenty girls in bikinis there. They were obviously a bit bored because they invited us onshore. I think it's rather nice: a lot of young people having a lovely time and enjoying the island.' But then David does admit that he finds some of Osea's dereliction a little distressing. 'There were the most beautiful paths around the island, Hilary's garden has gone to waste, and the orchard overgrown.' Some of his trees have been cut down. 'Still,' he says, recovering his unquenchable optimism, 'these are ephemeral things. It won't hurt the island. The island is eternal.'

On a final perambulation through the overgrown fields of Osea, I venture into another hidden pocket of its interior. Past a large asbestos-roofed barn full of discarded furniture is an opening in a straggly hedge.

Here I discover a feral field, full of high grass and echoing to the cackle of a green woodpecker. We are unfamiliar with abandoned land. We haven't really seen it in Britain for a century or more. In the past, allowing cultivated land to be swallowed up by weeds was viewed as morally reprehensible, and perhaps we still judge it as such, but there's something thrilling about this dereliction. Abandoned in the field is a mildewed caravan with its door slung open, an Iveco camper van in a similarly unkempt state, and a 2005 Mercedes Vito van already weathered far beyond its years. Alongside them is a BMW motorbike dumped on a trailer and a Nissan Almera, sunshade smashed through its front window. There's also a pile of fridges and cookers, the cinders of a bonfire and, most bizarrely, a six-foot-long inflatable orca. Someone must have had a wild party and howled at the moon. Someone's been playing with an air rifle, too. The vehicles all have their windows shot out, apart from a 2002 Volvo estate in metallic gold abandoned at a rakish angle, its tyre tracks sketched in mud around the field. It's been taken for a spin quite recently. The key is in the ignition, I slide into its smart leather seats and the door closes with a satisfying clunk. I turn the key. Nothing. The ignition is rusted up; its last driver neglected to close the electric windows.

Apart from the miraculously inflated orca, every man-made contraption in this field is broken. But the land is not. The hedges are exploding, brambles and blackthorn marching outwards to colonise the meadow, where teasels and thistles grow tall. There are seeds galore for the goldfinches and great handfuls of blackberries and hawthorn berries for everybody else. Here, decay is only seasonal. The rattling stands of bare elm and elder look dead, but they are resting, smudged with lichen and inhabited by beetles. Peeping from the hedge are the rusty nose and cab of an old Ford tractor, its exhaust pipe rising through the billowing green like a periscope. Where the farmer would sit twist a thousand leaves of joyriding bramble, pressing themselves against the glass. The human visitors are not the only ones to enjoy the absence of human controls on Osea island – so does every other species. Here they are, wild and free, behaving as they will, growing with abandon.

11

An Island for One

Ray Island, Essex, 110 acres; population 0

'An island is a nest which holds one egg, and one only.
This egg is the islander himself'
'The Man Who Loved Islands'

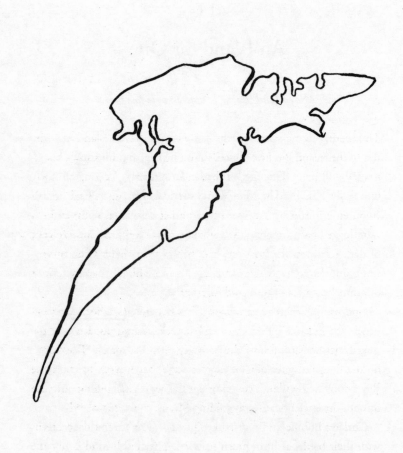

Thundering in my car across the causeway to Mersea Island with the rest of the rush hour, I nearly miss my destination until I spy a black-headed gull perched on a sign for a nature reserve. Veering abruptly into a pot-holed lay-by, I look across the vast expanse of salt marsh coloured crimson by a carpet of autumnal glasswort, tempted by a waterlogged path wiggling through a maze of creeks to a low crescent of dark scrub on the horizon. Irresistibly, great shafts of an unseen sun point through cavities in the clouds to highlight this mysterious hummock in a sea of mud and marsh: the Ray.

Confusingly, there's a sign saying 'Private – no unauthorised access' beside the Essex Wildlife Trust sign for Ray Island, but I ignore the mixed message and follow the pathway onto the marsh. The tide is on the flow and will soon be high enough, 5.1 metres, to make the Ray a convincing island, covering the glasswort and spilling onto the Strood, the ancient causeway joining Mersea to the mainland.

Curlews bubble and redshank pipe as I cross several deep creeks with their banks of lurid green seaweed. The marsh mud is not the despondent brown of a ploughed field, but dances with whorls of silver, purple and magenta. Worms have excavated blue-grey mud from below the surface that is washed copper and gold, or pink and yellow like the sky at sunrise. One ditch was dug deliberately by a previous owner of the Ray to enisle himself, but each creek is now spanned by narrow, railless footbridges of rough-hewn oak. Ancient wooden poles, previous iterations of one bridge, are sunk deep in the ooze. The island begins beyond the deepest creek, a fissure the height of a human. A little egret in Pure Brilliant White rises from the bottom.

Most of Ray's 110 acres are salt marsh, but a small oval of solid ground, barely 15 acres, is delineated by a fringe of silver-purple sea purslane. This grows where the highest tides deposit a matt of reeds decorated with the thousand shells of tiny crabs, as delicate as porcelain. Then there's an imperceptible rise and a 25-metre strip of wiry, bouncy grassland. Beyond, more than a metre above sea level, is a dark tight tangle of hawthorn, elder and blackthorn, its suckers striding across the spongy sward to do battle with the tides.

Cars still roar over the Strood a mile behind me, but here, at last, I am alone on an island, and here I will stay, for a night anyway. Camping is forbidden on the Ray but I've obtained special permission. This small island is my version of the man who loved islands' final retreat, the ultimate cocoon in which to contemplate the individual's relationship to society and the edge's connection to the centre. Was D.H. Lawrence correct? Is the solitary island-seeker on an enormous ego trip, doomed to misanthropy and insanity? Or can a spell on the periphery enlighten life in the middle of things?

I put down my pack, disconcerted that I can just abandon it on the ground, and set off to explore this perfect little world. The broad creeks that make the Ray an island are filling with water, which sloops slowly as it meets the muddy clay edge. Beyond the island to the west and north are flat fields reclaimed from salt marsh, the church towers of Peldon and Great Wigborough on distant higher ground. To the south rises Mersea Island, a caravan park and a thicket of masts by the sailing club. I follow a dapper set of fox prints on the sand. I could quickly walk around the Ray in ten minutes, but small-islanders don't do anything quickly. After twenty minutes' strolling, I see some fresh boot prints and start, and then deduce that I've completed a circuit and, like Pooh and Piglet in *Where the Woozle Wasn't*, I'm pursuing my own tracks. There are older human traces on the island, though. Rolls of old wire fencing show it was once grazed. Elder grows where people and livestock once lived, and hawthorns possess matronly skirts of old nettles, a shadow of the sheep or cows that once huddled beneath. There are several tiny freshwater ponds, unkempt old apple and plum trees, and one extremely pitiful Leylandii, which must have been planted fifty years ago but is stunted and ill-at-ease in such a wild place.

I twist my way into a thicket. It's dark inside. Decrepit elder pocked with mustard-coloured lichen is dank and rotting and falling down. Everything seems to have collapsed. The hawthorns cast knobby limbs over sandy soil where nothing grows except for moss and nettles. These are tall and stringy at the end of the season, their stings so feeble that they only gently tingle. Further on is a huge blackthorn, with great curtains for boughs. The ground is a Jenga game of dead twigs. Over a scraggy pond is a huge dead tree, the nettles beneath whitewashed by the birds that perch on its outstretched limbs. This island feels derelict, just like Osea, and it reminds me that the messiness of Osea is not the responsibility of its owner. People who love islands make no impression on the essence of places such as these. This Essex coast is wild, and will always be so.

Sunset approaches. It's time to set up camp. In the middle of Ray's thicketed high ground are glades of long yellow grass and great ant mounds. Each glade is the size of a tennis court but circular, like a nest. In one are hundreds of soft white feathers from the egrets that roost here every night. Sleeping in a glade with egrets sounds like paradise, but as I stand here, tent in hand, it doesn't feel quite right. In a glade, I am overlooked by a dark thicket, which makes me jumpy.

Robinson Crusoe spends the early weeks on his shipwrecked island frantically constructing fences. Our desire for security must be universal. I'm not spooked by the Ray, not yet, but I become very particular about my campsite. I don't want to be in a glade or on the open shoreline. I dive into a mess of plum trees. Inside is enough space to pitch my tent. I'm secluded, with a view out to shore and a creek beyond. This kind of campsite has probably been humankind's sweet spot of security for millennia.

I sit by my tent and watch the sun go down. A pheasant karks, an ash tree rattles as drily as a eucalyptus, and golden dust rises from a distant tractor ploughing a harvested field. It's been a parched autumn in a dry region. Under the trees are curious circular eruptions, like a giant pushing his fist up through the clay – old anthills, subsided, the earth dry and cracked around them.

I assumed the island took its name from the rays of sunlight that so often seem to spotlight it from the Strood, but Ray, *rey*, or *reisa* in Old Norse, means a raised mound, and this coast has many other similar alluvial deposits of clay with sandy tops, created in the days of Doggerland when the River Thames wound this far north. Rat Island, nearby, may be a corruption of 'ray' too. The Anglo-Saxon Chronicle records how Norsemen camped on Mersea in winter after a summer raiding the villages of Essex, and there are old ditches and mounds at Ray's northern end that could be Norse fortifications. Archaeologists say that every east coast island has similar legends, but Ray's mysterious ditches have yet to be scientifically excavated.

An 1819 map shows no settlement on Ray, but cattle and sheep were grazed on it for centuries and bricks have been found dating from the fifteenth century. Beneath an elder thicket is a midden containing fragments of red pantiles, old bones and pottery dating from the eighteenth century. So there was once a farmstead on Ray. Like many other small islands, its unpopulated state is a relatively recent phenomenon.

Ray Island is reputed to be haunted. I'm not too worried about the story told by two carloads of visitors returning to the mainland from Mersea one Saturday night. They were puzzled to see a man in fancy dress – a Roman centurion – pacing across the Strood in torrential rain. One car turned around to offer him a lift but the centurion had vanished. Another, or the same, Roman soldier said to haunt the causeway is usually only seen from the waist up. There are also stories of schoolchildren being spooked on the Ray by the thundering hooves of phantom horses. The only local legend that really troubles me concerns the former publican of the Peldon Rose who camped on Ray Island one evening. As he was settling down for the night, he heard the trudge of footsteps across the marsh. They crunched over the beach, nearer and nearer, and continued on right through his tent.

Dusk falls. A swan flies headlong up the creek, its neck wobbling like David Gray singing 'Babylon'. There's a curlew, a crescent moon, and clods of clay crumbling onto the beach, and then a gorgeous swoosh through the air as a small posse of dunlin fly down onto the darkening carpet of seaweed. Planes descending into Stansted fly low against the vanishing orange of the western horizon. By 7.30 p.m. the Ray is lit by the moon, in the sky and on the water, and I retreat to my tent to read *Mehalah*, the Victorian melodrama for which this tiny island is known.

It was a bestseller after its publication in 1880 and is well known today: everything from a restaurant to local wines pay tribute to the tragic heroine with an unusual name. Mehalah is a beautiful, passionate and courageous young islander with gypsy blood who struggles to support her mother on their rented farm on the Ray, which has been bought by a scheming farmer called Elijah Rebow who obsessively desires to possess her. The novel was written by a Victorian vicar called Sabine Baring-Gould, the last and perhaps most extreme of my eccentric islanders.

Baring-Gould is best known for composing the hymn 'Onward Christian Soldiers', and he makes Compton Mackenzie look like he suffered from writer's block. Baring-Gould wrote – standing up, like T.S. Eliot – 159 books and collected English folksongs. He had a pet bat that clung to his gown when he taught pupils at a school, and cultivated various gothic fascinations for werewolves, shapeshifters and berserkers. He was a man who didn't like islands, or at least the islands of the Essex marshes.

Born in 1834 to parents who owned a 3,000-acre estate in Devon, Baring-Gould was a sensitive and sickly child, taken on Grand Tours by his father when young. He was fluent in five languages before he eventually went to school, aged fifteen, but was bullied by fellow students at Cambridge because he set up a 'Holy Club' to help the poor. He remained a loner for the rest of his life, railing against everyone from the peasantry to the Church hierarchy. After training as a vicar, he was thirty when he fell in love with Grace Taylor, a millworker's daughter half his age, who met George Bernard Shaw later in life and may have been the inspiration for *Pygmalion*. Grace was trained in upper-middle-class mores before marrying Baring-Gould. The happy couple had fifteen children.

In 1871, he was offered the peripheral parish of East Mersea, possibly because the Church was already suspicious of this free-thinking young vicar. He accepted gratefully because the vicarage was large and his rapidly expanding family was so cramped in their current quarters that he had considered buying a 'van' to serve as his own bedroom. For ten years, the family lived on the island of Mersea. 'I cannot say that I either liked the place or became attached to the people . . . The Essex peasants were dull, shy, reserved and suspicious,' he wrote in his memoirs. 'I never managed to understand them nor they to understand me.' Mersea was only nine miles from Colchester but the road was unmetalled, impassable in winter, and there was no gentry to entertain. 'London muck' – sewage sweepings from the streets –

was applied to the fields and 'the stench was horrible', he complained. Mosquitoes gathered in the autumn in 'such swarms that the trees appeared to be on fire'. He hated the incessant wind.

But something about this difficult landscape, and the Ray, moved him. As he wrote in *Mehalah*:

A more desolate region can scarce be conceived, and yet it is not without beauty. In summer, the thrift mantles the marshes with shot satin, passing through all gradations of tint from maiden's blush to lily white. Thereafter, a purple glow steals over the waste, as the sea lavender bursts into flower, and simultaneously every creek and pool is royally fringed with sea aster. A little later, the glasswort, that shot up green and transparent as emerald glass in the early spring, turns to every tinge of carmine.

I am halfway through *Mehalah*: our heroine's house on the Ray has just burned to the ground, which was probably Baring-Gould retelling a real story he'd heard about the fate of the island's original farm. John Fowles considered *Mehalah* a flawed novel, with its interminable speeches, intermittent wooden dialogue and moments of implausibility; and yet it is also a story of great power, pitting the blind will of Elijah Rebow against the blind pride of Mehalah. I'm gripped, as Mehalah's rent money is stolen, her sweetheart disappears, presumed dead; and then, homeless, she is forced to move herself and her sick mother into Elijah's farm, where his mad brother is imprisoned in the basement. 'When I hold, I hold fast' is Elijah's family motto; now he's got Mehalah in his clutches, he won't let go.

Inside my tent, my inflatable mattress expires with a sigh and won't reinflate, so I lie on the hard sandy ground of the Ray, its discarded twigs prodding me like bones. Outside, the tightly packed ash and plum trees squeak and scrape in the breeze, rubbing each other up the wrong way like feuding neighbours. I jump at a human-sounding complaint among the trees. Curaarrrrck, guraarrrrk – the egrets have come down to roost above me, and their grumbling sounds like 'Oh, for goodness' sake'.

The gothic tragedy of *Mehalah* deepens. The scandal of living in Elijah's house forces Mehalah to marry him, although she swears their marriage will remain unconsummated. During a fight, she accidentally blinds him with acid. Guilt-ridden, she swears to look after him for the rest of her life. When her childhood sweetheart returns, I'm urging Mehalah to break her promise. I won't totally spoil it, but the ending is not what I expect. Sabine Baring-Gould does not believe in fairytales on the islands of Essex.

I lie in the pitch black on the rough ground of the Ray, and think about *Mehalah*. There's the scurry of a mouse by my ear, but no footsteps. Perhaps this is a late-night fancy, but I see Elijah Rebow embodying the relentlessness of life, the grip of a vice, a grander force that individuals – Mehalah – cannot escape. Her island life is childhood, an idyll from which we are banished as adults and cannot return to. The Ray, representing innocence, or not-knowing, is as good as it gets. Perhaps small islands are a similar paradise lost for all of us.

I can imagine what Lawrence would have made of Ray, a blank place that a man with an island fixation could make his own. When Lawrence's Mr Cathcart shuns all human contact and moves onto his island for one, he ends up despising even the non-human inhabitants – sheep, seagulls, his cat. He is glad there are no trees because they stand up, assertively, like people. His island grows eerie. The Ray is eerie too. I'm acutely aware of my status as the only human being here and yet I do not feel alone. This presence is not a hallucination, however, and I don't believe it is a ghost, but simply a heightened awareness of other animals and plants. They feel unusually close. I am keenly, gratefully, constantly conscious of our coexistence on this small patch of land. It seems a shared endeavour.

It's curious that despite all the egotism that Lawrence detected in

Compton Mackenzie, Monty never fulfilled the trajectory of 'The Man Who Loved Islands'. For all Monty's infatuations with grand island projects, his desire to feel significant and his love of mastery over a small place, I don't believe he ever spent a night by himself on an island, not even on the uninhabited Shiants which he owned for a decade. While some of his activism on Barra looks like a self-conscious repudiation of Lawrence's charge that the man who loved islands preferred an empty rock to people, the fact was that, as Lawrence hinted, an island for one was too threatening a proposition for a man such as Monty. From early childhood, Monty appears rather like an island, conspicuously alone, ignored by his father and deserted, he felt, by his mother. As an adult, he never allowed himself to have children. His 'family' was a succession of mother figures from Faith to Chrissie to Lily, who also played the role, as Lawrence so caustically observed, of loyal staff. Like many lonely people, Monty appears to have been terrified of being alone. He swerved real intimacy by constantly surrounding himself with company. It saved him from himself. He always needed a witness, even during the solitary business of writing when secretary–lovers would take down his dictation or play records, further noise to blot out his inner life. As well as providing creative inspiration, a small-island community, such as Barra, served his emotional needs perfectly. To the very end, as when parties of admiring schoolchildren clustered around his bed in Edinburgh, Compton Mackenzie assembled an audience wherever he went. Small inhabited islands were the warm home he never had, but tiny uninhabited islands were to be shunned, for they were the self.

At 5.45 a.m., the egrets start admonishing each other again, like geese with sore throats. The Strood, Mersea's umbilical cord, is already echoing with vehicular traffic. A mouse, or something else, darts past my tent, in a light dash. My appearance on the strand line causes oyster-catchers and redshank to fly up, crying out, and I'm pricked by my own intrusiveness. Perhaps I'm less in the way within the Ray's scrub, busy with small birds. A robin watches me, surprised. A chaffinch carries something in its beak. A wren hops through the brambles, travelling where I can't hope to go. Hummocks of sparsely flowering gorse still carry the coconutty warm scent of the summer past. I become embroiled in blackthorn, as stupid as a sheep, and tear my jacket, depositing a tuft of white down like wool on a snag. I'm trying to thread myself into the weft of the land but I'm too big. I don't mind, though: we're familiar with not belonging in a world of other animals; not belonging in the human world is much harder to take.

There are four sets of fox pads on the beach this morning: my fellow islander was roaming while I slept. I grab breakfast, a couple of apples from one of the trees. Their thick skin has a bitter aftertaste and although the sour flesh is a fresh palate-cleanser, the mainland supermarket apple in my rucksack tastes far nicer.

Even uninhabited islands are owned by someone, or inhabited, physically or mentally, by people, and any growing possessiveness I may feel about Ray is banished when I meet up with David Nicholls for a stroll. Born in Colchester, David trained as a gunsmith, attended Camberwell Art School in the swinging sixties and then taught at Colchester School of Art. He lives on Mersea, and since 1979 he's been Essex Wildlife Trust's volunteer warden for the Ray.

The Ray comes alive under his gaze. John Fowles once said the Essex marshes are 'set to the key of winter', and we admire the first winter migrants coming in: a flock of widgeon, slender ducks with a hint of sickle in their wing. Their call is a poignant whistle. David's favourite is the chatty cronk-cronk of the other visitors from the high Arctic, the brent geese. A snipe zigzags up from the long grass, as if fired from a loose canon. We clamber slowly over pouffe-sized anthills – where the dragons sit before they fly off, according to one young visitor overheard by David. The ant mounds are also a sign that the Ray remains untouched by the pesticides of modern farming.

'This place kept me sane after all the nonsense you get in education,' says David. He's had many magical-sounding experiences here. One time he came out for a walk with his lab-collie cross at sunset to admire the new moon under Venus. As dark fell, he heard a click: the talons of a long-eared owl grasping the branch of a dead tree as it landed. It took off again and flew, silent and low, over the head of his dog. The dog jumped up, maddened, and the owl turned and repeated its tormenting flyover. He's admired grass snakes swimming in the creek and spotted rarities like goshawks, a black tern and, blown in from Scandinavia, a visiting butterfly, a Camberwell Beauty. 'That's what the lads in Peckham used to call the art students,' he says.

There's always less-magical business for any protector of a wild place. When David took over, locals used to bring boats up the channel from Mersea and set fire to them on the Ray. 'You'd have the entire contents of the White Hart pub up here having a whale of a time,' he says. As well as feral beach parties, there's been drug-taking, kids smashing up bridges, poachers shooting foxes, people offering to 'tidy up' and chop down dead trees and, perhaps most alarmingly, discarded root vegetables carved with occult symbols. David is more upbeat than many nature reserve wardens, though. 'The local people, not just the local locals but the boatie people and the incomers here, love Ray Island. They absolutely love it.' He shows me a postcard from 1911 showing a very well grazed Ray surrounded by picnickers and elegant yachts. On a good tide in summer, there'll still be a hundred people picnicking on the north side. Kids make mudslides on the creek banks or learn to sail, and the next day there's not a scrap of litter. 'There's not many places where you can say that.' Some outsiders are less enamoured of it. The Ray is owned by the National Trust and 'every so often bigwigs from the Trust turn up,' he says. 'We took a group of them out one year and they had a look around and on the way back I said, "It's a pity you don't buy more of the Essex coast", and one of them said,

"Well, David, the aesthetic appreciation of Essex saltmarsh is very much an acquired taste."'

It takes me a while to realise that this unobtrusive, artistic man has been quietly responsible for the Ray's physical and cultural character in modern times. The old wire fencing is his work, so is the hand-painted sign warning of a fire risk, and so too is the big dead tree: a weeping willow that he obtained permission to kill because it was both incongruously suburban and sucking up the fresh water. The glades are only there because for twenty years he and his wife ran a flock of Soay sheep on the island. These famously tough beasts lived wild as they do on St Kilda, but they were eventually too much labour and the regulations were too arduous, so they sent them off, by boat, to a country park.

I've felt the Ray's uniqueness, but only grasp its rarity when David points out that its wonderfully subtle gradation – from mudflat to saltmarsh to coarse saltwater grassland to freshwater meadow to scrub to woodland – is actually half of all that remains of what ecologists call the 'natural transitional coastline' of Essex. Ray Island is tiny, and the Essex coast is as long as Holland's, but almost all of it has been intruded upon by humans who've erected sea banks and sea walls and drained the marshes. Ray Island is the last fragment showing how the coast looked half a millennium ago.

As well as the protector of its physical uniqueness, David has been a guardian of the Ray's cultural identity over the last four decades. He's researched the life of Sabine Baring-Gould – this remarkable Victorian is overdue for a revival, he thinks – and has gently debunked the island's ghost stories. He once spoke to the granddaughter of the pub landlord supposedly spooked by footsteps, who insisted he never camped on the Ray; the footsteps are a common urban myth, and this particular iteration was propagated by James Wentworth Day, a twentieth-century author who made a fine living from retelling East Anglian folk tales. 'You take anything he writes with a pinch of salt,' says David. Back in the early 1980s, he was having a drink in a local pub when he saw Wentworth Day in action, buying a man in his nineties a beer and a scotch. They talked, and Wentworth Day kept the beers and scotches coming for an hour before scurrying off. The old man turned to David, laughed, and said: 'I told him a tale or too. All bloody lies of course.'

Sabine Baring-Gould is 'loved and hated' by the locals, says David, for his portrayal of Essex 'peasants' as insular and introverted. David thinks he has a point. He mentions the old saying: 'Essex men with their feet of clay, slow to warm, many say.' But Baring-Gould's creation, *Mehalah*, is more universally loved. Fans of the book who seek out the Ray most commonly ask: Was she real? The answer is yes. David has discovered there was a young woman called Mahalah living on Mersea when Baring-Gould arrived there in 1871. The daughter of a couple who lived on an old barge and ferried people across the River Colne from Mersea to Brightlingsea, Mahalah worked as a domestic servant; Baring-Gould would almost certainly have met her when he took tea on the barge. He also immortalised her drunk stepmother in *Mehalah*. The real Mahalah married an Irishman based at Colchester's barracks and died of consumption in 1893, aged just thirty-five.

After David heads home, I sit on a dragon's pouffe and watch a dumpy little dunlin dibbing for the tiny jumping bugs that live under the carpets of green weed. By my foot is a fine pile of poo from a fox who's been eating blackberries. Daydreaming, I ponder the red berries of a half-fallen hawthorn on the beach. Soon, I'm counting them: bunches of seventeen, eleven, eight; 218 on a stem as long as my forearm; ninety-two similar stems on the tree; 20,056 berries, on one small hawthorn. I wonder how many hawthorns there are on the island, and if I can count every berry. A rattle of small-arms fire from nearby Fingringhoe Ranges breaks my reverie and reminds me what a predictable island trap I'm falling into: Crusoe was an obsessive cataloguer. Over on Runmarö, so is Fredrik Sjöberg. Mr Cathcart, the man who loved islands, set himself the task of recording every flower and plant on his island. Compton Mackenzie collected butterflies.

D.H. Lawrence made many astute observations in his parable of the futility of escaping to a small island, but Ray Island does not feel to me like an I-land, a monstrous creation of my own ego. I do not and could not dominate this place, even if I desired to. Being here is not about me, and I don't feel alone either. I'm living alongside other islanders: snipe, dunlin, foxes, mice. I don't dislike or feel divorced from humanity as represented by the ever present hum of tyres on the causeway along the horizon. I watch a double-decker bus crossing the Strood, and from this distance the marsh conceals its wheels so it appears to be floating. This image is as surreal as the human universe seems from this vantage point, a busy irrelevance to this world of water, wind, moon and tide.

Like Rousseau on his tiny Swiss island, I will never tire of the fresh drama of the sea and the ever changing colour of the marsh. Then again, I'm not sure it would do me or any individual much good to enisle ourselves for ever. To be apart from the world entirely is to grow estranged from it. We have obligations to the natural world and to the human world too.

On the Ray, I start to imagine a small-island manifesto that's been handed to me over the past two years – by bonxies and Orkney voles and Mairi Ceit MacKinnon and Sarah Boden and Georgi Kondakov and geranium narcissi and Kathleen MacLeod and the St Kilda wren and Liam McFaul and David Cole and Edward Montague Compton Mackenzie and all the other small-islanders I've encountered. The periphery is not simply a refuge from a centre in crisis. As the writer and Eigg rejuvenator Alastair McIntosh believes, small islands can be a pattern and an example for the mainland. It's not a given, but I've found these smaller societies arranged on a human scale more nurturing for humans, and more nurturing for the rest of the natural world. A small-island manifesto for larger islands might begin with the realisation that we need to treat other people more carefully. Be open to outsiders and to the world. Live as generalists, not as super-sclerosed specialists. Spend more time outside. Reduce our consumption. Make our own energy or, at worst, buy it by the sack, and then we will use less. Consider animals and plants as well as people. Live more intimately with our place, for it is a complex living organism too.

The centre needs the periphery as a source of inspiration and renewal, just as the periphery relies on the centre. The centrifugal forces that continue to deposit money and power in global corporations or global cities such as London seem stronger than ever. We must maintain the edginess of the periphery against their onslaught. Small islands are a useful repository of many memories, histories and half-forgotten ideas. They are a useful repository for many species too. I don't believe an apocalypse is coming, but if the human race did self-destruct, small islands would probably prove to be the last redoubt for human life too. We would be wise to remain open to the alternatives they offer. Small-island life can be inspiring, healing or a reproach, and I hope it endures.

When I return to my mainland home from the Ray, my bed feels indulgently soft compared with the island's hard dry ground. I spent less time there than on any other island but it possessed a peculiar intensity. The Ray does not diminish as I expect it to. I didn't spend a night *on* the Ray, I spent a night with it. This experience lingers with the vivid physicality of a love affair. Even after a shower, the smell of its mud stays in my scalp and on my skin. I did not detect it much when I was there, but its scent seeped into me. As I slept on its ground, those dead twigs digging into me like tiny elbows, the Ray was changing me.

I feel infatuated like poor, foolish Fanny Price in *Mansfield Park*, scorned for thinking 'of nothing but the Isle of Wight' which she calls 'The Island, as if there were no other island in the world'. For days afterwards, I can't escape the conviction that the Ray is not an empty space but a living thing, as distinct as any animal. It's a powerful, person-like place, deep and strange and full of intrinsic qualities, a life-force pulsing with vitality, integrity and perhaps even agency. It keeps popping into my head, nudging me, demanding things of me. I have not become an island-person, but I see the Ray as a person-island.

Perhaps my vivid sense of this small island is only my response to the natural world's version of a music festival or a one-night stand, an indulgent experience that delivers flashes of pleasure, nostalgia or regret. But I hope my feelings are more genuinely transformative. I admire the Ray as a discrete arena of great power, but I wonder if I now understand the sensation felt by other islanders such as Adam Nicolson on the Shiants – a fleeting sense that there is no gap between me and the Ray, that it is me, and I it. There is no trace of me on the Ray, but I carry a little bit of it inside me.

Perhaps we can all have more of this small-island healing in our lives. Are there enough to go round? I do a back-of-the-envelope calculation: every thirty years, I reckon, every individual in Britain could be guaranteed twenty-four hours alone on a small island or islet or tidal rock. 'Can't think of anything less appealing,' says Lisa when I tell her how it feels to be alone on the Ray. She likes people around her. But I think people-persons will love the experience of being an islander too. We welcome antidotes for our estrangement from the non-human world. We are happier being one of many species. How can we not be enchanted and enriched, when finding ourselves on a ring of dry ground surrounded by saltwater, mud, seven redshank, fifteen egrets, twenty thousand hawthorn berries, silence, the sun setting, a crescent moon rising: the alchemy of a small island.

ACKNOWLEDGEMENTS

Those inclined to nausea should skip this voyage around the Thankful Islands. Or at least put on your sea bands . . .

I'd like to thank islanders everywhere who generously shared their time to chat with an intrusive castaway. Thank you to everyone I've quoted. I've been inspired and helped to see the world anew by so many people, but particularly Mairi Ceit MacKinnon; also, Johnny Crellin, Kathleen MacLeod, Freda Norquay, Babette Barthelmess, Alastair McIntosh, Sarah Boden and Johnny Lynch, Brian and Camille Dressler, Liam and Alison McFaul, Daph Perkins, Stephen MacDonald, Christine Evans, David Cole and David Nicholls.

Some islanders have contributed greatly to this book while maintaining a lower profile. Thank you to Gail Jeffcoate for her generous enthusiasm, expertise, books and accommodation on the Isle of Man. There, I'd also like to thank Peter McEvoy, 'the bright young Irish civil servant'; Alistair Ramsay; Liz Charter and Tim Earl; and Terry Cringle, the veteran Isle of Man journalist and self-described 'celebrity (Isle of Man only)'. Thanks to Amy Colvin of RSPB Northern Ireland; Martin Batt, Moira Sleeman and Emma Odoli on Alderney; Derek Gordon and his witty assistant Nicola Boulton of Go To St Kilda; Nigel Frieda and Lily Frieda on Osea; and thanks to the Essex Wildlife Trust for granting me special permission to camp on Ray Island.

I'd like to sincerely thank the following people for reading drafts of chapters – commenting, criticising and helping me correct errors.

ACKNOWLEDGEMENTS

Their scrutiny has been vital: Sarah Boden, Brian Bonnard, Julian Branscombe, David Cole, Andrew Cordier, Jo Crellin and Johnny Crellin, Camille Dressler, Christine Evans and Colin Evans, Rachel and Robin Hamilton, Viv Jackson and Helen Smith, Gail Jeffcoate, Rob and William Jeffcoate, Alison and Liam McFaul, Alastair McIntosh, Mairi Ceit MacKinnon, Kathleen Macleod, Freda Norquay, David Nicholls and John Barkham. Thank you.

I must also thank Magnus Linklater and Adam Nicolson for opening up their fine minds over lunch. Others gave me contacts, book recommendations or ideas, some of which I've subsumed as my own and forgotten the originator; I'm sorry. Full credit, though, for tips from Clare Margetson, Andrew Clarke, Seán Clarke, Ian Jack, John Sutherland, Robert Macfarlane, David Simmonds, Hugh Aldersey-Williams, Martin Graebe and Rebecca Tope. I'd also like to thank Madeleine Bunting: two very different books she wrote a long time apart about two very different places have been key texts for me.

Thanks to Anna Jury, Ruth Chandler, Kitty Corrigan and Kate Langrish at *Country Living*; and Suzie Worroll, Emily Wilson, Andy Pietrasik, Jane Dunford, Malik Meer and John Crace at the *Guardian*.

A special thank you to Jeanie Feneron for generously providing two crucial writing retreats in her caravan by the beach at Eccles, and to Eliska Cheeseman for arranging them.

Huge thanks to the great brains at Granta including Sigrid Rausing, Iain Chapple, Sarah Wasley, Christine Lo, Katie Hayward, Lamorna Elmer; and copyeditor Sue Phillpott for doing a superb job. Thanks to illustrator Emily Faccini and cover designer Dan Mogford. Most of all, thank you, once again, to Laura Barber, my brilliant and incredibly dedicated editor, and to my legendary agent, Karolina Sutton at Curtis Brown.

Finally, I'd like to thank the archipelago around me for providing the love, shelter, peace and freedom required to write: thank you

Suzanne Barkham, John Barkham, Henrietta Barkham, Jan and Rob Palmer, Lisa Walpole, Milly, Esme and Ted. I would be washed away without you.

Notes

Introduction

p. 7   *a raven shot on its nest*: Eric Linklater, *The Man on My Back* (1941).

p. 8   *not to revisit places I've written about*: Lovers of Scolt Head Island, Lindisfarne, Inner Farne, Northey, Lundy and Brownsea might want to read my previous book, *Coastlines* (2015), which explores these marvellous places.

p. 9   *the popularisation of Jean-Jacques Rousseau's . . . the solitary self*: Peter Conrad's *Islands: A Trip through Time and Space* (2009) is an excellent global tour of the island in literature and thinking.

1. Man Is an Island

p. 13   *There was something exotic . . . youthful imagination*: Compton Mackenzie, *Unconsidered Trifles* (1932), p. 144.

p. 13   *Steamships carried more . . . in 1933*: S.P.B. Mais, *Isles of the Island* (1934).

p. 16   *driving into Douglas . . . (the dark and the light)*: George Broderick, 'Some Island Names in the Former "Kingdom of the Isles": a reappraisal', *Journal of Scottish Name Studies* 7 (2013), 1–28, republished online: http://www.clanntuirc. co.uk/JSNS/V7/JSNS7%20Broderick.pdf.

p. 18   *The arrival . . . helped transform its fortunes*: Roger Rawcliffe, *No Man Is an Island: 50 Years of Finance in the Isle of Man*

(2009), is a recent history of Man's economy from its own perspective. The veteran Isle of Man journalist Terry Cringle was also a good source of tales – some unprintable – from Man's Wild West years.

p. 17   *A joke from the 1930s . . . bending to England*: S.P.B. Mais, *Isles of the Island*, p. 212.

p. 21   *the only home . . . Lesser Mottled Grasshopper*: John F. Burton, 'The Mystery of the Isle of Man's Endangered Grasshopper', *British Wildlife* 2.1 (1990), and an update in *British Wildlife* 25.4 (2014) found the grasshopper 'in good numbers' in 2012.

p. 23   *he read Treasure Island in one glorious gasp*: Compton Mackenzie, *Unconsidered Trifles*.

p. 23   *I saw the rose-leaf complexion . . . she remembered*: From Faith Compton Mackenzie, *As Much As I Dare* (1938). Faith is a good memoirist who paints a vivid, wry portrait of Monty. She's not as open as we might wish about her relationship with him, or about her own affairs, but she imbues real people with more life than her husband could manage in his recollections.

p. 23   *He seriously considered . . . a playwright, an actor*: These and many other biographical details are found in Andro Linklater's excellent biography, *Compton Mackenzie: A Life* (1987).

p. 24   *It's all so simple . . . in a dreamy, sepulchral voice*: Compton Mackenzie, *My Life and Times, Octave Four 1907–1914* (1965).

p. 32   *fallen off . . . amnesiac in the road to progress*: Gill in full flow shows a certain kind of unsurpassed journalistic artistry, wit and invective (although less pleasant if you are the victim). You can read the full account of his time on the Isle of Man (shock: he kind of liked it) in *Table Talk: Sweet and Sour, Salt and Bitter* (2007).

p. 32 *the haunted wing of the Manx statute book*: This phrase was told me by the veteran Manx journalist Terry Cringle.

p. 33 *Mackenzie loved Man*: Compton Mackenzie, *My Life and Times: Octave Six 1924–1930* (1967), p. 218.

2. The Tomb of the Eagles

p. 46 *She paired with a male but he disappeared in 1908*: The disappearance of Britain's last sea eagle is well told in *Raptor* by James Macdonald Lockhart (2016).

p. 51 *archaeologist John Hedges reveals . . . for its situation*: In *Tomb of the Eagles* (1984), p. 128.

p. 53 *Bizarrely . . . the invention of the travel visa*: Andro Linklater, *Compton Mackenzie: A Life*, p. 154.

p. 53 *There was also a significant exodus of writers escaping Britain*: From *Abroad: British Literary Travelling between the Wars* by Paul Fussell (1980). On Corfu in 1936 and writing home for news, Lawrence Durrell exclaimed: 'IS THERE NO ONE WRITING AT ALL IN ENGLAND NOW?'

p. 54 *after Marlon Brando filmed* Mutiny on the Bounty *in French Polynesia*: Peter Conrad, *Islands*.

p. 54 *Hearing of Monty's impulsive decision, Lawrence wrote from Italy*: James T. Boulton and Andrew Robertson, *The Letters of D.H. Lawrence*, vol. III, *October 1916–1921* (2007).

p. 55 *organise something out of nothing*: Faith Compton Mackenzie, *More Than I Should* (1940), p. 78. Faith, again, pens a better portrait of an infatuated Monty than Monty does in his own memoirs. His woes on Herm and then Jethou are rather more honestly treated too. Just a shame Faith couldn't write more openly about their own strange relationship.

p. 56 *He sent Monty a series of postcards*: Boulton and Robertson, *Letters of D.H. Lawrence*, vol. III, *October 1916–1921*.

p. 57 *The island-hopping . . . gave rise to the theory of evolution*: This section is very much informed by David Quammen's *Song of the Dodo* (1997).

p. 59   *co-wrote a fascinating paper on the Orkney vole*: Julian Branscombe and Keith Dobney, 'The Mystery of the Orkney Vole', *British Wildlife* 27.5 (June 2016): 340–48.

p. 63   *Perhaps a dance-hall . . . I'm not sure yet*: Faith Compton Mackenzie, *More Than I Should*.

p. 67   *Orkney is prose*: Eric Linklater, *Man on My Back*, p. 303.

3. An Island Home

p. 74   *a volume of Barra essays*: John Lorne Campbell (ed.), *The Book of Barra* (1936).

p. 76   *the faraway nearby . . . in her recent history*: Madeleine Bunting, *Love of Country: A Hebridean Journey* (2016).

p. 77   *Monty turned fifty in 1933 and finished the year . . . Old Bailey*: Monty's woes are well examined in Andro Linklater, *Compton Mackenzie: A Life*.

p. 79   *riding along the horizon like snowy galleons*: Monty's ecstasy about living on Barra took shape in his 1936 BBC radio broadcast, *Living Off the Map*, and was repeated in his memoirs.

p. 80   *the view of Jean Cocteau*: From Peter Conrad, *Islands*.

p. 80   *I say that The Coddy was the outstanding character*: A memorable line from Compton Mackenzie's *My Life and Times, Octave Seven 1931–1938* (1968), p. 67.

p. 81   *a sloe-eyed young beauty from the Outer Hebrides*: Veronica Maclean, *Past Forgetting* (2002).

p. 82   *The Daily Record likened him to Robert Louis Stevenson in Samoa*: Compton Mackenzie, *My Life and Times, Octave Seven 1931–1938*.

p. 82   *Lawrence can enshrine . . . in one charmed sentence*: Compton Mackenzie, *My Life and Times, Octave Seven*, p. 36.

p. 83   *Monty's reinvention began . . . John Lorne Campbell*: You can experience John Lorne Campbell's generosity and good sense in his two essays, 'Our Barra Years – Memories of Compton Mackenzie', in *Scotland Magazine* (1974–5), available in one volume in the British Library. Ray Perman's fine biography, *The Man Who Gave Away His Island* (2010), clearly explains Monty and John Lorne Campbell's friendship.

p. 84   *After Monty's death . . . Campbell praised his friend's farsightedness*: John Lorne Campbell, 'Our Barra Years – Memories of Compton Mackenzie' (1974–5).

p. 92   *Monty clearly relished . . . and sustained his creative output*: Peter Conrad, *Islands*, also suggests that an island is a 'uterine shelter' surrounded, like the foetus, by fluid. Islands can be umbilical, he writes: Homer calls Calypso's island home the navel of the ocean, a nutritious bud from which all else grows, and the nymph detains Odysseus there for seven years.

p. 92   *Robert Louis Stevenson (Treasure Island) . . . had dalliances with the Hebrides*: As pointed out by Madeleine Bunting, *Love of Country*, p. 43.

p. 92   *In 1940, Monty urged George Orwell to retreat there*: Gordon Bowker's biography of George Orwell reveals Mackenzie met Orwell at an annual Charles Dickens conference in London. Monty was president; Orwell gave the key speech (and was excited by Mackenzie's islomania).

p. 92   *I like islands, wrote Will Self more recently*: Will Self, 'Inching along the Edge of the World', *New York Times* (23 October 2008), https://self.blogs.nytimes.com/2008/10/23/inching-along-the-edge-of-the-world/. Also quoted by Madeleine Bunting, *Love of Country*, p. 52.

p. 92   *In the 1870s, Rimbaud fled France*: Peter Conrad, *Islands*.

p. 93   *The places I have loved best I have always tried to avoid revisiting*: Compton Mackenzie in *Echoes* (1954), a collection of essays.

p. 93 *I felt as if the island itself had floated away like St Brendan's isle*: Compton Mackenzie, *My Life and Times, Octave Ten* (1971). St Brendan reportedly landed on this island in the Atlantic west of Africa in 512, but it is one of many imaginary islands given shape by cartographers but never found again by mariners.

p. 93 *In 1941, the SS Politician ran aground on rocks off Eriskay*: Roger Hutchinson, in *Polly: The True History behind Whisky Galore*, has written the definitive book on this subject.

p. 95 *denouncing my Popery*: Compton Mackenzie, *My Life and Times, Octave Ten, 1953–1963* (1971).

p. 95 *Alasdair Alpin MacGregor*: Quoted in Roy Calderwood, *Times Subject to Tides*.

p. 97 *sleeping until afternoon . . . Magnus Linklater remembers*: The academic and writer John Sutherland has similar memories to Magnus Linklater's of being taken in a group for an audience with bedridden Monty in Edinburgh. He told the young Sutherland: 'As a child, I sat on the knee of a veteran of Waterloo. I can see him more clearly than I can see you.' The veterans in Monty's childhood would hawk themselves and their medals around public houses, begging for money.

4. The Island for Idealists

p. 106 *The island doctor described . . . being able to shoot the bugger*: This brief résumé of Eigg's history is taken from Camille Dressler's thorough, witty and fair-minded account, *Eigg: The Story of an Island* (2007).

p. 106 *Legend has it that Schellenberg . . . a blind auction for Eigg approaching*: As told by Alastair McIntosh in *Soil and Soul* (2001).

p. 107 *By the summer of 1979, Eigg was open for business:* Dressler, *Eigg*, p. 157.

p. 108 *Keith actually wears . . . noise and clouds of dust*: As guests told the *Daily Mail*, and re-reported in various histories of the island.

p. 108 *devised war-games with yellow . . . Jacobites versus Hanoverians*: Sarah Boden remembers islander kids gaining a competitive advantage by arming themselves with potatoes to participate in the war games. When a girlfriend of one of Schellenberg's sons was hit in the face with a spud, the games were halted.

p. 108 *the laird's aristocratic Scottish guests . . . half-baked socialists*: Dressler, *Eigg*, p. 170.

p. 111 *Maggie Fyffe . . . soon it was £30,000 per bag*: As told to me by Maggie Fyffe.

p. 111 *owners even decided which . . . could eat Eigg's seaweed*: Patrick Kingsley, 'Eigg: the Answer to Britain's Housing Crisis?', *Guardian*, 17 September 2012.

p. 116 *sustaining their laidback lifestyles with mainland subsidies*: Many other nations also support island life with grants or subsidies. Fredrik Sjöberg acerbically writes in *The Fly Trap* of enthusiastic newcomers to his Swedish island: 'Many come and leave again quickly, always with some equally idiotic project for which they're hoping to get a government grant, since the island is so sparsely populated that no project is too hare-brained to get official support.', p. 44.

p. 127 *aristocrats of the democracy*: My favourite Monty quote, from his autobiography, and cited again by Andro Linklater, *Compton Mackenzie*, p. 255.

5. Isle of Seabirds, Isle of Stories

p. 138 *The corncrake had hoped . . . We never heard from him again*: Liam and Alison believe that a corncrake bred successfully on Rathlin in 2016, the summer after my visit, but the chicks of this secretive bird were never actually spotted.

p. 139 *a huge elongated skull*: Travel articles in newspapers and magazines are most prone to flights of fancy about the shapes of islands. The excellent travel writer Christopher Somerville considered Bardsey to be shaped like a sleeping otter. David Foster, writing in *The Times* in 1996, made the Alderney skull comparison.

p. 141 *If we were serious . . . this was how it must be*: In Nicolson's autobiography, quoted in Madeleine Bunting, *Love of Country*, p. 162.

p. 141 *Ian Mitchell, a travel writer who visited Rum in the 1990s*: Ian Mitchell, *Isles of the West: A Hebridean Voyage*, 1999.

p. 149 *Letitia Stevenson . . . member of the Anglo-Irish Protestant elite*: Letitia S. Stevenson, *The Guttering Candle, or Life on Rathlin 1920–1922* (self-published, collected letters edited by Patric Stevenson). I obtained a copy from the library of Liam and Alison McFaul.

p. 155 *John Lorne Campbell, Gaelic scholar . . . vertical plane*: This is nicely explained in Chapter 15 of Ray Perman's biography, *The Man Who Gave Away His Island*.

p. 156 *I had realised by now how much psychology . . . to literature*: Compton Mackenzie, *My Life and Times, Octave Seven 1931– 1938*, p. 166.

p. 156 *does not kiss and tell*: Compton Mackenzie, *My Life and Times, Octave Eight 1939–1946* (1969), p. 138.

p. 157 *like a mirror turned to face another mirror*: Andro Linklater, *Compton Mackenzie*, p. 180.

6. Prison Island

p. 167 *Victor Hugo described the Channel Islands . . . the mother hen*: Peter Conrad, *Islands*.

p. 167 *It is the boundedness of the smaller island, encompassable in a glance*: John Fowles and Fay Godwin, *Islands* (1978).

p. 168 *greater white-toothed shrew . . . dead rabbit carcasses after dark*: Curiously, the Isles of Scilly are home to the almost indistinguishable lesser white-toothed shrew, which also lives on the Channel Islands of Jersey and Sark.

p. 168 *The words of Alexei Ikonnikov*: As quoted on p. 171 of Madeleine Bunting's history of the Channel Islands under German rule, *The Model Occupation* (1995). I found this a superb history, but when I visited Alderney more than twenty years after the publication of Bunting's book, I was surprised to find islanders there still hostile to her account, which details the extent of Channel Island collaboration in what I consider a compassionate and judicious way.

p. 170 *An Island Story . . . Alderney's evacuation and homecoming*: Written by Ray Parkin to mark the seventieth anniversary of the return.

p. 170 *remembers George Baron, who was sixteen*: Brian Bonnard later updated me: George died at home with his family on 23 July 2016, aged ninety-one. He was active to the end. The church was packed at his funeral.

p. 172 *Hell couldn't look any worse, remembered Joyce Buckland*: This quote is taken from Charlie Gauvain's excellent documentary, *Alderney – The Homecoming*, which was crowd-funded and made for the seventieth anniversary. It contains a series of excellent interviews with local people who remembered the evacuation and the return. Joyce was particularly eloquent about the impact – unfortunately she wasn't at home when I called round!

p. 173 *Or, as another islander, Royston Raymond, put it*: Royston Raymond was another islander who wasn't at home when I stayed on Alderney, so his words too are from Gauvain's documentary.

p. 174 *I read of Georgi Kondakov's plight . . . islander called Brian*

Bonnard: Brian Bonnard (ed.), *Island of Dread in the Channel: The Story of Georgi Ivanovitch Kondakov* (1991).

p. 176   *Das Arschloch der Welt*: From Brian Bonnard, *Alderney at War 1939–49* (2009).

p. 176   *By 1944, German officers were . . . Inselwahn – island madness*: *Hitler's Island Madness* (2012), a documentary directed by Chris Denton and written by Martin Morgan.

p. 178   *Another old German soldier, Gustav Dahmer. . . scavenged food waste*: Bonnard, *Alderney at War*.

p. 178   *le rocher maudit*: I've used Bunting, *Model Occupation*, and Bonnard, *Alderney at War*, as my main sources.

p. 179   *Alderney witnessed . . . on British soil in modern times*: Bunting, *Model Occupation*, p. 289, calls it 'mass murder'. Other historians, including Bonnard, argue that many of the deaths were from terrible ill-treatment, overwork and poor diet, and therefore not intentional. Either way, it was an appalling crime.

p. 183   *His older brother Peter . . . whispering, Nazi, no good*: Interviewed in Gauvain's documentary.

p. 186   *Four men were prosecuted for war crimes on Alderney*: From Bunting, *Model Occupation*, pp. 152–8.

7. The Family Archipelago

p. 196   *Scilly is not the Cassiterides*: R.L. Bowley, *The Fortunate Islands* (1990).

p. 196   *Greek and Latin mythology persistently points . . . Straits of Gibraltar*: This is John Fowles's theory, and I love his quote about the Isles of Scilly being 'an eternal stone armada of over a hundred ships, aloofly anchored off England'. Both are taken from Fowles and Godwin, *Islands*. Fowles's mother was Cornish. He was definitely a man who loved islands, and the Isles of Scilly inspired him, as his excellent meditation on island existence shows.

p. 198   *that great nesomane Daniel Defoe*: 'Nesomane' is John Fowles's word too.

p. 206   *which might compete one day with Tresco . . . the finest garden in Europe*: Compton Mackenzie, *Unconsidered Trifles*, p. 236.

p. 206   *When he switched to Jethou . . . temperate garden, inspired by Tresco*: From Compton Mackenzie, *My Life and Times, Octave Six, 1924–1930*.

p. 207   *Scilly was poverty-stricken . . . primogeniture didn't operate on the islands*: Scilly's history is well written about and I'm grateful to Helen Smith and Viv Jackson for allowing me to peruse their library. I found Ernest Kay, *Isles of Flowers*, 1956, and particularly R.L. Bowley, *The Fortunate Islands*, 1990, most useful for a quick tour of Scilly's human history.

p. 208   *Eccentricity permeates the place, noted the Financial Times*: Jane Owen, 'At Home: Robert Dorien-Smith', *Financial Times*, 17 May 2013, https://www.ft.com/content/1da057f8-bbc5-11e2-82df-00144feab7de.

p. 210   *The first Scillonians . . . homes on the outer islands*: Andrew Cooper makes this observation in his *Secret Nature of The Isles of Scilly* (2006).

p. 211   *The Day the Tide Went Out . . . and out . . . and out*: A picture book by David McKee, first published in 1976, which I vividly remember as a child and still have on my shelves. Overdue a rediscovery by the climate-change generation.

p. 212   *regarded wrens as the tutelary creatures*: Compton Mackenzie, *Unconsidered Trifles*.

8. Lost Land

p. 217   *Tourists jostled into . . . bore the St Kilda postmark*: The historic scene I've chosen to open the St Kilda chapter is mostly taken from Tom Steel, *The Life and Death of St Kilda*, an excellent, accessible popular history. Steel is regarded as a reliable source although, as I mention in the chapter, he is challenged by contemporary Scottish historians who argue that he was too critical of the role of religion in the demise of St Kilda's community.

p. 218 *May God forgive those that have taken us away from St Kilda*: Finlay MacQueen was a senior member of the St Kildan society and something of a spokesperson, sought out by outsiders in the months and years following the island's evacuation. Finlay and several other older islanders returned to camp on the island in the summers afterwards. I suspect it was from him that Compton Mackenzie obtained his view that the islanders didn't want to leave their home.

p. 219 *as much a place of the imagination as a physical reality*: Bunting, *Love of Country*, p. 262.

p. 219 *there's no phone signal and no means of contact with the wider world*: There is no WiFi on St Kilda, except for QinetiQ workers and conservationists employed seasonally on the island. Just not for visitors like me or you.

p. 221 *has probably had more triumphs . . . sea of similar size in the world*: Compton Mackenzie, *My Life and Times: Octave Six 1924–1930*, p. 144.

p. 221 *a wild corner of fairyland*: Compton Mackenzie, *My Life and Times: Octave Six*, p. 89.

p. 222 *The expected price was £1,000 . . . his secretary Nelly, to bid up to £500*: Adam Nicolson, writing in *Sea Room*, offers the best account of Monty's auction, p. 341.

p. 223 *the secrets of my heart*: Faith Compton Mackenzie, *More Than I Should*, p. 34.

p. 224 *When he read it in a newspaper . . . with an injunction*: Compton Mackenzie, *My Life and Times: Octave Six 1924–1930*, p. 132.

p. 224 *During an interview . . . Lawrence deployed a trick . . . Monty argued*: Interviewed by Harry T. Moore, researching *The Intelligent Heart: The Story of D.H. Lawrence* (1954), p. 240.

p. 229 *arrived on the first steamships in 1834*: Angela Gannon and George Geddes, *St Kilda: The Last and Outmost Isle* (2015), p. 198.

p. 229 *If this island is not the Eutopia so long sought, where will it be found?*: Widely quoted, and in Tom Steel, *The Life and Death of St Kilda*, p. 34.

p. 230 *Martin Martin, in 1697 one of the first visitors . . . life on St Kilda*: Martin Martin, *A Description of the Western Islands of Scotland: A Voyage to St Kilda*, introduction by Charles W.J. Withers (1999), is still read and widely requoted in Steel, *The Life and Death of St Kilda*, and elsewhere. Unlike almost every other visitor, Martin Martin at least spoke Gaelic.

p. 230 *Everything smells of feathers*: Quoted in Steel, *Life and Death of St Kilda*, p. 54.

p. 231 *he pitched up in June 1930, two months before the evacuation*: Compton Mackenzie, *My Life and Times: Octave Six 1924– 1930*, p. 216. Monty is at odds with most other contemporary commentators who claimed a unanimity among the St Kildans over their exodus. It seems logical to deduce that Monty obtained his dissenting view from Finlay MacQueen, but I can't prove it!

p. 232 *drunk with spaciousness*: Quoted in Bunting, *Love of Country*.

p. 233 *Recently, though, a revisionist view . . . close connection to the Western Isles*: This perspective can be found in Bob Chambers (ed.), *Rewriting St Kilda* (2010), Lawson, Love, Randall and Robson, *St Kilda: Myth and Reality* (2010), and in Donald John Gillies's long-lost memoir, *The Truth about St Kilda*, edited by John Randall. The latest beautifully illustrated and very comprehensive history of St Kilda by Gannon and Geddes, *St Kilda: The Last and Outmost Isle*, accepts this view too.

p. 234 *Their government is strictly a republic*: Another quote about St Kilda, so widely used that it is probably vastly overstated, reflects the prevalent belief of writers such as Tom Steel in *The Life and Death of St Kilda*.

p. 241 *Many a fiddle . . . desirable for salvation*: Quoted in Steel, *Life and Death of St Kilda*, p. 99.

p. 242 *In a recent essay, Donald Meek*: Donald E. Meek, '"The Remote Islanders of the Sea"? Towards a Re-examination of the Role of Church and Faith in St Kilda', in Chambers, *Rewriting St Kilda*, attacks the credibility of Sands's accounts of the island. Sands certainly changed his mind about its minister. His portrait of a people oppressed by religion in the 1870s has a certain veracity but does appear to be sensationalised.

p. 243 *One islander, Lachlan MacDonald, later explained*: Gannon and Geddes, *St Kilda: The Last and Outmost Isle*, p. 218, quoting from D.A. Quine, *St Kilda Portraits*, Downland Press (1988).

9. The Saintly Tadpole

p. 251 *Lindisfarne began as a franchise . . . Godless north-east England*: See Kate Tristram's *The Story of Holy Island* (2009).

p. 254 *We have not enough young men to row boats off . . . the cattle*: Love Pritchard was quoted in the *Daily Sketch* in 1925, from the introduction to the locally produced Enlli guidebook.

p. 254 *a small island occupied by some extremely devout monks*: From the local guidebook. Most of my history of Enlli is taken from Mary Chitty's careful and interesting two-part history, *The Monks on Ynys Enlli* (1992).

p. 255 *Men and women took up an ascetic form of Christianity*: The historian Kate Tristram, in *The Story of Holy Island*, explains this well.

p. 255 *Richness in extremis . . . Celtic church*: Nicolson, *Sea Room*, p. 160.

p. 257 *In 1964, an eighty-six-year-old islander . . . they ploughed the fields*: Jennie Jones, *Tomos the Islandman* (1999).

p. 258 *He first visited the island . . . to see its newly opened bird observatory*: Byron Rogers, *The Man Who Went into the West – The Life of R.S. Thomas* (2006).

p. 258 *In November 1957, a meeting . . . hermetic life on Ynys Enlli*: My account is drawn from the direct testimony of islanders and Jenny Farwell's fascinating account, 'The Nun, the Priest and the Prophet: The Revival of the Eremitical Life in Enlli and Llŷn', in *Trivium* 39 (2010).

p. 263 *grew into a great sense of discernment and liberty of spirit*: From Farwell, 'The Nun, the Priest and the Prophet'.

10. After the Party

p. 274 *Northey is much smaller*: I explored Northey in my previous book, *Coastlines* (2015).

p. 275 *The secret island where the A-list go . . . party all night*: *Daily Mail*, 7 September 2013, http://www.dailymail.co.uk/news/article-2414481/Osea-The-secret-island-A-list-drink-strip-party-night.html.

p. 276 *A judge described the company . . . shame a Third World country*: Care Quality Commission, 'Regulator Successful in Causeway Retreat Prosecution', 19 November 2010, http://www.cqc.org.uk/content/regulator-successful-causeway-retreat-prosecution.

p. 276 *Osea's idealistic moment came in 1903 . . . £1 million, bought the island*: Guy Thorne's 1913 hagiography of Charrington is entertaining, and available online.

p. 278 *when he lodged at another favoured bolt-hole . . . started on his next*: As recalled in Alison Symons's *Tremedda Days* (1992), her enjoyable memoir of growing up on the Penrith Peninsula.

p. 279 *Old Bill, as his family . . . the British Empire Exhibition*: As well as David's stories about Major Allnatt, gleaned from the Osea employees he inherited, there is a short biography of Allnatt in Peter Kilgarriff, *A Matter of Trust: A Brief History of the Lankelly Chase Foundation* (2012), http://lankellychase. org.uk/wp-content/uploads/2015/07/Matter_of_Trust.pdf.

p. 290 *Someone's been playing with an air rifle, too*: I later discover that this was probably one of David Cole's grandsons on a summer visit to the island.

11. An Island for One

p. 293 *Ray Island, Essex, 110 acres; population 0*: I made a mistake by walking onto Ray Island. There is no public access on foot because the marsh immediately south of the Strood is privately owned. Ray Island is open to the public as a nature reserve, but you will have to sail, cruise or kayak there from Maldon.

p. 298 *Robinson Crusoe spends the early weeks . . . frantically constructing fences*: Adam Nicolson writes about this with characteristic panache in *Sea Room*.

p. 298 *rey, or reisa in Old Norse, means a raised mound*: P.H. Reaney, *The Place-Names of Essex*, Cambridge University Press, 1935.

p. 299 *I'm not too worried about . . . the mainland from Mersea one Saturday night:* I'm indebted to the Ray Island warden David Nicholls for the ghost stories.

p. 300 *Baring-Gould is best known for . . . Onward Christian Soldiers*: The full life of Baring-Gould is well worth retelling, and a new biography is due shortly. I used the biography recommended by the Sabine Baring-Gould Society: Bickford H.C. Dickinson, *Sabine Baring-Gould: Squarson, Writer and Folklorist 1834–1924* (1970).

p. 300 *I cannot say that I either liked . . . he wrote in his memoirs*: Further reminiscences, widely quoted, from John Fowles's excellent introduction to the reissue of Sabine Baring-Gould's *Mehalah* (1969).

p. 303 *As an adult, he never allowed himself to have children*: Andro Linklater's biography of Compton Mackenzie records that Faith was persuaded not to try for another child by Monty. She later tried to adopt several children and fell pregnant by a lover but – deliberately, says Linklater – miscarried. Monty barely mentioned his stillborn son, except to 'make the best of it' by declaring that he never wanted a son because they would suffer for having a father with an 'excess of personality'. Linklater, *Compton Mackenzie: A Life*, p. 96.

p. 304 *John Fowles once said the Essex marshes are set to the key of winter*: in introduction to Baring-Gould's *Mehalah*.

p. 307 *David has discovered there was a young woman . . . there in 1871*: The Ray Island warden David Nicholls is also the de facto local historian of the Ray and has written a two-part essay on the island's links with Baring-Gould: 'Ray Island and the Legacy of Mehalah', published in the *Mersea Courier* 506 (27 May 2011) and 507 (8 June 2011), and updated online: http://www.merseamuseum.org.uk/mmresdetails. php?tot=1&cat=&col=&typ=ID&hit=0&pid=COR2_016.

p. 309 *not as super-sclerosed specialists*: Charles Foster in *Being A Beast* (2016) writes brilliantly, in his chapter on being an urban fox, of the constraints humans have put themselves under. In *Echoes*, Compton Mackenzie wrote: 'One of the handicaps of contemporary existence is the continuously rapid expansion of human knowledge which drives people into specialisation and therefore constricts their outlook.'

p. 309 *infatuated like poor, foolish Fanny Price in Mansfield Park*: Quoted in my book, *Coastlines* (2015), p. 223.

BIBLIOGRAPHY

General

Austen, Jane, *Mansfield Park*, Wordsworth Editions, 1993 (originally published 1814)

Baker, Timothy C., 'Collecting Islands: Compton Mackenzie and *The Four Winds of Love*', *Scottish Literary Review* 2.2 (2010): 85–106

Boulton, James T., and Andrew Robertson, *The Letters of D.H. Lawrence*, vol. III, *October 1916–1921*, Cambridge University Press, 2007

Boulton, James T., and Lindeth Vasey (eds.), *The Letters of D.H. Lawrence*, vol. V, *March 1924–1927*, Cambridge University Press, 1989

Bowker, Gordon, *George Orwell*, Little, Brown, 2003

Bullough, Oliver, 'On the Rocks: The Fall of Jersey', *Guardian*, 8 December 2015: https://www.theguardian.com/uk-news/2015/dec/08/fall-of-jersey-how-tax-haven-goes-bust

Bunting, Madeleine, *Love of Country, A Hebridean Journey*, Granta, 2016

Clayton, Matthew, and Anthony Atkinson, *Lundy, Rockall, Dogger, Fair Isle*, Ebury Press, 2015

Conrad, Joseph, *The Mirror of the Sea*, Little Toller, 2013

Conrad, Peter, *Islands: A Trip through Time and Space*, Thames & Hudson, 2009

Defoe, Daniel, *A Tour Through the Eastern Counties of England, 1722*, Cassell & Company, 1891

—, *A Tour Through the Whole Island of Great Britain*, Penguin, 1978 (first published in 3 vols.,1724–7)

—, *Robinson Crusoe*, Wordsworth, 1995

Fogle, Ben, *Offshore: In Search of an Island of My Own*, Penguin, 2007

Foster, Charles, *Being a Beast*, Profile, 2016

Fowles, John, *The Magus*, revised edition, Triad/Granada, 1977

— and Fay Godwin, *Islands*, Jonathan Cape, 1978

Fraser Darling, F., and J. Morton Boyd, *The Highlands and Islands*, Collins New Naturalist, Fontana, revised edition 1969

Fussell, Paul, *Abroad: British Literary Travelling between the Wars*, Oxford University Press, 1980

Golding, William, *Pincher Martin*, Faber & Faber, 1956

Gross, John, *The New Oxford Book of Literary Anecdotes*, Oxford University Press, 2006

Houellebecq, Michel, *The Possibility of an Island*, tr. Gavin Bowd, Phoenix, 2006

Kerrigan, John, 'Louis MacNeice among the Islands', in Peter Mackay, Edna Longley and Fran Bearton (eds.), *Modern Irish and Scottish Poetry*, Cambridge University Press, 2011

Kingshill, Sophia, and Jennifer Westwood, *The Fabled Coast*, Random House, 2012

Lawrence, D.H., 'The Man Who Loved Islands', in *The Collected Short Stories of D.H. Lawrence*, Book Club Associates by arrangement with William Heinemann, 1974

—, 'Two Blue Birds', in *The Collected Short Stories of D.H. Lawrence*, Book Club Associates by arrangement with William Heinemann, 1974

—, *The Rainbow*, Penguin, 1989 (first published 1915)

Link, Victor, 'D.H. Lawrence's "The Man Who Loved Islands" in the Light of Compton Mackenzie's Memoirs', *D.H. Lawrence Review* 15.1–2 (1982): 77–87

Linklater, Andro, *Compton Mackenzie: A Life*, Chatto & Windus, 1987

Linklater, Eric, *The Man on My Back*, Macmillan, 1941

Lockhart, James Macdonald, *A Journey through Birds*, Fourth Estate, 2016

McIntosh, Alastair, *Soil and Soul*, Aurum Press, 2001

—, *Island Spirituality: Spiritual Values of Lewis and Harris*, Islands Book Trust, 2013

—, *Poacher's Pilgrimage: An Island Journey*, Birlinn, 2016

Mack, John, *The Sea: A Cultural History*, Reaktion Books, 2011

Mackenzie, Compton, *My Life and Times, Octave One 1883–1891*, Chatto & Windus, 1963

—, *My Life and Times, Octave Two 1891–1900*, Chatto & Windus, 1963

—, *My Life and Times, Octave Three 1900–1907*, Chatto & Windus, 1964

—, *My Life and Times, Octave Four 1907–1914*, Chatto & Windus, 1965

—, *My Life and Times, Octave Five 1915–1923*, Chatto & Windus, 1966

—, *My Life and Times, Octave Six 1924–1930*, Chatto & Windus, 1967

—, *My Life and Times, Octave Seven 1931–1938*, Chatto & Windus, 1968

—, *My Life and Times, Octave Eight 1939–1946*, Chatto & Windus, 1969

—, *My Life and Times, Octave Nine 1946–1953*, Chatto & Windus, 1970

—, *My Life and Times, Octave Ten, 1953–1963*, Chatto & Windus, 1971

—, *The Heavenly Ladder*, Cassell & Company, 1924

—, *Unconsidered Trifles*, Martin Secker, 1932

—, *The South Wind of Love*, Rich & Cowan, 1937

—, *Whisky Galore*, introduction by Roger Hutchinson, Birlinn, 2012 (first published 1947)

—, *The Rival Monster*, Chatto & Windus, 1952

—, *Echoes*, Chatto & Windus, 1954

—, *Butterfly Hill*, Kaye & Ward, 1970

Mackenzie, Faith Compton, *As Much As I Dare*, Collins, 1938

—, *More Than I Should*, Collins, 1940

—, *Always Afternoon*, Collins, 1943

—, *The Crooked Wall*, Jonathan Cape, 1954

Maclean, Veronica, *Past Forgetting*, Headline Review, 2002

McMahon, Elizabeth, 'The Gilded Cage', in Rod Edmond and Vanessa Smith (eds.), *Islands in History and Representation*, Routledge, 2003

Mais, S.P.B., *Isles of the Island*, Putnam, 1934

Massie, Allan, 'The Magnum Opus of Compton Mackenzie', *Spectator*, 26 August 2007: https://www.spectator.co.uk/2007/09/the-magnum-opus-of-compton-mackenzie/

Mitchell, Ian, *Isles of the West: A Hebridean Voyage*, Canongate, 1999

Moore, Harry T., *The Intelligent Heart: The Story of D.H. Lawrence*, Penguin, 1954

Nicolson, Adam, *Sea Room: An Island Life in the Hebrides*, HarperCollins, 2001

—, *Atlantic Britain*, Harper Perennial, 2004

Oates, Matthew, *In Pursuit of Butterflies*, Bloomsbury, 2015

Plomer, William, review of Compton Mackenzie's *The Darkening Green*, *Spectator*, 6 July 1934: http://archive.spectator.co.uk/article/6th-july-1934/30/fiction

Quammen, David, *The Song of the Dodo: Island Biogeography in an Age of Extinctions*, Scribner, 1997

Raban, Jonathan, *Coasting*, Collins Harvill, 1986

Richards, Eric, *The Highland Clearances*, Birlinn, 2013

Rintoul, M.C., *Dictionary of Real People and Places in Fiction*, Routledge, 1993

di Robilant, Andrea, *Venetian Navigators: The Mystery of the Voyages of the Zen Brothers*, Faber & Faber, 2011

Shelden, Michael, *George Orwell: The Authorised Biography*, William Heinemann, 1991

Sjöberg, Fredrik, *The Fly Trap*, tr. Thomas Teal, Particular Books, 2014

Wills, Dixe, *Tiny Islands*, AA Publishing, 2013

Wood, Jenny, *Herm, Our Island Home*, Linton, 1986

The Isle of Man

Broderick, George, 'Some Island Names in the Former "Kingdom of the Isles": A Reappraisal', *Journal of Scottish Name Studies* 7 (2013): 1–28, republished online: http://www.clanntuirc.co.uk/JSNS/V7/JSNS7%20Broderick.pdf

Burton, John F., 'The Mystery of the Isle of Man's Endangered Grasshopper', *British Wildlife*, 2.1 (1990): 37–42

Chappell, Connery, *Island of Barbed Wire*, Robert Hale, 1984

Duncan, Peter, 'Crustacean and Mollusc Fisheries of the Isle of Man', *Proceedings of the Isle of Man Natural History and Antiquarian Society* XII.4 (April 2011–March 2013): 744: http://www.manxantiquarians.com/media/Proc/Proc%20XII-4.pdf

Freke, David, 'History', in Vaughan Robinson and Danny McCarroll, *The Isle of Man: Celebrating a Sense of Place*, Liverpool University Press, 1990

Fyson, Robert, 'Gladstone in the Isle of Man', *Proceedings of the Isle of Man Natural History and Antiquarian Society* XII.4 (April 2011–March 2013): 684

Kinvig, R.H., *The Isle of Man: A Social, Cultural and Political History*, Liverpool University Press, 1975

Mais, S.P.B., *Isles of the Island*, Putnam, 1934

Raban, Jonathan, *Coasting*, Collins Harvill, 1986

Rawcliffe, Roger, *No Man Is an Island: 50 Years of Finance in the Isle of Man*, Manx Heritage Foundation, 2009

Webber, David T., *An Illustrated Encyclopedia of the Isle of Man*, Manx Experience, 1997

Orkney and South Ronaldsay

Barthelmess, Ilse Babette, *A Celebration of Sunrise at The Tomb of the Eagles*, Orkney Museums and Heritage, 2004

Branscombe, Julian, and Keith Dobney, 'The Mystery of the Orkney Vole', *British Wildlife* 27.5 (June 2016): 340–48

Foster, Sally, *Maeshowe and the Heart of Neolithic Orkney*, Historic Scotland, 2015

Hedges, John W., *Tomb of the Eagles: Death and Life in a Stone Age Tribe*, New Amsterdam, 1984

Liptrot, Amy, *The Outrun*, Canongate, 2016

Sackville, Amy, *Orkney*, Granta, 2013

Towers, Roy, Nick Card and Mark Edmonds, *The Ness of Brodgar*, Ness of Brodgar Trust, 2015

Barra

Calderwood, Roy, *Times Subject to Tides: The Story of Barra Airport*, Kea Publishing, 1999

Campbell, John Lorne, 'Our Barra Years – Memories of Compton Mackenzie', *Scotland Magazine*, 1974–5

— (ed.), *The Book of Barra*, George Routledge & Sons, 1936, republished Acair, 1998

Hutchinson, Roger, *Polly: The True Story behind Whisky Galore*, Mainstream Publishing, 1998

MacKinnon, Mairi Ceit, *Vatersay and Its People*, Mairi Ceit MacKinnon, 2016

MacPherson, John, *Tales from Barra, Told by the Coddy*, 1960, republished Birlinn, 1992

Perman, Ray, *The Man Who Gave Away His Island: A Life of John Lorne Campbell*, Birlinn, 2010

Shaw, Margaret Fay, *From the Alleghenies to the Hebrides: An Autobiography*, Canongate, 1993

Eigg

Dinshaw, Minoo, *Outlandish Knight: The Byzantine Life of Steven Runciman*, Allen Lane, 2016

Dressler, Camille, *Eigg: The Story of an Island*, Birlinn, 2nd edition 2007

Forsyth, Tom, Bob Harris and Alastair McIntosh, 'Open Letter of Beseechment to Keith Schellenberg, "Laird" of Eigg', 1992: http://www.alastairmcintosh.com/articles/1992_beseechment.htm

McIntosh, Alastair, 'The Isle of Eigg Trust Launch Address', 25 October 1991: http://www.alastairmcintosh.com/articles/1991_eigg_address.htm

—, 'Colonised Land; Colonised Mind: People of the Island of Eigg Celebrate Their Freedom', *Resurgence* 184 (1997): 28–30. Republished online: http://www.alastairmcintosh.com/articles/1997_eigg_resurgence.htm

—, *Soil and Soul*, Aurum Press, 2001

Riddoch, Lesley, *Blossom: What Scotland Needs to Flourish*, Luath Press, 2013

Rixson, Denis, *The Small Isles: Canna, Rum, Eigg and Muck*, Birlinn, 2001

Rathlin

Gage, Patrick, *Memories and Tales of Rathlin Island* (self-published), 2011

Gage, Robert Conolly, 'A List of Birds Found in Rathlin Island', *Proceedings of the Natural History Society of Dublin*, III, December 1861: 91–3

Gorman, Damian, *A Place Apart – Island Voices, A Creative Baseline Evaluation for Rathlin*, 2010

Kohl, Johann Georg, *Travels in Ireland* Part 4 (1844), Clachan Publishing, 2012

Murphy, Michael J., *Rathlin: Island of Blood and Enchantment: The Folklore of Rathlin*, Dundalgan Press, Dundalk, 1987

Stevenson, Letitia S., *The Guttering Candle, or Life on Rathlin 1920– 1922* (collected letters ed. Patric Stevenson; self-published)

Waugh, Edwin, *The North Coast 1869*, Dalriada, 1990 (from *Rambles & Revelries*, 1874)

Alderney

Bonnard, Brian, *Alderney at War 1939–49*, History Press, 2009

— (ed.), *Island of Dread in the Channel: The Story of Georgi Ivanovitch Kondakov*, Alan Sutton, 1991

Bunting, Madeleine, *The Model Occupation: The Channel Islands under German Rule 1940–1945*, HarperCollins, 1995

Edwards, G.B., *The Book of Ebenezer Le Page*, Moyer Bell, 1981

Gander, Terry (ed.), *Alderney: An Introduction to the Delights of This Very Special Channel Island*, Barnes Publishing

Morris, Alex, Jason Hazeley, Joel Morris, Robin Halstead, *More Bollocks to Alton Towers*, Penguin, 2008

Thomas, Leslie, *Some Lovely Islands*, Arlington Books, London, 1982

The Isles of Scilly

Bowley, R.L., *The Fortunate Islands: The Story of the Isles of Scilly*, 8th revised edition, 1990

Cooper, Andrew, *Secret Nature of The Isles of Scilly*, Green Books, 2006

Fowles, John, and Fay Godwin, *Islands*, Jonathan Cape, 1978

Gibson, Frank, *My Scillonian Home*, Beric Tempest, 1980

Kay, Ernest, *Isles of Flowers: The Story of the Isles of Scilly*, Alvin Redman, 1956

Marsden, Philip, *Rising Ground*, Granta, 2014

Perkins, Gladys, *Times Remembered . . . A Scillonian's Story*, Signal Row Publishing, 2014

Taylor, Colin, *The Life of a Scilly Sergeant*, Century, 2016

St Kilda

Bartlet, Leslie, 'Roderick the Imposter and the St Kilda Cult', *History Scotland* 14 (January/February 2014): 16

Boddington, David, *St Kilda Diary: A Record of the Early Re-occupation of St Kilda*, Islands Book Trust, 2010

Chambers, Bob (ed.), *Rewriting St Kilda: New Views on Old Ideas*, Islands Book Trust, 2010

Clutton-Brock, Tim, and Josephine Pemberton, *Soay Sheep: Dynamics and Selection in an Island Population*, Cambridge University Press, 2004

Gannon, Angela, and George Geddes, *St Kilda: The Last and Outmost Isle*, Historic Environment Scotland, 2015

Gillies, Donald John, *The Truth about St Kilda: An Islander's Memoir*, ed. John Randall, Birlinn, 2010

Lawson, Bill, 'Hiort in Pre-1930 Writings – An Overview', in Bob Chambers (ed.), *Rewriting St Kilda: New Views on Old Ideas*, Islands Book Trust, 2010

—, John Love, John Randall, Michael Robson, *St Kilda: Myth and Reality*, Islands Book Trust, 2007

Love, John A., *A Natural History of St Kilda*, Birlinn, 2009

Macaulay, Margaret, *The Prisoner of St Kilda*, Luath Press, 2009

Maclean, Charles, *The Island on the Edge of the World: The Story of St Kilda*, revised edition, Canongate 1996

Martin, Martin, *A Description of the Western Islands of Scotland: A Voyage to St Kilda*, introduction by Charles W.J. Withers, Birlinn, 1999

Meek, Donald E., '"The Remote Islanders of the Sea"? Towards a

Re-examination of the Role of Church and Faith in St Kilda', in Bob Chambers (ed.), *Rewriting St Kilda: New Views on Old Ideas*, Islands Book Trust, 2010

Self, Will, 'On Charles Maclean's St Kilda: Island on the Edge of the World', *New Statesman*, 27 November 2000: http://www.newstatesman.com/node/152462

Steel, Tom, *The Life and Death of St Kilda* (revised edition) HarperPress, 2011

Bardsey

Anon., '"The Way the Saints Went" . . . And Why the Pilgrims Followed Them. A study of Bardsey Island', Z0214593 Theology BA Hons paper, 2004

Chamberlain, Brenda, *Tide Race*, Seren Books, 2007

Chitty, Mary, *The Monks on Ynys Enlli*, Part One, *c.500 AD to 1252 AD*, W. Alun Jones, 1992

—, *The Monks on Ynys Enlli*, Part Two, *1252 AD to 1527 AD*, W. Alun Jones, 2000

Evans, Christine, and Wolf Marloh, *Bardsey*, Gomer Press, 2008

Farwell, Jenny, 'The Nun, the Priest and the Prophet: The Revival of the Eremitical Life in Enlli and Llŷn', *Trivium* 39 (2010)

Jones, Jennie, *Tomos the Islandman*, Carreg Gwalch, 1999

Rogers, Byron, *The Man Who Went into the West: The Life of R.S. Thomas*, Aurum, 2006

Tristram, Kate, *The Story of Holy Island*, Canterbury Press, 2009

Osea

Caton, Peter, *No Boat Required: Exploring Tidal Islands*, Matador, 2001

Fautley, M.P.B., and J.H. Garon, *The Essex Coastline: Then and Now*, 2004

Kilgarriff, Peter, *A Matter of Trust: A Brief History of the Lankelly Chase*

Foundation, 2012: http://lankellychase.org.uk/wp-content/uplo ads/2015/07/Matter_of_Trust.pdf

Pretty, Jules, *This Luminous Coast*, Full Circle Editions, 2011

Symons, Alison, *Tremedda Days*, Tabb House, 1992

Thorne, Guy, *The Great Acceptance: The Life Story of F.N. Charrington*, Hodder & Stoughton, 1913 (Project Gutenberg ebook, 2012)

Yearsley, Ian, *Islands of Essex*, Ian Henry Publications, 1994

Ray Island

Baring-Gould, Sabine, *Mehalah*, introduction by John Fowles, Boydell Press, 1969

Canton, James, *Out of Essex, Re-imagining a Literary Landscape*, Signal Books, 2013

Caton, Peter, *No Boat Required: Exploring Tidal Islands*, Matador, 2001

Day, J. Wentworth, 'The Sea-Country of Mehalah', *Geographical Magazine* 34 (1961): 431–6

Dickinson, Bickford H.C., *Sabine Baring-Gould: Squarson, Writer and Folklorist 1834–1924*, David & Charles, 1970

Nicholls, David, 'Ray Island and the Legacy of Mehalah', *Mersea Courier* 506 (27 May 2011) and 507 (8 June 2011); updated online: http://www.merseamuseum.org.uk/mmresdetails.php? tot=1&cat=&col=&typ=ID&hit=0&pid=COR2_016

Yearsley, Ian, *Islands of Essex*, Ian Henry Publications, 1994

Index

agriculture: Barra, 76–7, 83; Isle of Man, 36–7; St Kilda, 230

Albert, Prince Consort, 169

alcohol, 93–5, 122–5

Alderney: economy, 185; history, 167, 168–70; landscape, 163, 167–8; location and political status, 166–7; overview, 161–87; Second World War and aftermath, 163–4, 170–87; shape, 139, 321; travelling to, 165; LANDMARKS: Bibette Point, 163–4; Fort Tourgis, 181; Longis Bay, 181; 'the Odeon', 181; St Anne, 165–6; Sylt concentration camp, 178, 187

Alderney – The Homecoming (documentary), 323

Allchin, Revd Donald, 262, 263

Allnatt, Major Alfred, 279–81, 329

Allnatt diamond, 280

Angell, Norman, 274

animal farming, 76, 131–2, 200

Anita, Oblate Sister, 260

Antrim, 1st Earl of, 149

archaeology, 43–52, 64–8

Arran, Isle of, 66

Ashford, Rodney, 202, 203–4, 205, 206, 209

Austen, Jane, 309–10

Bardsey *see* Ynys Enlli

Bardsey Island Trust, 252, 253, 263

Baring-Gould, Grace, 300

Baring-Gould, Sabine, 299–302, 306, 307, 329–30

Barkham, Esme: holiday on St Martin's, 195, 197, 209, 210; relationship with twin, 214; travelling to St Martin's, 191, 193

Barkham, Milly: holiday on St Martin's, 197, 209; relationship with twin, 214; travelling to St Martin's, 191, 193

Barkham, Ted, 191–4, 206, 209

Baron, George, 171, 172, 173, 184–5, 323

Barra: books inspired by, 93–5; conviviality, 80–1, 86; economy, 87–8; history and culture, 76–7; landscape, 73–4, 79, 95–6; Linklater on, 67; Mackenzie's time on, 67, 71–2, 77, 79–86, 88–98, 103, 225; overview, 69–98; travelling to, 71–3; LANDMARKS: Castlebay, 73–5, 85; Eoligarry Peninsula, 95–6; Suidheachan, 71, 88–92, 98

Barrie, J.M., 8, 92

Barthelmess, Babette, 49–50, 64

Beauly River, 63, 77, 79

Beauman, Sally, 89

Bective, Earl of, 281–2

Bell, Allan, 19–20, 25–6, 30–1

birds: conservation on Rathlin, 137–8, 142–6; conservation on Ynys Enlli, 267–8; Ray Island, 303–5; reasons for decline in seabird numbers, 239–40; St Kilda's, 219, 226, 228, 230–1, 236–40; *see also individual birds by name*

Bismarck, Count Gottfried von, 276

Blackwater, 274–5

Boateng, Paul, 283

Boden, Sarah: life on Eigg, 115, 120, 129–33, 320; on Schellenburg, 108, 109

Bonnard, Brian, 174–5, 176, 177, 178–80, 323